IMAGES OF THE DIVINE AND CULTURAL ORIENTATIONS

For Mona Siddiqui
with respect and admiration,
Michael Welker

Michael Welker | William Schweiker (Eds.)

Images of the Divine and Cultural Orientations

Jewish, Christian, and Islamic Voices

EVANGELISCHE VERLAGSANSTALT
Leipzig

Bibliographic information published by the German National Library
The Deutsche Nationalbibliothek lists this publication in the Deutsche Nationalbiographie; detailed bibliographic data are available in the Internet at http://dnb.dnb.de

Printed in Germany · H 7940

This book was printed on ageing resistant paper.

Cover: Kai-Michael Gustmann, Leipzig
Cover image: © persephone3d / www.fotosearch.com
Typesetting: Hajo Kenkel, Heidelberg
Printing and Binding: Hubert & Co., Göttingen

ISBN 978-3-374-04109-1
www.eva-leipzig.de

Content

Introduction 7
William Schweiker and Michael Welker

Part I
Divine Invisibility and Power

Invisibility and Power in Islamic Religion and Culture 15
The Ambiguity of Veiling
Baber Johansen

In the Image of the Invisible 51
Kathryn Tanner

Is Seeing Believing? 67
'Visibility' and 'Self Concealment' of God in Jewish Theology after the Holocaust
Alfred Bodenheimer

Part II
Spiritual Transformation and the Divine

Images of the Divine and Spiritual Transformation in Judaism 79
Michael Fishbane

Between Sensual and Heavenly Love 95
Franz Rosenzweig's Reading of the Song of Songs
Paul Mendes-Flohr

God Sharing in the Conditio Humana 103
Reflections on the Potential of Christian Imagery from a Lutheran Perspective
Friederike Nüssel

Image of the Divine and Spiritual Presence 115
In What Ways Can Christology Provide Cultural Orientations?
Michael Welker

The Forces of Good and Evil in 'Islamic' Comic 125
Susanne Enderwitz

Re-Thinking Jewish/Christian Divergence on the "Image of the Divine" 133
The Problem of Intra-Divine Complexity and the Origins of the Doctrine of the Trinity
Sarah Coakley

Part III
The Divine and the Elevation of Life

'God as Light' in the Christian Moral Imagination 153
William Schweiker

Paradise as a Qur'anic Discourse 167
Late Antique Foundations and Early Qur'anic Developments
Angelika Neuwirth

"So that he could not bear the sweetness" 187
Imagining the Unimaginable in Medieval Ashkenaz
Johannes Heil

Islam as a Cultural Orientation for Modern Judaism 197
Susannah Heschel

Christology 215
The Images of the Divine in USA and South African Black Theology
Dwight Hopkins

Introduction

William Schweiker and Michael Welker

This book documents results of a research project which was meant to explore fruitful commonalities and fruitful differences among the Jewish, the Christian and the Islamic traditions. Over against conventional doctrinal and comparative religious explorations, we wanted to explore the impact that the basic contents of faith and practice have on cultures and their forms of ethos. This approach was chosen to relate different traditions of research to each other–one more dominant in the European contexts (the so-called *Geistesgeschichte*) and the other in the Anglo-American world, one based on cultural and social studies. When we started the project the majority of our group voted for the title "Images of the Divine and Cultural Orientations." An introduction to the chapters that follow can be usefully isolated through attention to the title of the volume, the problems it implies, and the challenge it puts to the study of the religions, including theology.

1. Image and Culture

In marked contrast to the contemporary globalized media and the flood of images that saturate, inform, and orient people's imaginations around the world, the Jewish, Christian, and Muslim traditions share in different forms and degrees the rejection of what is called "image-worship." We read: "You shall not make for yourself a graven image, or any likeness of anything that is in heaven above, or that is in the earth beneath, or that is in the water under the earth; you shall not bow down to them or serve them ..." (Ex 20:4f; cf. Dtn 5:8 and Dtn 4:16-19).[1] Yet, ironically, we also find in the Holy Scriptures a multitude of images of the Divine and the divine glory. In the *Tanach* (Hebrew Scripture) the human being is called the "image of God" (Gen 1:26f, 5:1, 9:6) and in the New Testament of the Christian Bible they receive the promise that they will bear the image of the "second *anthropos*" (or the second Adam) from heaven (1Cor 15:49; cf. Rom 8:29), namely, Jesus Christ, "who reflects the glory of God and bears the very stamp of his nature" (Heb 1:3). Likewise, in the Qur'an, there is a strict prohibition of making images of the divine even as Allah has a hundred names and human beings are the "viceregents" of God on earth.[2]

---

1 All biblical references in this chapter will be from the Revised Standard Version.

2 See *Humanity Before God: Contemporary Faces of Jewish, Christian, and Islamic Ethics*, eds. W. Schweiker, K. Jung, and M. Johnson (Minneapolis, MN: Fortress Press, 2006).

Within these religious tradtions, how does one relate the criticism of images with the diverses names and images of God in Holy Scripture, and with claims about God's revelation? Jews, Muslims, and Christians must think about, pray to, and worship a reality which, in any precise sense, cannot be adequately imagined or concieved, and, yet, also think, pray, and worship within the context of the religious life teeming with a multitude of names and images: God as one, God as power, God as the merciful and most high one, the outpouring of the Holy Spirit, a pillar of smoke leading the people out of Egypt, Christ as the Son of God, Moses the Law-giver, and Muhammed the "seal of the prophets," and on and on. In the face of this paradox of the criticism of images but their proliferation, how is one to avoid falling into a deafening silence about the divine or skepticism about God's reality and power? This challenge we can call "the iconic problem" of theology.

However, the "iconic problem" is not only a theological puzzle. It can also be raised with respect to any call for religious "cultural orientation" and brings us to the second major term in the title of this book, namely, "culture." Is culture a powerful icon or regulative ideal meant to provide orientation to human personal and social life? Kathryn Tanner, Terry Eagleton and others alerted us to the enormous complexity of the phenomenon of culture, which explains the fascination and enthusiasm with this topic in the academy and in the media.[3] 'Culture' offers a realistic and a constructivist dimension. It can also be a descriptive (say, American culture) or an evaluative and even a normative term (say, high or low or pop culture). Culture includes the actual and the desirable notion of reality and–at least in a vague way–a vision or visions of perfection. Who wants to be "un-cultured?" The idea of culture is often and understandbly related to claims about education and its importance in human existence. Culture is not only seen as a complex human activity, but as a complex state of actual and possible human affairs. And culture concentrates not only on natural reality, but also on spiritual and symbolic realities. Not surprisngly, in eighteenth-century Europe, 'culture' became equated with 'civilization' and correlated with all kinds of modern progress.

Since J. G. Herder in the nineteenth century, one witnesses social developments that have led to changes in ideas about culture, especially in our global age: the pluralisation of cultures, the critique of Eurocentric ideas of culture, and the emergence of a multicontextual ways of thinking about it. A nuanced approach towards different cultures across the globe and a continuous growth in the awareness of the social and cultural differentiations in complex societies is now, thankfully, the standard for all relevant investigations of the the idea of culture and also actual cultures. As Terry Eagleton noticed laconically, "The complexity of the idea of culture is nowhere more graphically demonstrated than in the fact that its most eminent theorist in post-war Britain, Raymond Williams, defines it at various times to mean the standard of perfection, a habit of mind, the arts, general intellectual development, a whole way of life, a signifying system, a structure of feeling, the

3 Kathryn Tanner, *Theories of Culture: A New Agenda for Theology*, (Minneapolis, MN: Fortress Press, 1997) and Terry Eagleton, *The Idea of Culture* (Oxford: Blackwell, 2000).

interrelations of elements in a way of life and everything from economic production and the family to political institutions."[4]

Granting the problems with ideas about culture, problems that now characterize our global age, most of the definitions and theories of culture seem to agree, explicitly or implicitly, on the fact that culture serves to secure continuities in the communication among human beings via memories and expectations. With the help of their culture(s) peoples develop amazing abilities to connect and to disconnect, to share and to differentiate, memories and expectations. People anticipate, reproduce and reconstruct in memories and imaginations what others remember, anticipate, and expect. Moving in the realms of memory and imagination, people can attune individual and communal emotions as well as thoughts and practices in powerful ways. In this way, cultures allow people to respond to the perceptions of their lives by others even as their perceptions reflectively shape those whom their engage. The reflexive dynamic of the mutual shaping of self-perception would seem to be basic to the communicate logic of culture, especially in our global media age. Among the religious, how one is seen by others shapes, for good and for ill, the self-understanding of peoples, a shaping power that is, sadly, too often resisted through violent reactions driven by fundamentalistic ideologies or, conversely, the deluting of traditions into vague patterns of thought, practice, and spirituality.

Despite all of these problems and challenges, it must still be said that the enormous individual and communal power to create worlds of memories and imaginations, to store, select, connect, and shape them, and to process and attune powerful streams of information, illumination, thoughts and emotions discloses the human spirit in and through cultural forms. And this same spirit can and does shape the consciousness of others through cultural communictation even as one is being shaped by this same reflexive process. For this reason, the interpretation and assessment of culture(s), one task of this book, is a means to examine human existence itself, the structures of lived human reality in real and imagined worlds, and thus also to understand people's capacities to create meaningful worlds.[5]

The challenge to understand the many processes of cultural memory and the many forms of imagination and their impact on the different societal systems is enormous.[6] This challenge is heightened by the awareness that the global flux of cultural forms has to wrestle with enormous local and global distortions: massive injustice, poverty and ecological destruction in the contemporary world; the threat of relativism, cynicism, and apathy; the weakening and distortion of cultural and canonical memory by the enormous powers of the market, the media, and technology; the long term crisis and the potential restitutions of the ideologies of

---

4 Terry Eagleton, *The Idea of Culture*, 36.

5 See William Schweiker, *Theological Ethics and Global Dynamics: In the Time of Many Worlds* (Oxford: Blackwell, 2008).

6 Cf. Michael Welker, "Kommunikatives, kollektives, kulturelles und kanonisches Gedächtnis," in: *Jahrbuch für Biblische Theologie, Bd. 22: Die Macht der Erinnerung* (Neukirchener: Neukirchen-Vluyn 2008), 321-331.

the nation state in the context of the current crisis of the monetary system; and, the different speed of the shift from the modern to the post-modern paradigms and mentalities across the globe.

2. The Tasks of this Book

Mindful of the complexity of ideas about images within religious tradtions and also culture as a human reality, the context of this book is the current global reality where images and cultures interact with increasing speed and intensity. However, our purpose in the following chapters is not only to explore the great monotheistic religions (Judaism, Christianity, Islam) through the framework of the interactions among "images," the iconic problem, and "culture(s)." While that is indeed one of the tasks of this book, a task that, to be honest, alone would justify the scholarly labor found in the book's pages. Yet beyond the work of interpreting the exceedingly complex ways that the monotheistic religions have provided orientation to human cultures in and through their images of the divine, two other tasks define the purpose of this book.

Another task of this book beyond exploring the religions within different historic-social contexts is decidely "constructure." That is to say, some of the authors represented in this book, but by no means all of them, seek to show that the monotheistic faith with their specific forms of the iconical problem in giving people cultural orientation, have, nevertheless, surprising power to speak to the global situation marked by a whirlwind of images transgressing and ingressing into cultures. This whirlwind both facilitates understanding among cultures but also blocks and distorts mutual understanding. In this situation, the constructive religious thinker must sort through distortions in his or her own tradition and its reflexive relations to other religious and non-religious global cultural forms. Additionally, the constructive thinker is audacious enough to seek to show that the resources of his or her religious tradition can provide decisive cultural orientation amid global cultural flows that are missing in other interpretation of the current situation: say, economic, political, media, non-governmental, environmental, scientific, or sociological forms of interpretation. This constructive task is the most daring purpose of this book and yet it arises organically out of the materials studied and the context in which we now live and think.

The third and final task of this book compliments its analysis of religious traditions and its forays into constructive religious thinking. This third task is modeled in the book as a whole more than finding explicit expression in any of its parts. That is to say, the book seeks to model a way for Muslims, Christians, and Jews to interpret and live out their faiths and practices in a global context that too often circulates images of the divine and religious orientations in life in their most violent, inhumane, and destructive forms. Is there a way to be religious that is deeply steeped in and committed to a religious tradition and yet avoid amid the challenges of the global age both fundamentalistic ideologies and vague spiritualities? By answering to that question, the book provide examples of being

Christian, being Muslim, and being Jewish that demonstrate the cultural orienting power of these three great religions in a time when global realities too often and too powerfully thwart human understanding and flourishing. In this way, the book is a testimony to the cultural orientation now possible for religious people who are fully mindful of the challenges of global times.

These three tasks undertaken in and through the examination of religious traditions, cultural contexts, and the "iconic problem" help to explain the sturcture of this volume. We begin in **Part I** with articles that explore features of the "iconic problem" itself as well as its forms and uses in Judism, Christianity, and Islam. Longstanding debates about the knowableness and also invisibility of the divine are approached historically and also constructively. In our global age marked by the whirlwind of images shaping human consciousness through the medial system, it is remarkable the insights these ancient religions bring to explore the place of "images" in human thought and life.

Part II explores "spiritual transformation" of human life in relation to images of the divine in Judaism, Islam, and Christianity. These chapters seek to understand the operative power of the divine to transform and orient human life. Importantly, the chapters show the depth and richnessness of these traditions to orient and empower spiritual transformations in ways radically distinct from vague, popular forms of "spirituality" or fundamentalistic ideologies.

Part III of the book examines a more specific form of human life, namely, the elevation of human life in relation to the divine. Here one can see how "images of the divine" are used by these traditions to think about the dyanmics of human existence and the highest human good. This process of elevation is not to a condition contrary to the meaning of being human, it is not a denial of one's humanity, as many of the critics of religion contend. Quite the inverse is the case. The elevation of live in and through divine power is in fact an elevation into true humanity; it is to be fully and profoundly alive. Taken together, the Parts of the book provide incisive examinations of the monotheistic traditions within the framework of the problems and challenges denoted by the title of this book.

3. Acknowledgements

This book would not have been possible without the support of many persons and institutions. We especially thank all of the contributors both for their incise contributions to the meetings in Heidelberg, Berlin, and Chicago within which their articles originated and also for the splendid writings that bear the fruit of our common labor. The colleagues involved came from the USA, Germany, Switzerland, and Israel. They brought in inspirations from Jewish and Christian faith traditions and Islamic Studies. Their academic fields were Jewish Studies, Jewish History and Literature, Modern Jewish Thought, Islamic Studies, Islamic Religious Studies and Sociology, Arabic Philology and Cultural Studies, Systematic Christian Theology, Christian Theological Ethics, Constructive Theology, Ecumenical Theology.

We want to thank the various institutions that supported this project. Foremost, we thank the Ministerium für Wissenschaft, Forschung und Kunst, Stuttgart, in general, and Dr. Heribert Knorr in particular for its great support in the framework of the Zukunftsoffensive IV (Winning the Future IV). Next, we express our gratitude to the Martin Marty Center for the Advanced Study of Religion at the University of Chicago Divinity School, the Research Center for International and Interdisciplinary Theology (FITT), and the Internationales Wissenschaftsforum (IWH) of the University of Heidelberg for providing financial and logistic support to this international and interdisciplinary project.

Finally, we thank those persons who gave decisive and necessary assistance to our work: Sabine Wagner und Dr. Nina Mützlitz who organized our meetings, and Charlotte Reda, David Barr, Willa Lengyel, Philip Geck, Corinna Klodt, Nick Yancey, Hajo Kenkel, and Dr. Annette Weidhas who paved the paths towards publication.

This book is also related to a larger research project now underway at the University of Chicago and Ruhr University Bochum. Through the generous support of the John Templeton Foundation, *The Enhancing Life Project*, directed by William Schweiker (Chicago) and Guenter Thomas (Bochum), is a three year research project dedicated to explore the religious, spiritual, scientific, and social meanings of "Enhancing Life." In this respect, *The Enhancing Life Project* continues and yet extends the work of this book. For further information, please visit the website *enhancinglife.uchicago.edu.*

Chicago and Heidelberg, January 2015 *W. S. and M. W.*

Part I
Divine Invisibility and Power

Invisibility and Power in Islamic Religion and Culture

The Ambiguity of Veiling

Baber Johansen

I want to draw attention in this chapter to the three levels in which the symbolic expression of power through invisibility has served, in the history of Islam, to establish links between revelation, political power and gender relations.

1. The *Qur'ān* on Jesus and Moses

On the first level, that of revelation, the *Qur'ān* discusses the relation between power and invisibility in the relation between God and His prophets. Its text refers to the Law and the prophets of Judaism as well as to Jesus' teaching as part of God's revelation to mankind. It has, in particular, focused on Moses' and Jesus' relation to God as examples for particular intimacy between God and His prophets on the one hand, the necessary respect of God's transcendence and invisibility on the other.

The *Qur'ān* recognizes Jesus as God's Word (*kalimatu llāh*), having his origin in God's word of creation[1] and being strengthened by the Holy Spirit.[2] An interpretation of Jesus as the logos of God is, therefore, possible. The *Qur'ān* underlines, on the other hand, that Jesus is made of clay[3] and that the Holy Spirit may be understood as the spirit of revelation that God sent to many prophets, Muhammad among them, but that it may be only for God to know what the Holy Spirit is.[4] The Qur'ānic Jesus emphatically denies the assumption that he claims

---

1 *Qur'ān*, Sūra 3 (Āl ʿImrān), 45, 48 and Sūra 4 (*al Nisāʾ*), 71; for a modernist interpretation of these verses see Muḥammad 'Abduh and Muḥammad Rashīd Riḍā, *Tafsīr al-Qur'ān al-ḥakīm al-shahīr bi-tafsīr al-Manār*, third edition (Cairo: 1367 h.) [henceforth *Tafsīr al-Manār*], *op. cit.* vol. III, pp. 297, 303-304, vol. VI, pp. 82-86.

2 *Qur'ān*, Sūra 2 (*al-Baqara*), 87, 253 and Sūra 5 (*al-Māʾida*), 110; see also *Tafsīr al-Manār, op. cit.*, vol. II, p. 376-377 for Sūra 2 (*al-Baqara*), 87 and vol. VII, p. 244 on Sūra 5 (*Al-Māʾida*), 110.

3 *Qur'ān*, Sūra 3 (*Āl ʿImrān*), 59.

4 *Qur'ān*, Sūra 16 (*al-Naḥl*), 2; Sūra 17 (*Al-Isrāʾ*), 85; Sūra 40 (*Al-Mu'min*), 15; Sūra 42 (*Al-Shūra*), 52.

to be God's son[5] or to participate in the divine right of being worshipped.[6] The *Qur'ān* states that Jesus was neither crucified nor killed by his enemies but rather removed to God and thus protected from persecution.[7] Jesus is thus recognized as God's Word, as being strengthened by the Holy Spirit and, at the same time, characterized as a human being, created by God from clay and being sent, like other prophets, with a revelation from his Lord. He is a prophet, a human being who does not participate in the divine except through the revelation and the signs that God gave to him.[8] Among the special signs that characterize his message is the one announcing "news of an apostle who will come after me whose name is Ahmad."[9] Proximity to, as well as distance from the Christian doctrines on Jesus are evident.

The ambition to see God, is, in the *Qur'ān*, attributed to Moses only. The Qur'ānic text takes into account the narrative of the Bible on Moses in *Exodus* and *Numbers*, but it chooses certain elements and omits others that do not seem to be acceptable in a Qur'ānic understanding of a prophet's relation to God. The chosen elements concern the spoken communication between God and Moses, the omitted elements the full or partial visibility of God. The burning bush of *Exodus* 3: 1-7 poses no problem. The *Qur'ān*, Sura 19 (*Maryam*), 51-52 tells the story as a sign for the special privilege granted to Moses, the prophet and messenger with whom God "communed in secret." *Numbers* 12: 6-8 specifies the privileged position that Moses enjoys among the Prophets in his verbal communication with God: "*Hear* these my words: When a prophet of the Lord arises among you, I make myself known to him in a vision, I *speak* with him in a dream. Not so with My servant Moses; he is trusted throughout My household. With him I *speak* mouth to mouth, plainly and not in riddles, *and he beholds the likeliness of the Lord*." *Exodus* 33: 11 uses similar terms: "The Lord would speak to Moses face to face, as one man speaks to another." The *Qur'ān* underlines this special privilege of Moses through contrasting God's general rule for His communication with His prophets to the intimacy and directness of Moses' relation to God.

God's general rule for the communication with His prophets is given in *Qur'ān*, Sura 42 (*al-Shūrā*), 51: "It is not vouchsafed to any mortal that God should speak to him except by revelation, or from behind a veil, or through a messenger sent and authorized by Him to make known His will." According to this rule, visible manifestations of God to His chosen persons do not figure among the elements through which He reveals himself.[10] Many interpretations of God's relations to His

---

5 *Qur'ān*, Sūra 19 (*Maryam*), 35-36; Sūra 5 (Al-Mā'ida), 116.

6 *Qur'ān*, Sūra 5 (*al-Mā'ida*), 116.

7 *Qur'ān*, Sūra 4 (*Al-Nisā'*), 157-58; Sūra 3 (Āl-'Imrān), 51-59.

8 *Qur'ān*, Sūra 3 (*Āl 'Imrān*), 49, 84; Sūra 4 (Al-Nisā'), 163-166, 171; Sūra 33 (Al-Aḥzāb), 7.

9 *Qur'ān*, Sūra 61 (*al-Ṣaff*), 6.

10 But see *Qur'ān*, Sūra 81 (*al-Takwīr*), 13 and Sūra 53 (*al-Najm*), 11. These verses could be read as parallels to Moses's vision of God. But they are not interpreted in this way in the exegetical texts; many commentators, among them the nineteenth-century Yemeni reformer Shawkānī, define revelation rather as "inspiration" (*ilhām)* than as vision. See

prophets that we find in the exegetical literature hold that God, while speaking to Moses directly, talked to him behind a veil. This seems rather a deduction from God's general rule than an interpretation of the Qur'ānic verses that depict God's relation with Moses. *Qur'ān*, Sura 4 (*al-Nisā'*), 164 states: "Of some apostles We have already told you, but there are others of whom We have not yet spoken. God spoke to Moses directly"[11] and *Qur'ān*, Sura 19 (*Maryam*), 51-52 refers to the story of the burning bush (*Exodus* 3: 1-7) in saying: "In the Book, tell also of Moses, who was a chosen man, an apostle, and a prophet. We called out to him from the right side of the Mountain. And when he came near We communed with him *(qarrab-nāhu)* in secret." Both verses do not refer to any veil between God and Moses.

But when it comes to the way in which *Exodus* discusses the visibility of God, the Qur'ānic text takes its distance. *Exodus* 19: 1-24 reports that when God came down on the mountain of Sinai He announced that: "I will come to you in a thick cloud, in order that the people may *hear* when I speak with you and so trust you ever after."[12] He threatened all those with death who would go up the mountain or touch the border of it "beast or man, he shall not live."[13] But in *Exodus* 24: 9-11 it is said that "Moses and Aaron, Nadab and Abihu, and seventy elders of Israel ascended; and they *saw* the God of Israel [...]. Yet He did not raise His hand against the leaders of the Israelites; they beheld God and they ate and drank." This vision of God by the Elders of Israel is not mentioned in the *Qur'ān*. Also the partial vision of God that He grants to Moses, according to *Exodus* 33: 21-23, has no place in the Qur'ānic text.

The Qur'ānic narrative of Moses vision of God rather focuses on *Exodus* 33: 17-23. On the Mountain of Sinai God promises Moses to lead the people of Israel to the Promised Land "for you have truly gained My favor and I have singled you out by name." Moses replies "Oh let me behold Your Presence!" And He answered, "I will make all My goodness pass before you, and I will proclaim before you the name LORD, and the grace that I grant and the compassion that I show. But–He said–*you cannot see My face, for man may not see Me and live.*" And the LORD said, "See, there is a place near Me. Station yourself on the rock and as My presence passes by, I will put you in a cleft of the rock and shield you with My hand until I have passed by. Then I will take My hand away and *you will see My back; but My face must not be seen.*"

Muḥammad b. ʿAlī b. Muḥammad b. ʿAlī al-Shawkānī, *Fath al-Qadīr al-jāmiʿ bayna fannay al-riwāya wa l-dirāya min ʿilm al-tafsīr* (Dār al-Wafā' li l-ṭibāʿ wa l-nashr wa l-tawzīʿ, 1415/1994) [henceforth Shawkānī, *Fatḥ*], vol. IV, pp. 522-23.

[11] Quoted from the translation of N. J. Dawood, *The Koran* (London: Penguin, 1956). The brackets in which the translator puts these words have no justification. The words are plain text in the *Qur'ān*. For a nineteenth-century interpretation see *Tafsīr al-Manār, op. cit.*, vol. IX, pp. 126-127 and vol. VI, p. 67.

[12] *Exodus* 19: 9.

[13] *Exodus* 19: 12-13, see also 19: 21-24.

The Qur'ānic narrative of this event–given in *Qur'ān*, Sura 7 (*al Aʿrāf*), 142-145–leaves no space for even a partial view of God granted to Moses. It reaches its climax in 7; 143-44:

> And when Moses came at the appointed time and His Lord talked to him, he said: "LORD, show me [Thyself] (*rabbī arīnī*) so that I may gaze at you" (*anẓur ilayka*). He replied: "You shall not see Me. But look upon the Mountain; if it remains firm upon its base, then only shall you see Me." And when the LORD manifested (*tajallā)* Himself to the Mountain, He leveled it into dust. Moses fell down senseless and when he recovered his senses, he said: "Glory be to You. Accept my repentance. I am the first of the believers." He replied: "Moses, I have chosen you of all mankind to make known My messages and My commandments. Take therefore what I have given you, and be thankful."

2. The Exegetical Literature on the Communication between God and His Prophets

The Muslim exegetical literature on these verses faces several problems. Implicit in the wish to see God in this world is Moses' attempt to make God an object of human vision. The wish to see God is interpreted, by the Muslim commentators, as a sign of disrespect for God's transcendence, a neglect of the difference between the created world and the realm of the creator. In the created world, communication between God and human beings has to rely on the words revealed by God. It is God's word through which He becomes accessible. The spreading and the interpretation of His word is, therefore, the task of the prophets. The human effort to see God implies an effort to make God an object of the human senses (other than the hearing of His words, which depends on God's choice of the hearer and leaves the human being in a passive, even if attentive role). Hearing, in Arabic as in many other languages, is linked to obedience. Such a distinction between hearing and seeing God is closely linked to obedience, is implicit in Exodus 33: 17-23 and in the *Qur'ān*. It has probably become more obvious with the growing influence of the natural sciences of Late Antiquity on Muʿtazilī and Shīʿī theology and in particular with the growing influence of Ptolemy's *Optics* on the exegetical literature.

Ptolemy's theory of vision is based on the notion of rectilinear rays sent out from the eyes until they meet their object. It depicts vision as a flux from the eyes to the external objects. In his "Introduction" to *Ptolemy's Theory of Visual Perception*, A. Mark Smith describes this flux as follows: "Issuing forth at enormous speed, the visual flux eventually strikes external objects and, in so doing, feels them visually. Thus, while it may not be an actual species of touch, sight is like touch in its basic operation [...]."[14]

---

[14] A. Mark Smith, *Ptolemy's Theory of Visual Perception. An English Translation of the Optics with Introduction and Commentary* (Philadelphia: The American Philosophical Society, 1996), vol. 86, part 2, p. 23. See also pp. 21, 25 and 37, and Smith's English translation of the Arabic text of Ptolemy's Optics, written by Amiratus Eugeny in the twelfth century,

Many Arab authors quote Ptolemy's Optics from the tenth century on.[15] Smith has suggested, with good reasons, that the founder of Arab philosophy, al-Kindī (d. 873), already used it in his optical treatise *De Aspectibus*.[16] Josef Van Ess, in his magistral work on *Theologie und Gesellschaft im 2. und 3. Jahrhundert Hidschra*, points out that the influence of Greek optics is already clearly traceable in the work of the eigth century Shīʿī theologian Hishām ibn al-Ḥakam (d. 796 in Kufa).[17] The notion that the gaze is equivalent to touching its object has thus received a scholarly grounding in theology and Optics during the eighth and the ninth century. It seems to be dominant in theology and in the exegetical literature of the ninth and tenth century. From the tenth century on, the influence of Muʿtazilī theology and Ptolemy' Optics on the Sunni exegetical literature clearly diminishes. This change is due in the first line to the increasing dominance of the Ashʿarī theology from the second half of the tenth century on. This theology upheld the hope for a vision of God by the elected in the hereafter and did not assign to science and optics a decisive role for its arguments.[18] The fact that Ibn al-Ḥaytham (965-1040) developed a new form of optics that gave more place to an intromission aspect to the theory of vision may have supported this exegetical development.[19]

---

pp. 63-64, 74-75, 81, 99, 103. For the study of vision and optics as a key to cultural history, see Gérard Simon, *Archéologie de la Vision. L'optique, le corps, la peinture* (Paris: Editions du Seuil, 2003). He also underlines "la palpation du regard antique" (pp. 68-69, 72), but with a view to understanding vision as a psychological and cultural phenomenon. He underlines, in this context, the importance to the approach of Ptolemy's Optics and vision as a means of accessing the supra-lunar sphere (pp. 86-87).

15 Smith, *Ptolemy's Theory, op. cit.*, p. 56.

16 *Ibid.*, p. 55.

17 Josef Van Ess, *Theologie und Gesellschaft im 2. und 3. Jahrhundert Hidschra vol. 1* (Berlin and New York: Walter de Gruyter, 1991), p. 345; see also Josef Van Ess, *Theologie und Gesellschaft im 2. und 3. Jahrhundert Hidschra vol. V* (Berlin and New York: Walter de Gruyter, 1993), pp. 69-70.

18 Daniel Gimaret, *La doctrine d'al-Ashari* (Paris: Cerf, 1990), chapter X: Que Dieu. est visible aux regards humains, et qu'il sera vu des croyants dans l'au-delà, pp. 329-344.

19 Ibn al-Ḥaytham (965-1040), whose optics (*manāẓir*) were translated into Latin under the title *De Aspectibus*, exerted a lasting influence on European scientists until the nineteenth century. He was the first author who brought together different strands of the theories of vision and perception in late antiquity, among them those of Ptolemy, to produce a new and coherent theory on the role of light in an intromission theory of vision and perception. See A Mark Smith, *Ptolemy's Theory of Vision, op. cit.*, pp. 6-9. In his book on *Alhacen's Theory of Visual Perception. A Critical Edition, with English Translation and Commentary, of the First Three Books of Alhacen's De Aspectibus, the Medieval Latin Version of Ibn al-Haytham's Kitāb al-Manāẓir*. Vol. One. Introduction and Latin Text (American Philosophical Society: Philadelphia, 2001), A Mark Smith has published a theoretical analysis of its cultural sources (see Introduction, pp. XV-CXVIII and Notes, pp CXIX-.CLIV) as well as a list of its Manuscripts and Editing (CLV-CLXXVII) as well as the Latin text (pp. 3-337). He shows the different models of Optics that go into Ibn al-Haytham's and Ptolemy's theories and, in particular, the role assigned to light in these theories and their sources.

Like most other exegetes, the eleventh-century Khurasani scholar Samʿānī (1035-1096), a Shāfiʿī jurist, admits that it is impossible for a human being to see God in this world: the sight would destroy not only mountains but also the human being.[20] The older exegetical tradition linked to Qatāda (d. 735) had in fact taught that Moses died at the moment when God manifested Himself to the mountain and later was resurrected.[21] Samʿānī, as before him the tenth-century exegetic authority al-Ṭabarī, holds that Moses fainted and–after having come back to his senses–repented.[22] It is implicit in his text that in this world the attempt to request the vision of God confronts the human being with a power that is extremely dangerous for him.

Samʿānī focuses on the means of communication with the divine that are licit and less risky. He interprets *Qurʾān*, Sura 7 (*al-Aʿrāf*), 143 as a meeting between God and His prophet, shielded off against the presence of Satan and the angels. In this meeting God spoke to Moses "so that He made him hear and understand" whereas Gabriel, who according to another transmission attended this meeting, did not hear anything.[23] Samʿānī focuses his interpretation on the problem of language: did God speak to Moses in His own language that neither the angels nor Satan–let alone human beings–understand but through which God and Moses could communicate, thus choosing a means of communication specific to these two and not accessible to others? One wonders how Samʿānī's interpretation of Sura 7 (*al-Aʿrāf*), 143 is connected to the theological conflict between Muʿtazilīs and Ashʿarīs on the question whether God's speech is created or uncreated.

To the moral question "How did he (Moses) ask God to see Him, knowing very well that God is not to be seen by mortals?" Samʿānī answers by quoting a religious scholar, Íasan, who said: "His desire stimulated him and so he asked the vision. Others said: he asked the vision of his LORD because he thought that it is admissible in this base world."[24] The question touches on another conflict between Ashʿarīs and Muʿtazilīs. The Muʿtazilīs use *Qurʾān*, Sura 7 (*al-Aʿrāf*), 143 as proof for their doctrine that human beings will not see God, neither in this nor in the next world, because he is unlike the human creatures and cannot become the object of their sense perception. Samʿānī holds that in the hereafter those saved in Paradise will enjoy the *visio beatifica*. He insists that God's answer "You shall

Gerard Simon, *Archeologie de la Vision, op. cit.*, pp. 80-164, has analyzed the differences between the cultural, psychological, and philosophical dimensions between Ptolemy's and Ibn al-Haytham's systems of optics and vision.

20 Abul-Muẓaffar Manṣūr b. Aḥmad b. ʿAbd al-Jabbār al-Marwazī al-Samʿānī, *Tafsīr al-Qur'ān* (ed. Abū Tamīm Yāsiribn Ibrāhīm) [Madār al-waṭan li l-nashr (maṭābiʿal-Fusṭāṭ) 1418/1997], vol. I (*min surat al-māʾida ila Hūd*), pp. 212-213.

21 Abū Jaʿfar Muḥammad b. Jarīr al-Ṭabarī, *Tafsīr al-Ṭabarī al-musammā jāmiʿ al-bayān fī taʾwīl al-Qurʾān* (Beirut: Dār al-kutub al-ʿilmiyya, 1992/1414h.), vol. VI, p. 53. See also Samʿānī, *op. cit.*, p. 213.

22 Ṭabarī., *Tafsīr, op. cit.*, vol. VI, p. 53.

23 Samʿānī, *Tafsīr, op. cit.*, vol. I (*min sūrat al-māʾida ilā Hūd*), p. 212.

24 *Ibid.*, p. 212. As to the Íasan quoted in the text, neither Samʿānī nor the editor of his work give any specification of this scholar's identity.

not see Me" does not imply a reproach made by God to Moses, but simply means "neither at present nor in this base world," but that it does not mean "I will not be seen by you" ever.[25]

The twelfth-century Maḥmūd ibn ʿUmar al-Zamakhsharī (1074-1143) who lived and worked in Khwarizm, produced an exegetical work on the *Qurʾān*[26] along the lines of Muʿtazilī theology that has been widely recognized in the Muslim tradition as a philological and intellectual masterpiece of exegesis[27] but strongly criticized for its theological leanings. In his exegesis Zamakhsharī explicitly uses arguments derived from Greek optics in order to support Mu'tazilī forms of reasoning. Like Sam'ānī he focuses on God's speech, God's invisibility and the moral justification of Moses' request.

Zamakhsharī interprets *Qurʾān*, Sura 7 (*al-Aʿrāf*), 142-45 first of all as a proof for the thesis that God created his own speech. He insists that God spoke to Moses "without intermediary, much as the king speaks."[28] That he spoke to him (implies) that He created the speech through which He speaks in some bodies much as He created it as writing on the tablet (referring to *Qurʾān*, Sura 85 [*al-Buruj*], 22). According to one recital, Moses heard the speech (of God) from all directions. According to Ibn ʿAbbās, "[...God] spoke to him for forty days and forty nights and wrote the tablets for him."[29] For the Muʿtazilī exegete, Zamakhshari, the Qurʾānic confirmation that God spoke to Moses is a proof that God created His own speech and thus also the *Qurʾān*, so that He could talk directly and without any intermediary with His prophet. The human sense of vision does not allow a communication between God and humans. Discussing vision as sense perception, Zamakhsharī bases his argument on *Qurʾān*, Sura 7 (*al-Aʿrāf*), 143 and the difference between "make me see" and "so that I may gaze at You." He argues that "make me see" means "manifest yourself" and is, in fact, the condition for Moses being able to gaze at God. His request is thus for a vision that leads to perception and not for a gaze that is not accompanied by perception. God has clearly answered Moses' request in the negative. Zamakhsharī then explains why: the objects of perception have to be material bodies or accidents related to these bodies, such as color, form or smell. As God is neither a body nor an accident on a body He cannot be perceived through the human sense of vision.[30]

---

[25] Ibid. Vol. I, p. 212.

[26] Abu l-Qāsim Maḥmūd ibn ʿUmar al-Zamakhsharī, *Al-Kashshāf ʿan ḥaqāʾiq al-tanzīl waiec-ʿuyūn al-aqwāl fī wujūh al-taʾwīl* (Beirut: Dār al-kitāb al-ʿarabī, 1947), verse 143, vol. II, pp.151-152.

[27] On Zamakhsharī's status in Muslim exegesis of the Qurʾān see Ignaz Goldziher, *Die Richtungen der Islamischen Koranauslegung* (Leiden: E.J. Brill, 1952), pp. 117-177.

[28] *Al-Kashshāf, op. cit.*, on verse 143, vol. II, p. 152.

[29] Companion of the Prophet, d. 686 or 688. He is considered to be the leading religious scholar of his generation and a pioneer in creating Qurʾānic exegesis, see Goldziher, *op. cit.* (note 27 above), pp. 32, 65-77.

[30] Zamakhsharī, Kashshāf, op. cit., vol. II, pp. 151-153.

Remains the question: if Moses knew all this, how could he ask for the privilege of visual perception of God, a privilege which he knew God could not and would not grant him? Moses, according to *Qurʾān*, Sura 2 (*al-Baqara*), 55, reproached the people of Israel for having asked to see God as a proof for Moses' mission. Zamakhsharī concludes from this verse that Moses–knowing well that God would never grant such a request–asked the Lord to enable him to see Him. God "spoke to Moses only and they [the elders of Israel] were listening. When they heard the speech of the Lord of Glory they wanted that He *show Moses His essence (dhātahu)* so that they could *see* it with him. *This desire was based on a wrong analogy* [between speech and seeing]." [31]Seeing is so different from speech that the one cannot be explained in the terms of the other. To see God is unconceivable, to hear His speech is a gift given to many prophets.

According to Zamakhsharī, Moses asked God the capacity to see Him, because he thought that God would refuse his request and once the elders of Israel would hear that this request was refused to a prophet, it would be clear to them that for the same reason their request also had to be refused, "because the messenger is the leader of his community and [the commands] addressed to him [...] return to them." The crude anthropomorphism that, according to Zamakhsharī, is contained in the demand "so that I gaze at you" shows that Moses only interprets their suggestion and quotes their utterance. As Zamakhsharī formulates, Moses was far above turning "God into a visible object facing the sense of vision," because he was by far superior to all the theologians in the knowledge of God. [32]

The negation of the future vision of God "You shall never see me" is, through its linguistic form, extended to eternity.[33] Moses, after he recuperates his consciousness, revokes his request to see God and declares himself to be the first one who believes that God is not an object of vision and not accessible to any sense perception. Through his response, God has manifested His majesty and the fact that he is not accessible to human vision and not willing to become its object. Zamakhsharī clearly assigns an important place to the argument, drawn from Greek Optics, that view presupposes direction and objects that are bodies or accidents. From this argument he draws the conclusion that human beings can never see God.

In the centuries that follow, the debates about the visibility of God remain focused on *Qurʾān*, Sura 7 (*al-Aʿrāf*), 142-145 and on the elements discussed between Zamakhshari and Samʿānī. The conclusions drawn from these elements differ. The fifteenth century Damascene Hanbali Ibn ʿĀdil draws, from Moses' request, the conclusion that God can be seen, because otherwise Moses would not have asked him for it.[34] He admits that the dissolution of the mountain into dust proves that "nobody can resist God's vision unless God fortifies him through His

---

31 Ibid., vol. II, p.153, on verse 143.

32 Ibid., vol. II, pp. 153-154, on verse 143.

33 *Ibid.*, vol. II, pp. 154-155, on verse 143.

34 Ibn ʿĀdil, *Al-Lubāb f ʿulūm al-kitāb* (Beirut: Dār al-kutub al-ʿilmiyya, 1998), vol. IX, p. 300.

help and support."[35] He interprets this part of the verse as an "exaltation of the importance of [God's] vision."[36]

Against Zamakhsharī–whom he quotes extensively–Ibn ʿĀdil defends, like other Ashʿari or Hanbali authors from the eleventh century on, the *visio beatifica* of God in the hereafter. Moses' repentance concerns only his demand to see God in this base world. He asks God to forgive him for having asked the privilege of seeing Him without first waiting for God's permission to ask such a favor. He is "the first to believe that God cannot be seen in this base world or that it is not admissible to ask Him such a favor without His permission."[37]

3. The Invisibility of Satan and the *Jinn*

It is not only the creator whose power requires invisibility. *Qurʾān*, Sura 7 (*al-Aʿrāf*), 27 states: "Children of Adam! Let not Satan deceive you, as he deceived your parents out of Paradise. He stripped them of their garments to reveal them their nakedness. He and his minions see you whence you cannot see them. We have made the devils the guardians over the unbelievers."

Ibn ʿĀdil summarizes the debate between Sunnīs and Muʿtazilīs in the following words:

> The adherents to the Sunna of the Prophet say: they see the human beings, because God, may He be exalted, created in their eyes a perception. The human beings do not see them, because God, be He exalted, did not create this perception in their eyes.
>
> The Muʿtazila said: the aspect [that allows to understand why] the human beings do not see the *jinn* lies in the thinness (*riqqa)* of the *jinns*' bodies and in their fineness (*laṭāfa)*. And the aspect [that renders comprehensible why] the *jinn* see the human beings lies in the solidity *(kathāfa*) of the bodies of the human beings. The aspect [that renders comprehensible why] the *jinn* see each other is that God, be He exalted, strengthens and reinforces the visual rays *(shuʿāʾ abṣār*) of the *jinn*. If He, be He exalted, would sharpen the strength of our gaze in the same way, we would also see them. According to this [proposition], the [capacity] of the humans to see the *jinn* depends, according to the Muʿtazila, either on an increase in the solidity of the *jinns*' bodies or an increase in the strength of the vision of the human beings.
>
> His [God's] saying "whence you cannot see them" points to [the fact that] the human beings do not see the *jinn* because His saying "whence you do not see them" comprises the future times.[38]

According to Ibn ʿĀdil's proposition the Sunni interpretation of *Qurʾān*, Sura 7 (*al-Aʿrāf*), 27 has no relation to Greek Optics. God creates in the eyes of the *jinn* a perception and does not do the same in the eyes of the human beings. The way in which perception is reached through vision is not discussed. It is the reference

35 *Ibid.*, p. 301.

36 *Ibid.*, p. 302.

37 *Ibid.*, p. 303.

38 *Ibid.*, vol. IV, p. 77.

to God's creation that determines and explains the whole process. Ibn ʿĀdil's presentation of the Muʿtazilī position describes it in terms of Greek optics. The human beings as objects of the *jinns*' vision are sufficiently solid to resist the visual rays of the *jinn* and Satan and thus to become perceptible. The thinness and the fineness of the *jinns*' bodies does not resist the visual rays of the human beings, therefore the *jinn* are not visible. As the visual rays of the *jinn* are stronger than those of the human beings they can also see each other. Within the framework of God's creation, visibility is the result of the relation between the strength of the visual rays and the solidity of the objects to be perceived. Greek optics seem to remain a dominant reference in the *Muʿtazili* position.

God's, Satan's and the *jinns*' invisibility shows that their power and their immaterial constitution make it impossible for human vision to perceive them in this world. If there is a protocol of the gaze concerning God, Satan and the *jinn*, it can be resumed in one proposition: under the conditions of this base world, human vision cannot aspire to make them their object. If human beings, be they God's preferred prophets and lawgivers, request to see Him they commit a transgression and consequently risk their life.[39]

4. The Invisible Ruler

Ibn Khaldūn in his *Muqaddima* describes the process in which rulers who come to seize power based on widespread tribal and ethnic solidarity tend, after their power has been established, to become inaccessible to the common people and restrict access to them to a small group of friends and counselors. His examples cover mostly caliphs and rulers of empires. My argument in this section also refers to this category of rulers, not to those whose rule remains restricted to one country or one ethnic group. Ibn Khaldun refers to the founder of the Umayyad dynasty, Muʿāwiya, and his successors as the first Muslim rulers who created a court ceremonial that excluded all those from the presence of the caliph who were not allowed by the chamberlain or "veiler" *(ḥājib)* of the caliph to visit him. Ibn Khaldūn states that these restrictions were reinforced under the Abbasids and finally ended in later dynasties in the seclusion of the ruler from his subjects. He attributes this development to the jealous intrigues of the small group of intimates of the ruler who tried to gain complete control over the prince so as to be able to manipulate him in their interest.[40]

Jean Sauvaget's studies of the link between Umayyad court ceremonial and the architecture of Umayyad Palaces and Mosques, and Gulru Necipoğlu's analysis of the relation between the Ottoman court ceremonial and the architecture of the

[39] It is true that Ibn Taymiyya (1263-1328), *Al-tafsīr al-kabīr* (Beirut: Dār al-kutub al-ʿilmiyya, no date), vol. IV, p. 284, holds that saints and pious Muslims may sometimes see them. But he does not give any explanation for his statement.

[40] Ibn Khaldūn, *The Muqaddimah. An Introduction to History*, trans. Franz Rosenthal (Princeton: Princeton University Press, 1967), vol. II, pp. 112-113.

Ottoman Topkapi Palace and its mosque, strongly support, extend and complete Ibn Khaldūn's intuitive thesis, as far as the relation of caliphs of Muslim empires are concerned. Jean Sauvaget's text on "The Mosque and the Palace"[41] shows how the Umayyad Palace architecture serves the organization and preservation "of a highly developed ceremonial which, from the early days of the dynasty, regulated relations between the Commander of the Faithful and his subjects."[42] Visitors had to receive the permission of the chamberlain (*ḥājib*) in order find access to the Caliph. "In the reception hall, the caliph sat at the end and along the axis of the room [...], facing the principal entrance [...]. In front of him hung a curtain and he spoke to his visitors from behind this curtain."[43]

When the Caliph left his palace for the mosque he would enter into a space that had the same structure: an apse with two aisles, a highly ritualized meeting space that was prepared for the central role to be played by the Caliph as speaker who sat on the *minbar* or as the sovereign who took his place in the *maqṣūra* that separated him from the mass of the mosque visitors and allowed him to receive selected guests in the space reserved for him. Sauvaget underlines "the similarities between the *maqṣūra* and the terminal apse of the audience hall" and he suggests that "we are justified in comparing it with the curtain suspended in front of the apse of the audience hall in order to 'separate' the monarch and his intimates from the rest of the gathering. [...] It seems to have been intended more as a means by which to enhance the majesty and prestige of the leader rather than to assure his security."[44] Sauvaget thus describes the mosque as the public analogy to the private audience hall, both structured in a way that allows the Caliph to control the ceremonial, to separate himself and his guests from the crowd, in a special order that underlines–through his seclusion–his majesty and his dominant role for the ceremonial.

In her magistral work on the Ottoman Topkapi Palace, built by Sultan Mehmet II after the conquest of Constantinople (1453), Gülru Necipoğlu shows how the architecture and the court ceremonial focus on the Sultan's segregation.[45] Under the influence of Persian and Byzantine models, the site of the Palace is chosen far from other buildings so as to render the imperial seclusion of the Sultan not only possible but meaningful.[46] Necipoğlu summarizes the argument of the sixteenth-century court historian Bidlisi for the ceremonial's focus on the seclusion of the Sultan in an isolated palace. Bidlisi underlines that the Sultan's isolation "was made necessary by the sacredness of the sultan, not for his safety:

---

41 Jean Sauvaget, "The Mosque and the Palace," in *Early Islamic Art and Architecture,* vol. 23, edited by Jonathan M. Bloom, in *The Formation of the Classical Islamic World,* general editor Lawrence I. Conrad (Aldershot and Burlington, VT: Ashgate, 2002), pp. 109-147.

42 *Ibid.*, pp. 116-17.

43 *Ibid.*, pp. 118-119.

44 *Ibid.*, pp. 140-141, see also p. 144.

45 Gülru Necipoğlu, *Architecture, Ceremonial, and Power: The Topkapı Palace in the Fifteenth and Sixteenth Centuries* (Cambridge, MA, and London: The Architectural History Foundation Inc., New York, New York and the MIT Press).

46 *Ibid.*, pp. 15, 247-49.

this spiritual being, endowed with divine light, could not possibly dwell among ordinary mortals in the populous center of the city. It was fitting that his dwelling place be a sanctified enclosure, cleansed of impurity and resembling the heavenly realm."[47]

Necipoğlu shows how, from the end of the fifteenth to the end of the sixteenth centuries, this ideal of a secluded and inaccessible Sultan was put into practice.[48] "By the last quarter of the sixteenth century–she writes–the principle of royal seclusion had been carried to an extreme with the expansion of the harem quarters, into which the sultan voluntarily retreated,"[49] and "Besides the eunuchs, the sultan was the only person who could move freely and mediate between the strictly drawn gender boundaries of the third court, a rule that accentuated his role as master of the house. The spatial, architectural, and functional organization of the royal household was unified under one principle: the omnipotence of the sultan."[50]

The court ceremonial, *the kanunname*, under which these sultans lived had been developed in its codified form, by Mehmet II, who is thus the author of the code and the builder of the palace.[51] The palace architecture and the ceremonial code correspond perfectly to Mehmet II's concept of the role of the secluded, omnipotent and omniscient ruler and controller of the empire's power elite. In the *kanunname* he institutes a "chamber of petitions" which would allow him to watch his *vezirs* and judges in the performance of their tasks, while he himself would be hidden from their view. He wrote: "First, let there be built a Chamber of Petitions. My sacred Majesty sitting behind the curtain, let my viziers and army judges and financial officers enter into my imperial presence with their petitions four times a week."[52]

Not only is the Ottoman sultan hidden from the view of the common people and the power elite, he cannot even be reached by their words. From the middle of the sixteenth century on, signs *(isharet)* replace spoken words in the communication of sultan and palace staff. The sanctification, invisibility, one-sided control of the sultan is underlined by the fact that words cannot be spoken to him but have to be replaced by signs.[53]

The protocol of the gaze formulated in the *kanunname* withdrew the sultan from the view of the common people as well as that of the highest dignitaries, it sanctified him through this invisibility, it drew a curtain between him and the rest of mankind and used this curtain to underline his rank as the invisible, omnipotent and omniscient controller of the empire's elite. At the rare occasion when the sultan showed himself to his subjects he rode in stately royal processions through

---

47 *Ibid.*, p. 16.

48 *Ibid.*, pp. 21-22, see also p. 26.

49 *Ibid.*, p. 95.

50 *Ibid.*, p. 96.

51 *Ibid.*, pp. 16-24.

52 *Ibid.*, p. 19, see also pp. 58-59, 85ff.

53 *Ibid.*, pp. 26, 28.

the city providing to the people the opportunity to see him in all his splendor and to submit petitions to him.[54] The court ceremonial clearly sees in the Sultan's isolation from his subjects an instrument to enhance his sacralization.

The Muslim court ceremonials, the Umayyad as well as the Ottoman, and Persian and their implicit reference to the problem of the visibility of God was used in sixteenth-century Europe as a justification of a French court ceremonial that withdrew the monarch from the view of the people and had a strong influence on the discussion of its political function in Early modern Europe. On this point, I am referring to the work of one of the most influential political thinkers of Europe in the sixteenth century, Jean Bodin (1530-1596).

Jean Bodin,[55] the great theoretician of the sixteenth century France state, not only suggested, for political reasons, a drastic reduction of contacts between the ruler and his subjects, but he did so in referring to the relation between God and Moses and in giving as good examples of invisible rulers the oriental kingdoms of his time. Bodin feared that if the ruler could be regularly observed by his subjects, they would follow his bad examples[56] and, even if he did not give them a bad example, the daily contact with them would diminish his awe and reputation.[57] The ruler should, therefore, follow God's example:

> It seems that this great God, this sovereign prince of the world, showed the [human] princes, who are His true images, how to communicate with [their] subjects: He only communicates with the human beings through visions and dreams and only to very small number of the elected and the most perfect. And when He published, *by His voice* His Decalogue He showed His fire [rising] up to the sky and He made tremble the mountains with his lightning and thunder with such a frightening sound of trumpets that the people, putting their faces on the ground, prayed that God might not speak to them any more [...]. If, therefore, the wise [human] Prince in the treatment of his subjects has to imitate the wisdom of God in the government of this world, he has to expose himself very rarely to the view of his subjects and [if he does so, he has to do it] with a majesty appropriate to his greatness and power. Nonetheless, he has to choose dignified men, necessarily in small numbers, in order to, in addition, declare his will and instantly to shower his subjects with his graces and favors.[58]

---

54 *Ibid.*, p. 30.

55 Jean Bodin, *Les Six Livres de La République* (Paris: Fayard, 1986), vol. IV, pp. 155-160.

56 *Ibid.*, vol. IV, pp. 155-56.

57 *Ibid.*, vol. IV, 157.

58 *Ibid.*, vol. IV, pp. 157-158. The original says: "Et semble que ce grand Dieu souverain Prince du monde, a monstré aux Princes humains, qui sont ses vrayes images, comme il se faut communiquer aux subjects: car il ne se communique aux homes que par visions et songes, et seulement à bien petit nombre des esleus, et plus parfaicts. Et quand il publia de sa voix le décalogue, faisant voir son feu jusqu'au ciel, et de ses foudres et tonnerres trembler les montaignes, avec un son si effroyable de trompettes, que le people pria se tapissant sur sa face, que Dieu ne parlast plus à eux [...]. Si donc le sage Prince doit au maniement de ses subjects imiter la sagesse de Dieu au gouvernement de ce monde, il faut qu'il se mette peu souvent en veuë des subjects, et avec une majesté convenable à sa grandeur et puissance: et néanmoins qu'il face chois des homes dignes, qui ne peuvent ester qu'en

Jean Bodin not only quotes the example of Moses on Mount Sinai, he also refers to the Oriental kings, "the great kings of Ethiopia, Mongolia (Tartarie), Persia, Turkey that do not even want their subjects to gaze at them directly, and still are not so much feared for their power as for the majesty they keep when they show themselves to their subjects." Rejecting the objection that such an isolation of the ruler from his subjects may be appropriate for Oriental peoples but is not appropriate for the peoples of the West, he states:

> If one objects that the peoples of the East and the South have to be governed in that way but not those of the West and the North, I answer that in this respect all is one (*que c'est tout un pour ce regard*). We know well enough that the kings of England, Sweden, Denmark and Poland preserve much more their greatness in face of their subjects than the kings of France. The king of Moscow does this even more than the others. In spite of this, they are not less but may be even more obeyed.[59]

The protocols of the gaze that regulate the subjects' gaze at their rulers in sixteenth-century France and the contemporary Ottoman Empire are based on a concept of majesty that is built on the Bible's and the *Qur'ān*'s representation of God's relation to Moses and on the admiration of Western courts for the political successes of the Ottoman and the Safavid courts. What is common to them is that they find a religious justification for the court practices in biblical narratives–reformulated in the *Qur'ān*–and a practical justification for focusing on the cult of the ruler in the references to the practice of Oriental courts. As Cornell Fleischer has shown, during the sixteenth century such common references of court cultures in France, the Ottoman Empire and Iran can be shown to represent new forms of a political universalism that transcends religious limits. What is obvious in all of them is the very conscious effort to construct a ceremonial practice that embodies an elaborate protocol of the gaze based on enhancing the majesty of the ruler through the diminution of their visibility for their subjects.[60]

---

petit nombre, pour declarer sa volonté au surplus, et incessamment combler ses sujets de ses graces et faveurs."

59 *Ibid.*, vol. IV, pp. 159-60. The original says: "Grands Rois d'Ethiopie, de Tartarie, de Perse, et de Turquie, qui ne veulent pas mesmes que les subjects jettent la veuë droit sur eux, et ne sont pas tant redoutez pour leur puissance, que pour la majesté qu'ils tiennent quand ils se montrent aux subjets. Et si on dit que les peoples d'Orient et de Midy se doyent ainsi gouverner, et non pas ceux d'Occident et de Septentrion: je dis que c'est tout un pour ce regard: car on sçait assez que les Rois d'Angleterre, Suede, Dannemarch, Polongne tiennent beaucoup plus leur grandeur envers les subjects, que les Rois de France: et le Roy de Moschovie plus encore que les autres, et ne sont pas moins, et peut ester plus obeïs."

60 Cornell H. Fleischer, "The Lawgiver as Messiah: The Making of the Imperial Image in the Reign of Süleymān", in Süleymân The Magnificent and His Time, edited by Gilles Veinstein (Paris: Ecole des Hautes Etudes en Sciences Sociales, 1992), pp.159-177, see in particular p. 167. See also Cornell Fleischer, "Ancient Wisdom and New Sciences. Prophecies at the Ottoman Court in the Fifteenth and Sixteenth Centuries" in *The Book of Omens*, edited by M. Farhad and S. Bagci (London: Thames and & Hudson, 2009), pp. 241-242.

5. The Gaze in Gender Relations: The Shame-Zone Construction

The classical *fiqh* created a protocol of the gaze for the seclusion, inaccessibility and ritual segregation of women. Does this approach imply that women, in analogy to the ruler and his subjects, represent a power the unveiling of which is dangerous for the women who are unveiled and the men who see them?

Because this approach sounds counterintuitive I will start with a description of the rules that constitute the protocol of the gaze concerning women. The *Qur'ān* gives three basic rules: in Sura 24 (*al-Nur*), 30-31 it tells men and women that if they fear temptation they should lower their eyes instead of ogling at persons of the other sex. The jurists of all schools render the sense explicit: if men or women fear temptation when looking too closely at the other gender, they should lower their eyes and look away. As an eleventh-century Central-Asian Hanafi jurist put it, the text of the *Qur'ān* requires men to preserve moral discipline in their gaze on the bodies of the other sex: "The gaze at these bodies [of unrelated women] is only licit if the man knows that he will not desire [her] if he looks and if he has no doubt that he will not [desire her]. But if he knows that he will desire [her] or if he thinks so, he is not allowed to look *because the covetous gaze is a sort of fornication (nauʿ zinā).*"[61] If, on the other hand, men and women can control their urges and emotions they can licitly look at each other.

In Sura 33 (*al-Ahzab*), 53 the *Qur'ān* underlines the claim of the Prophet's wives to social distance and distinction and commands believers who want to talk to them in the house of the Prophet, to do so from behind a curtain.
A general command is given to all Muslim women in Sura 33 (*al-Ahzab*), 59:

> O Prophet! Tell thy wives and daughters, and the believing women, that they should cast their outer garments over their persons (when outside the house): that is most convenient, that they should be known (as women of social standing) and not molested. And God is Oft-Forgiving, Most Merciful.

On the basis of these Qur'ānic verses, the Muslim jurists have construed a detailed system of rules that settles the way in which men and women may look at each other under different circumstances. In the following text I will describe this system based on the teaching of the generally recognized four Sunni law schools giving special preference to the Hanafi school, comparing it, whenever necessary, to the teaching of other schools of Sunni Islamic law.

The Hanafi school is the oldest and the most widespread of the Sunni law schools. Its jurists distinguish rules that apply to same-gender-relations (*mujānasa*) from those concerning relations between different genders. Same-gender-rules concern the gaze of men on men and of women on women. Men are

---

[61] Abū Bakr Muḥammad b. Aḥmad b. Abī Sahl al-Sarakhsī, *Kitāb al-Mabsūṭ* (Beirut: Dār al-maʿrifa li l-ṭibāʿa wa l-nashr, 1398/1978), vol. X, 148; see also Kasani, *Badāʾiʿ al-ṣanāʾiʿ*, *op. cit.*, vol. V, pp. 120-124 on this condition for most forms of the licit gaze of men on women and vice versa.

allowed to look at all parts of the bodies of other men, and women on all parts of other women, except on the zone between navel and knee. This zone is considered to constitute the shame zone (*'awra*) of both genders and ought, therefore, not to be visible neither to members of the same nor of the other gender.[62] The rare exceptions have to be justified through undisputable necessity (*ḍarūra*).[63] The general rule holds that what can licitly be seen can also licitly be touched and what ought to remain invisible also ought not to be touched.[64] Exceptions to this rule will be discussed below.

The same-gender rules suggest a fundamental similarity between the genders: they share the same shame zone that normally remains inaccessible to the gaze and the touching of all other persons. It seems as if the legal norm were based on a biological quality inscribed in the bodies. The only problem is constituted by the hermaphrodites: should they be integrated into the male gender or

---

62 For the shame zone between navel and knee see Sarakhsī, *Mabsūṭ, op. cit.*, vol. X, pp. 146-147; Kāsānī, *Badā'iʿ al-ṣanā'iʿ, op. cit.*, vol. V, pp. 123-124; Muḥammad Amīn al-shahīr bi-Ibn ʿĀbidīn, *Radd al-muḥtār ʿalā al-durr al-mukhtār sharḥ tanwīr al-abṣār* (Cairo: no date) (1307h.) vol. I, p. 296. The Shāfiʿī school of law holds that in same-gender rules the male and the female shame zone is basically identical (except for the integration of the navel in the shame zone), see Abū Zakariyyā' Yaḥyā Ibn Sharaf Al-Nawawī, *Al-Majmūʿ sharḥ al-Muhadhdhab* (Cairo: Maṭbaʿat al-ʿĀṣima, no date), publisher Zakariyyā ʿAlī Yūsuf, vol. I, p. 185, see also Muḥammad al-Shirbīnī, *Mughnī al-Muḥtāj ilā maʿrifat alfāẓ al-minhāj* (Cairo: sharikat maktabat wa-maṭbaʿa Muṣṭafāal-Bābī al-Ḥalabī, 1377h./1958 c.e.), vol. I, p. 185.

63 Kāsānī, *Badā'iʿ al-ṣanā'iʿ, op. cit.*, vol. V, p. 122, states that witnesses and judges are entitled to gaze at the face of free women to whom they are neither related by kinship nor by marriage, even if they assume that through the gaze they will be motivated to desire these women. This is a case of necessity, because otherwise women cannot be identified before the court. Kāsānī, *ibid.*, vol. V, p. 123 also states that circumcision and medical treatment of wounds situated in the shame zone, justify the circumciser's or the doctor's gaze on the shame zone between navel and knee. In vol. V, p. 124, Kāsānī states that the midwife who helps to give birth to a child or collects the evidence for the virginity of a woman who claims to be married to an impotent man or of a slave woman who has been bought under the condition that she be a virgin, has the right to gaze at the sex of women. It is only when no woman knowledgeable in the art of healing can be found for a woman patient whose life is in danger or who suffers unbearable pain, that a man can look at the female shame zone, but he is only allowed to uncover the situation of the wound and he has to turn away his gaze as much as possible. See also ʿUthmān ibn ʿAlī al-Zaylaʿī, *Tabyīn al-ḥaqā'iq sharḥ kanz al-daqā'iq* (Beirut: Dār al-maʿrifa li l-ṭibāʿa wa l-nashr [reprint of the Cairo edition of 1315h. (1313 h?)]), vol. VI, pp. 17-18.

64 Sarakhsī, *Mabsūṭ, op. cit.*, vol. X, pp. 146-147, 149, 153; Kasani, *Kitab badā'iʿ al-ṣanā'iʿ fī tartīb al-sharā'iʿ* (Cairo, 1356h), vol. V, pp. 123-124. This basic rule applies to the relations between husband and wife, master and slave concubine as well as between men and the slave women of other proprietors, see: Shaybānī, *Kitāb al-Aṣl, op. cit.*, vol. III, p. 50; Ibn al-Humām, *Sharḥ fatḥ al-qadīr* (Cairo, 1356 h.), vol. VIII, pp. 100, 102, 107.

the female gender? Both opinions are held by Hanafi jurists and some also hold that they belong to neither sex.[65]

6. The Seven Categories of Women

As soon as one enters the debate on how men and women are allowed to look at each other and how women have to prepare for men gazing at them, the simplicity of the same-gender-rules gives way to a normative system of confusing complexity. Simple analogies hardly exist anymore. The tenth-century Baghdadi Hanafi jurist, Abu l-Ḥusayn al-Karkhī (d. 981 in Baghdad) therefore, has put the rules on gazing and touching into a separate chapter on "Prohibition and permissibility" *(al-ḥaẓr wa l-ibāḥa)*. Hanafis of a later periods like the eleventh-century Sarakhsī and the twelfth-century Kāsānī follow him in this arrangement: they discuss the problems of gaze and touching (*al-naẓar wa l-mass*) in a special chapter under the title *istiḥsān*.[66] This word indicates "legal preference" and it is normally used to justify legal solutions that deviate from the dominant forms of analogy. It seems to me that the choice of this chapter title indicates precisely this: that the construction of legal norms by analogy, an otherwise widely recognized legal method, often has to be abandoned in this chapter for other normative solutions for which justifications have to be found case by case.

The male shame zone does not change when the jurists proceed from the same-gender-rules to those in which one gender gazes at the other. It remains the same for free men and for male slaves. But women cease to constitute one category in the rules on the gaze between genders. Kāsāni, the most systematic mind among the Hanafi jurists of the classical period has the following to say on this aspect of the gaze:

> As far as the [different] kinds of prohibited and permissible acts that are grouped together in this [book on Istiḥsān] are concerned, we say—and success resides in God-the prohibitions grouped together in this book are, in principle, two kinds. One kind [are those that] are to be respected with regard to men and women together (*nawʿun tathbutu ḥurmatuhu fī ḥaqqi l-rijāli wa l-nisāʾi jamīʿan*) and another kind [concerns those] to be respected with regard to men and from which women are excluded. As [to those] that have to be respected with regard to men and to women, some of them have already been mentioned in the appropriate places in the [preceding] books and we are not going to repeat them [here]. We will mention what has not been mentioned in the [preceding] books. We begin with the same issue with which Muḥammad [ibn

[65] Kāsānī, *Badāʾiʿ al-ṣanāʾiʿ*, *op. cit.*, vol. V, pp. 122-123 treats them as men; Ibn ʿĀbidīn, *Radd al-muḥtār*, *op. cit.*,vol. I, pp. 296-297 as women. Others hold that they cannot be integrated into any gender. Shirbīnī, *Mughnī al-muḥtāj*, *op.cit.*, vol. I, p. 230, holds that hermaphrodites have the same status as women concerning the public prayer: they should not be forbidden to attend the communal prayer but it is better when they stay at home.

[66] For Karkhī and Sarakhsī see Sarakhsī, *Mabsūṭ*, *op. cit.*, vol. X, p. 145; see also Kāsānī, *Badāʾiʿ al-ṣanāʾiʿ*, *op. cit.*, vol. V, p. 118.

> al-Ḥasan] al-Shaybānī[67] began the book: the respect for [the rules on] the gaze and the touching. The discussion of it (*wa l-kalām fīhā*) is divided in three parts. One of them on that what is permissible and forbidden for the man [to see and touch] of the woman and for the woman of the man. The second [part] concerns the explanation of that which is permissible and forbidden for the man [in seeing and touching] another man. The third [part] [treats] what is permissible and forbidden for the woman to see and touch of another woman. As far as the first one is concerned, one cannot reach knowledge of it before one knows the [different] types of women. We say—and success resides in God—in this chapter women consist of seven kinds.[68]

Kāsānī's seven different categories of women are distinguished through their social and legal status, through their legal relations (kinship, in-laws, slaves etc.) with the men who look at them, and through the situations in which the gaze takes place. In other words, these categories define women through their relations to men. I change the sequence in which Kāsānī enumerates the seven categories[69] so as to begin with women whose kinship degrees to men prohibit marriage and sex between them. I continue with distant relatives whom men can marry and then introduce the category of "unrelated women" (*ajnabiyyāt*) who have no kinship relation to the men who look at them and from among whom men, therefore, can freely choose their marriage partners. I conclude with the women who are slaves of other owners. These slave women may qualify as marriage partners for free men and male slaves.

1. Men are forbidden by law to marry women who are closely related to them by blood relationship. Forbidden women (*maḥārim*) of this kind are the mother and her female ancestors, the sisters, the daughters, the aunts on the maternal or the paternal side, the son's and the daughter's daughters and their descendents. These women, if free, continue of course to be marriage partners for other men to whom they are "unrelated" (*ajnabiyyāt*).

---

67 Muḥammad ibn al-Ḥasan al-Shaybānī (d. 805) is one of the three jurists who are considered to be the founders of the Hanafi school of law, the other two being Abū Ḥanīfa and Abū Yūsuf.

68 Kāsānī, *Badāʾiʿ al-ṣanāʾiʿ*, *op.cit.*, vol. V, p. 118.

69 Kāsānī, *ibid.*, pp. 118-123 lists the seven categories of women in the following sequence: 1. Married women, pp.118-119; 2. slave women (and concubines), pp. 119-120; 3. women who are so closely related to men by blood relationship that they cannot marry them, pp. 120-121; 4. women who for other reasons (kinship resulting from foster relations, affinity) are so closely related to men that they cannot marry them, p. 121; 5. slave women of other male or female owners p. 121; 6. free women *(ajnabiyyāt)* unrelated to the men who look at them, 121-123; 7. women whose kinship relation with the men who look at them are not close enough to forbid marriage between them, p. 123. Other Hanafi authors list only women that free men are forbidden to marry, such as the list of 'Uthmān ibn ʿAlī al-Zaylaʿī, *Tabyīn al-ḥaqāʾiq sharḥ kanz al-daqāʾ iq* (Beirut: Dār al-Maʿrifa, re-impression of the Cairo edition of 1315 h.), vol. II, pp. 101-102. But see also the list of 21 categories of women given by Abū Muḥammad Maḥmūd ibn Aḥmad al-ʿAynī, *Al-Bināya fī Sharḥ al-Hidāya* (Beirut: Dār al-Fikr, 1414h./1990 c.e.), vol. IV, pp. 504-507.

2. Relations between men and women that are based on foster relationship *(riḍāʿa)* also render marriage illegal not only "between foster brothers and sisters but also between the foster mother and her relatives on the one side and her foster children, their spouses and their descendents on the other side."[70]

3. Women related to men through affinity are not licit marriage partners for them.

4. Female relatives, such as cousins, whose kinship degree does not forbid them to marry their male relatives, are licit marriage partners. The marriage with the daughter of the father's brother has been a popular practice and was widely recommended in the literature related to marriage and family.

5. Free women who are neither related to men through close kinship relations based on blood relationship, nor through affinity or foster relations are "unrelated women" (*ajnabiyyāt*) and as such marriage partners par excellence.

6. Men may marry the slave women of other owners or buy them to use them as concubines, licit sex partners.

7. The wives of other husbands are, of course, forbidden marriage and sex partners for other men. This situation changes when they are divorced by their husbands.

The seven kinds of women thus serve to distinguish women who are licit marriage partners from those women who are either forbidden or the marriage with whom needs, in the case of slave women, their owner's permission. Under this aspect and from a purely legal point of view they can be reduced to four categories: women belonging to the first three categories are not only forbidden marriage partners but also forbidden sex partners. In order to acquire licit sexual or marriage partners among women belonging to category six, men have either to buy them and make them their concubines or, with the permission of their owner, to marry them. If they marry them, the slave owner keeps his property of the slave woman and acquires automatically the property of her children. Consequently, he keeps an important authority over her and her children. If these slave women are bought from their proprietor they are licit sex partners, many jurists, though, question their capacity to become licit marriage partners.[71] Free women

---

70 N.J. Coulson, *Succession in the Muslim Family* (Cambridge: Cambridge University Press, 1971), p. 14.

71 Zaylaʿī, *Tabyīn al-ḥaqāʾiq, op. cit.*, vol. II, p. 109; Sarakhsī, *Mabsūṭ, op. cit.*, vol. V, p.130; Saḥnūn ibn Saʿīd al-Tanūḫī, *Al-Mudawwana al-Kubrā* (Cairo: Maṭbaʿat al-Saʿāda, 1323h.), vol. IV, pp. 52, 55 holds that it is only permissible to marry one's slave women, if one fears that otherwise one would commit fornication; the Shāfiʿī doctrine is stricter: Nawawī, *Al-Minhāj*, vol. III, p. 183 at the margin of Muḥammad al-Shirbīnī al-Khaṭīb, *Mughnī al-muḥtāj ilā maʿrifat alfāẓ al-minhāj* (Cairo: Maṭbaʿat al-Bābī al-Ḥalabī, 1958), vol. III, p. 183 holds that a marriage between a proprietor and his slave woman is valid only if he is not already married to a free woman. Shirbīnī, *ibid.*, p. 183, holds the same opinion and explains it, much as the Hanafi Zaylaʿī, through the argument that marriage is built upon sharing the fruits of marriage between husband and wife and that this principle speaks for the prohibition of marriage between a slave and a free person because a slave cannot ask her or his master for an equal sharing in fruits common to them.

of categories four and five are licit candidates for marriage: the same norms apply to both categories. Nobody has a right in these marriages to interfere between husband and wife.

This categorization of women determines the right of men and of women to gaze at the other gender. No restrictions exist in the rules of gaze and touching between husbands and wives on the one hand, men and their slave concubines on the other. The category of shame zone *('awra)* does not apply to their relationships. Husbands can look at the naked bodied of their wives and concubines, wives and slaves can look at the naked bodies of their husbands or masters. The same holds true for the relationship between men and their concubines. In both cases the rules governing the right to gaze and to touch are practically unlimited and gaze and touch are seen as reciprocal rights.[72]

Men are not allowed to see the naked bodies of their "forbidden women" (*maḥārim*). But, because these women are unmarriageable members of the family and not potential marriage or sex partners, the rules of their covering in the presence of the men of their family are much more relaxed than the rules applying to categories of "unrelated women" (*ajnabiyyāt*). According to the Hanafi doctrine, when the free woman is at home, among her close kin, her male relatives may licitly look at her head, her face, her hair, her neck, her chest, her upper arms, forearms, palms, legs and feet, but not at her belly and her back and they may touch what they can licitly see. Women, when facing their close male relatives may, therefore, dress in a reduced negligee. The legal reason for this privilege is that the law forbids men to marry women to whom they are related by descent, foster relationship, uterine kinship or alliance. Men and women within such a degree of kinship form the group of *maḥārim*, of forbidden marriage partners. Among them, according to the jurists, one does not have to fear illicit desires and, therefore, the rules of gazing and touching do not have the same importance as between men and their possible marriage or sex partners. Men and women of this category have access to each other's rooms if they share the same building. They may also travel together without being accompanied by third persons because, the jurists say, illicit sexual approaches are normally not to be feared from the gazing and touching between men and women who are so closely related that they are forbidden to marry. But if men fear that such gaze or touching would kindle desire in them, they are told not to look at those parts of the related women.[73]

---

72 Sarakhsī, *Al-Mabsūṭ*, op. cit., vol. X, p. 148; Zaylaʿī, *Tabyīn al-ḥaqāʾiq*, op. cit., vol. II, p. 18. While these authors support this legal rule, they still alert their readers to the medical dangers that such a gaze on the naked body of one's wife or concubine entails: they risk to lose their memory if they gaze at the naked female body. This alert is not taken seriously by all legal authorities: the son of the caliph ʿUmar, ʿAbdallāh ibn ʿUmar, is quoted as having encouraged men to fully enjoy the gaze at their wives and concubines during the sexual act, see Sarakhsī, *Al-Mabsūṭ*, vol. X, p. 149; Zaylaʿī, *Tabyīn al-ḥaqāʾiq*, op. cit., vol. II, p. 19. For the Shāfiʿī discussion on the same idea see Shirbīnī, *Mughnī al-muḥtāj*, vol. III, p. 134.

73 Abū ʿAbdallāh Muḥammad ibn al-Ḥasan al-Shaybānī, *Kitāb al-Aṣl* (Hydarabad, 1969), vol. III, p. 49-50; Sarakhsī, *Mabsūṭ, op. cit.*, vol. X, pp. 149-150; Sarakhsi *ibid.*, p. 148

The Hanbali scholars discuss a number of different norms concerning the "forbidden women". They quote Qur'an 24,31 in which women are enjoined "not to display their finery (*zaynatahunna*) except to their husbands, their fathers, their husbands fathers, their sons, their step-sons, their brothers, their brothers' sons, their sisters' sons, their women-servants, and their slave-girls; male attendants lacking in natural vigour and children who have no carnal knowledge of women".[74] Some of them try to opt for a very narrow interpretation of these verses. Others hold that the rules of the gaze between male and female *maḥārim* should be those that govern the same-gender rules for men and women. Ibn Qudāma holds that it is licit to look at those parts of the female *maḥārim* that are ordinarily visible and not to look on those that do not normally appear to the observer.[75]

The Shāfiʿī doctrine is formulated succinctly by the famous Damascene jurist Al-Nawawi: "He should not look at the 'forbidden woman's' body between her navel and her knee, everything else is permitted [to look at] for him. It is also said that he is allowed only to look at what is visibly when she is in her work dress."[76] Jurists from different schools of law support this rule through the argument that women have to sweep and clean the house and do other home works. They, therefore, have to dress in their "working dress" (*thiyāb mihnatihā*). It would too much to ask that she cover her whole body from head to foot while engaging in this kind of work.[77]

The Mālikī-s hold, concerning the gaze of male and female *maḥārim* on each other, the doctrine with the largest range of opinions professed by any Sunnī school of law. One of their doctrines assigns to the gaze of the female *maḥram* the same range as that of the same gender rule for men or women, i.e. it assigns to her the same right to see the whole body of her close male relative except the zone between navel and knee[78]. According to another opinion this privilege is restricted to the free women among the "forbidden women" and does not apply to the slave woman[79] . The slave woman should not see more from her male relative than his face and his limbs, whereas he is entitled to see her whole body except the zone between navel and knee.[80]

---

criticizes as too extensive the Shāfiʿī position according to which the gaze of men on "forbidden women" (*maḥārim*) should be regulated by analogy to the same-gender rule; Kāsānī, *Badāʾi al-ṣanāʾiʿ, op. cit.*, vol. V, pp. 120-121; ʿUthmān ibnʿAlī al-Zaylaʿī, *Tabyīn al-ḥaqāʾiq sharḥ kanz al-daqāʾiq* (Cairo, 1313h.), vol. VI, p. 17.

74 Translation by N.J. Dawood, *The Koran with a Parallel Arabic Text* (London, England: Penguin Classics).

75 Muwaffaq al-Din Ibn Qudāma, *Al-Mughnī* (Beirut: Dār al-Kutub al-ʿilmiyya, no date), vol. vii, pp. 454-456.

76 Nawawī, *Majmūʿ, op. cit.*, vol. III, p. 129; see also Shirbini, *op. cit.*, vol. iii, p. 129.

77 Sarakhsī, *Mabsūṭ, op. cit.*, vol. X, p. 149; for the Shāfiʿī school see Shirbīnī, *op. cit.*, vol. I, p. 185.

78 Khurashi, op. cit., vol. I, p. 248.

79 Ibid., op.cit., vol. I, p. 248.

80 Khurashī, op. cit., vol. I, p. 248.

But as soon as these free women go out into the public sphere, such as streets, markets, or mosques their shame zone, like that of all other free women, extends to their whole body, "from head to feet" as all jurists say. Therefore, they have to be covered entirely. Only their face, their hands and -according to the Hanafis– the back of their feet can be seen uncovered. These rules apply to all free women who enter the public sphere. In other words, while for men and for female slaves the shame zone (from navel to knee) seems to be inscribed in their bodies and not to change when they transit from the private (house) to the public realm (prayer, streets, markets), for free women it is the gaze of other persons that determines the shame zones they have to cover. While at home, under the eyes of their close male relatives, they can dress informally, in a sort of domestic *négligée*, when they go out their shame zone extends over their whole body, "from head to feet" as all jurists say, and has to be covered entirely. Only the women's face and hand can licitly be seen uncovered. Some jurists add to the visible parts the back of the women's feet and their forearms. [81]

The jurists distinguish four kinds of gaze on other persons: the gaze of men on men, women on women, women on men and men on women.[82] The first two forms of gaze are regulated by the "same-gender rule" (*mujānasa*). The same-gender rule states that one may touch those parts of another person's body of the same gender that one is allowed to look at.[83] The rules on same-gender gaze thus

---

81 Shaybānī, *Kitāb al-Aṣl, op. cit.*, vol. III, pp. 56-59, 67; Sarakhsī, *Mabsūṭ, op. cit.*, vol. I, 198; in vol. X, p. 145 he states that, according to the obvious analogy (*qiyās ẓāhir*) a woman is shame zone from head to feet but that because of need and necessity the permission to look at her and to touch her was granted under certain circumstances. This deviation from the obvious analogy is called "legal preference" *(istiḥsān)* because it is more compassionate for the humans; Kāsānī, *Badāʾiʿ al-ṣanāʾiʿ, op. cit.*, vol. I, p. 199, vol. V, pp. 121-122; Zaylaʿī, *Tabyīn al-ḥaqāʾiq, op. cit.*, vol. VI, p. 17; Ḥaṣkafī, *Al-Durr al-mukhtār sharḥ tanwīr al-abṣār* (printed at the margin of Ibn ʿĀbidīn, *Radd al-muḥtār ʿalā al-durr al-mukhtār* [Cairo 1307]), vol. I, p. 297.

For the Maliki law school see Abū al-Walīd Sulaimān al-Bājī, *Kitāb al-Muntaqā sharḥ muwaṭṭaʾ Mālik ibn Anas* (Cairo: Maṭbaʿat al-Saʿāda, 1331 h.), vol. I, p. 251.

For the Shāfiʿīs see Muḥammad al-Shirbīnī al-Khaṭīb, *Mughnī al-muḥtāj ilā maʿrifat al-minhāj* (Cairo: Sharikat maktab wa-maṭbaʿat Muṣṭafā al-Bābī al-Ḥalabī, 1377/1958), vol. III, pp. 128-129.

For the Hanbali position and a discussion of the doctrine of the other Sunni law schools on this matter see Muwaffaq al-Dīn Abū Muḥammad ʿAbdallāh ibn Aḥmad ibn Muḥammad Ibn Qudāma, *Al-Mughnī* (Beirut: Dār al-Kitāb al-ʿarabī [offset reprint 1403h./1983]), see vol. VII, pp. 454-465, see also vol. I, pp. 636-637. Voir aussi, Baber Johansen, "La traduction du Coran et les mantes des musulmanes", in *Revue des mondes musulmans et de la Méditerranée* ("Enquêtes dans la bibliographie de Jacques Berque. Parcours d'histoire sociale"), 1997, no. 83-84, pp. 195-201.

82 Sarakhsī, *Mabsūṭ, op. cit.*, vol. X, p. 146.

83 Sarakhsī, *Mabsūṭ, op. cit.*, vol. X, pp. 146-150, 153. This basic rule applies to the relations between husband and wife, master and concubine, in the "same-gender rule" (*mujānasa*) between men and men and women and women as well as between men and the

render visible and touchable all parts of the body that do not have to be constantly covered in the presence of persons of the same gender. This part of the body constitutes the "shame zone" (ʿawra). Accordingly, men may see and touch every part of another man's body except the shame zone between navel and knee. The same holds true for a woman looking at another woman.[84]

Women gazing at men can look at every part of the body except the male shame zone between navel and knee. This rule indicates that the male shame zone does not change with the onlooker. The licit gaze of men on women is divided into four parts: (1) the gaze of the husband on his wife and of the owner on his female slaves, (2) the gaze of the man on his female relatives whom, for reasons of close kinship, he is not allowed to marry (*maḥārim*), (3) a man's look on the slave women of another owner, and (4), the man's gaze at free women to whom he is not related via kinship (*ajnabiyy*āt).[85]

The gaze of the husband or the owner of female slaves on his wife or his concubines is not limited by any shame zone "because touching and sex are more important than the gaze and they are licit between them (ḥalāl)."[86] His gaze on his female relatives whom he cannot marry is restricted to the body beyond their shame zone between navel and knee and–in addition–the back and the belly.[87]

The basic same gender rule of the gaze is that one is allowed to touch what one is allowed to see. According to this rule, the face and the hands of "unrelated women" (*ajnabiyyāt*) should be touchable by unrelated men (*ajānib*). But the

---

slave women of other proprietors: Shaybānī, *al-Aṣl, op. cit.*, vol. III, p. 50; Kāsānī, *Badā'iʿ al-ṣanāʿiʿ, op. cit.*, vol. V, pp. 120-21.

84 Sarakhsī, *Mabsūṭ, op. cit.*, vol. X, pp. 147-148; for the Shafiʾī-s see Nawawī, *Al-Minhāj, op.cit.*, vol. I, p. 129; for the Mālikīs see Khurashī, *sharḥ, op. cit.*, vol. I, p. 246; Al-ʿAdawī, *op. cit.*, vol. I, p. 246.

85 Sarakhsī, *Mabsūṭ, op. cit.*, vol. X, pp.148. We have discussed the first two forms of gaze above, see notes 73 and note 74. For the gaze on the slave women of other owners see for the Hanafis Sarakhsi, *Mabsūṭ, op. cit.*, vol. X, p. 151; for the Mālikīs see Khurashī, *op. cit.*, vol. I, p. 246 and ʿAdawī, *op. cit.*, vol. I, p. 246; for the Shāfiʿīs see Nawawī, *Minhāj*, op. cit., vol. I, p. 185, Shirbīnī, op. cit., vol. I, p. 185. Nawawī explains in *Majmūʿ*, op. cit., vol. III, p. 173 that there are deviant opinions about this question, but that the dominant opinion of the Shāfiʿī school is that the slave woman's shame zone is the zone between navel and knee and thus clearly distinguished from the shame zone of the free woman. This opinion is also held by the Hanbali Ibn Qudāma in his *Mughnī, op. cit.*, vol. I, pp. 639-640 who underlines that she has the same shame zone as the men. For the gaze of the man on the "unrelated free woman" (*ajnabiyya*), see for the Hanafis, Sarakhsī, *Mabsūṭ, op.cit.*, vol. X, pp. 152-154 and Kāsānī, *op. cit.*, vol. V, pp. 121-123; for the Hanbalis, Ibn Qudama, *al-Mughnī, op. cit.*, vol. I, pp. 637-638, see also the commentary of his nephew ʿAbd al-Raḥmān ibn Muḥammad ibn Aḥmad Ibn Qudāma, *Al-Sharḥ al-kabīr* (printed at the margin of the *Mughnī*) (Beirut Libanon: *Dār al-kutub al-ʿilmiyya*, no date), vol. I, p. 456; for the Malikis, see Khurashī, op. cit., vol. I, 247; for the Shāfiʿīs see Nawawī, *Majmūʿ, op. cit.*, vol. III, p. 172.

86 Sarakhsī, *Mabsūṭ, op. cit.*, vol. X, p. 148.

87 See notes 73 for the Hanafis, notes 74 and 75 above for the Hanbalis and note 76 for the Shāfiʿī schools of law.

jurists stress that no man is entitled to touch the hands or the face of unrelated women, not even when he is sure that he will not be tempted by desire.[88]

In fact, the extent of the shame zone is not inscribed in the body. It is always produced by the licit social relations between the individuals who gaze at each other. That holds true for free women as well as for free men and male slaves. The rules of the gaze always answer the question: under which conditions is a man or a woman A entitled to gaze at a man or a woman B? It is the gaze of A that determines the shame zone of B. As husbands, men may gaze at the naked bodies of their wives without any restriction, and the wives enjoy the same right of gazing at their husbands' naked bodies. The same holds true for the gaze between masters and concubines.[89] Between husbands and wives, masters and concubines there are no legal obstacles to this gaze. Those jurists who are opposed to the unrestricted gaze between husband and wife, master and concubine, cannot muster legal arguments for their opposition. They have to use a pseudo-medical references to suggest restrictions: they tell their readers that a look at the naked body of the other may cause the loss of memory. Needless to say, most of the legal authorities do not take such an argument seriously.[90]

Because shame zones depend on the legal and social relations between men and women or free and enslaved persons they are not inscribed in the bodies of the persons concerned. They are, to a large extent, determined by the social relations between persons. But the shame zone of the male body–as well as that of the female slave–adapts less to changing encounters than the shame zone ascribed to free women. Men may: (1) look at other men, following "the same genre rule" (*mujānasa*), looking licitly at every part of other men's body except the zone between navel and knee and, following the general rule that one may licitly touch what one is allowed to see, they may touch every part of other men's body except the zone between navel and knee;[91] (2) A man who wants to marry a woman may licitly look at her, even with desire, but is not allowed to touch her;[92] (3) Once having married, or having made one of his enslaved women his concubine, he may gaze at the naked body of his wife and concubine without any restriction; (4) Men

[88] Unrelated men may look at a woman's face and her hands and also at her cloths. But they are, contrary to the general rule, not allowed to touch what they see: Sarakhsī, *Mabsūṭ, op. cit.*, vol. X, p. 154. This holds also true for the man who wants to marry a woman. He may look at her face and her hands, but he may not touch them: Zaylaʿī, *Tabyīn al-ḥaqā'iq, op. cit.*, vol. VI, pp. 18-19.

[89] Shaybānī, *al-Aṣl, op. cit.*, vol. III, p. 69; Sarakhsī, *Mabsūṭ, op. cit.*, vol. X, p. 148-149; Ibn al-Humām, *FAQ, op. cit.*, vol. VIII, pp. 103-06; Shirbīnī, *Mughnī al-muḥtāj, op. cit.*, vol. III, p. 130; Zaylaʿī, *Tabīn al-haqā'iq, op. cit.*, vol. VI, p. 19.

[90] For the Hanafis see note 86 above. For the Shāfiʿīs see Shirbīnī, *op. cit.*, vol. III, p. 134; for the Mālikī-s see Khurashi, op. cit., vol. III, p. 166.

[91] *Mujānasa*-rule: Sarakhsī, *Mabsūṭ, op. cit.*, vol. X, pp. 146-47, vol. II, p. 41; Kāsānī, *Kitāb Badā'i*, vol. V, pp. 120-121; Ibn al-Humām, *FAQ, op. cit.*, vol. VIII, pp. 100-102; Zaylaʿī, *Tabyīn al-haqā'iq, op. cit.*, vol. VI, p. 18.

[92] Mens' gaze at the women they want to marry: Sarakhsī, *Mabsūṭ, op. cit.*, vol. X, p. 155; Zaylaʿī, *Tabyīn al-haqā'iq, op. cit.*, vol. VI, p. 18.

are allowed to look at the bodies of the women whom they are forbidden to marry within the limits described above. While most of these exchanges of the gaze are reciprocal, it is the gaze of men on "unrelated women" (*ajnabiyyāt*) that requires –according to the jurists–the complete covering of the body of the women as soon as they leave the family house.

Free women, in order to protect their shame zone from being violated by the illicit gaze of unrelated men (*ajānib*), have to cover their whole body–with the exception of the face and the hands–so that no gaze can reach it. There are discussions whether free women may show the back of their feet or their forearms, but that hardly changes the rules of the game. The women have to make sure that they render their shame zone inaccessible to the gaze of unrelated men. The man also has to protect his shame zone, but the minimal requirement is for him to cover his backside and his sex, normally he is required to cover the zone between navel and knee. As a man he is never completely identified with his shame zone that only covers a part of his body.

Free women, on the other hand, are identified with their shame zone. It covers their whole body in public and in prayer. "The woman is shame zone (ʿawra)" writes the seventeenth-century Mālikī jurist al-Kharashī, "because one expects corruption from her view and from hearing her voice, (this is) not (derived) from the meaning of the verb 'to blind' in the sense of ugliness (*qabḥ*), because that does not apply to the beautiful among the women, because the souls feel attracted to them. But maybe someone might object [and say]: 'what is meant by ugliness is what the sacred law considers to be ugly, even if nature inclines towards it'".[93] In a much less emphatic but equally clear way, the famous twelvch-century philosopher and jurist, Ibn Rushd, the Latin Avverroes, states: "Most of the jurists maintain that her entire body constitutes shame zone, except for the face and the hands."[94] The famous twelfth-century Transoxanian jurist Marghīnānī, over the centuries commented upon in other regions of the Muslim world, states in equally clear words:" The body of the free woman is in its entirety shame zone, except her face and her two palms." [95]

Only through proving that their body submits entirely to the commands of the law can women keep their reputation, perform their prayers validly, and thus protect the honor of their family. But as the law of all Sunni law schools imposes different rules on covering their bodies in public, the female gender is–as far as the rules of the gaze are concerned–divided by the law into free women and slaves. In this, the female gender differs from the male gender. Free and enslaved men are according to the law one gender as far as the rules of the gaze are concerned. Their shame zone is the body part between the navel and the knee. The slave woman shares with them the same shame zone. The free women alone have

---

93 Khirshī, *Sharḥ*, *op.cit.*, vol. I, p. 244.

94 Ibn Rushd, *The distinguished Jurist's Primer* (*Bidāyt al-Mujtahid*) (Reading: The Center for Muslim Contribution to Civilization, 1994), vol. I, p.126.

95 ʿAlī ibn Abī Bakr al-Marghīnānī, *Fatḥ al-Qadīr*, printed at the margin of Ibn al-Humām, *Sharḥ Fatḥ al-Qadīr* (Beirut: Dār al-Kutub al-ʿilmiyya, 1995), vol. I, p. 266.

to cover their whole body with the exception of the face and the palms of their hands.

Free women are thus clearly discernible from slave women. Their difference in social ranking is underlined by the fact that the free woman has to cover her whole body, whereas the slave woman is not entitled to do so. Through their way of dressing the free women stress their claim to social distance to unrelated men (*ajānib).*

The male gaze at the female slaves of other men is regulated quite loosely. The debased status of the slave women is underlined by the fact that she is not entitled to veil herself. In her relation to all unrelated men, the slave woman has to follow the same dress code that applies to the "forbidden women" (*maḥārim*) in their relations with men to whom they are related through kinship, foster relationships or affinity. In other words, all men can not only see her unveiled body but also touch it. Sarakhsi informs his readers that "practical jokes" with slave women of other owners are permissible, because they were customary among the Arabs before Islam. "Therefore, God ordered the free women to take the *jilbāb*, a loose, shirtlike garment, so that they could be distinguished from slave women. This indicates that slave women would not take the *jilbāb*. If [the caliph] ʿUmar saw a veiled slave he would take off the veil with his whip and say: Throw off this head scarf, you stinker. ʿUmar said that the slave woman has thrown off her horns behind the wall, i.e. that she does not veil. Anas [a companion of the Prophet] said: [the caliph] ʿUmar's slave women served his guests, their heads uncovered and their bodies [cloths] in disorder. The slave woman has to go out and fetch the things her master needs and so she goes out in her work dress and her status with all men concerning the tribulation of gaze and touch is like the status of man with women forbidden to him in marriage (maḥārim). Muḥammad ibn Muqātil al-Rāzī[96] said: "He cannot look on her body between navel and knee, but everything above that he may licitly gaze at." Ibn ʿAbbās [famous companion of the Prophet] has said: "Whosoever wants to buy a slave woman should look at her whole body except under her loin cloth."[97] But Sarakhsī holds that this report should be interpreted more cautiously: that the slave woman closes her cloth above her breasts and that then one may touch what one can see.[98] The gaze on the uncovered body parts and on the cloths of unrelated free women (*ajnabiyyāt)* is permitted but does not entail a right to touch these parts.

The gaze of free women at unrelated men follows *Qur'ān*, Sura 24 (*al-Nūr*), 31 in that the woman, if she is sure not to experience temptation (*fitna*) and desire can look at women's and men's bodies in the same way that a man looks at a man's body "because in what does not belong to the shame zone men and

---

96 Muḥama ibn Muqātil al-Rāzī was an important Hanafi scholar of the eighth century.

97 Zaylaʿī, *Tabyīn al-haqā'iq, op. cit.*, vol. VI, pp. 19-20.

98 Sarakhsī, *Mabsūṭ, op. cit.*, vol. X, p. 151. Sarakhsī, *Mabsūṭ, op. cit.*, vol. X, p. 157; Ibn Qudāma, *Mughnī, op. cit.*, vol. I, pp. 639-40; Shirbīnī, *Mughnī al-muḥtāj, op. cit.*, vol. I, p. 131.

women are equal." If she fears to experience temptation and desire it is better (*yastaḥibbu*) that she lower her eyes or look away.[99]

In the Hanafi school of law, in contrast to the Shāfiʿī doctrine, the illicit lustful gaze of men on the body of a free unrelated woman (*ajnabiyya*) produces far reaching legal consequences. It is, says the eleventh-century Transoxanian jurist, Sarakhsī, "an illicit sexual appropriation."[100] It entails the prohibition, for all male relatives of the perpetrator, to marry the female ascendants and descendants of that woman.[101]

This rule knows exceptions: the magistrate who identifies women,[102] the medical doctor who practices a surgical operation on a woman,[103] the man who practices female circumcision[104] are all justified by the purpose they are pursuing, if they look full of desire at the face and the body of the women whom they identify or treat. Their gaze does not count as illegal and illicit gaze.

7. Fitna

Over the centuries, Muslim jurists have constantly enlarged and extended the norms that prohibit the gaze on and restrict the visibility of free women. One of their preferred tools for the justification of these prohibitions and restrictions is the fear that temptation may result in sedition (*fitna*) with increasingly disastrous consequences not only for individual men but also for the public order. Temptation, in this reasoning, originates in women, men are defenseless victims of women's temptation and, therefore, women have to be controlled to protect men and the public order.[105] I give a few examples of this form of reasoning.

---

[99] Zaylaʿī, *Tabyīn al-haqā'iq*, *op. cit.*, vol. VI, p. 18. This author adds that women are mostly dominated by their desires and that therefore the legal assumption is that she is dominated by desire if she looks.

[100] Sarakhsī, *Mabsut*, *op. cit.*, vol. X, p. 148.

[101] Sarakhsī, *Mabsut*, *op. cit.*, vol. X, pp. 150, 154; Maḥmūd ibn Aḥmad al-ʿAynī, *Al-Bināya fī sharḥ al-hidāya* (Beirut: Dār al-Fikr li-l-ṭibāʿa wa l-nashr wa l-tawzīʿ, 1990), vol. IV, pp. 530-35; Chafik Chehata, *Etudes de droit musulman* (Paris: Presses Universitaires de France, 1971), vol. I, pp. 62-63.

[102] Shaybānī, *al-Aṣl*, *op. cit.*, vol. III, pp. 59, 66; Sarakhsī, *Mabsut*, *op. cit.*, vol. X, pp. 154-55; Zaylaʿī, *Tabīn al-haqā'iq*, *op. cit.*, vol. VI, p. 17; FAQ, vol. VIII, p. 99.

[103] Shaybānī, *al-Aṣl*, *op. cit.*, vol. III, pp. 66-67; Sarakhsī, *Mabsut*, *op. cit.*, vol. X, p. 155.

[104] Shaybānī, *al-Aṣl*, *op. cit.*, vol. III, pp. 66-67; Sarakhsī, *Mabsut*, *op. cit.*, vol. X, pp. 156-57; Zaylaʿī, *Tabīn al-haqā'iq*, *op. cit.*, vol. VII, pp. 17-18.

[105] Sarakhsī, *Mabsut*, *op. cit.*, vol. X, pp. 152-53, see also p. 158; Kāsānī, *Kitāb Badā'i*, *op. cit.*, vol. I, 155; vol. V, pp. 121-122, 124-125; Zaylaʿī, *Tabyīn al-haqā'iq*, *op. cit.*, vol. VI, p. 17 (*fitna* and *ghadd al-naẓar*); Shirbīnī, *Mughnī al-muḥtāj*, *op. cit.*, vol. I, pp. 135, 230, also vol. III, pp. 128-29, 131; Burhan ad-din 'Ali b. Abi Bakr al-Marghīnānī, *al-Hidaya sarh bidayat al-mubtadi'* (printed at the margin of Ibn al-Humam *Fath al-qadir*, Cairo, 1356), vol. I, p. 637.

The eleventh-century Transoxanian jurist, Sarakhsī, explains why touching what one is allowed to see does not apply to the gaze of men on unrelated women:

> This is due–he says–to the fear of *fitna*. If the woman is old and no longer desires [men], *fitna* is non-existent. That holds true also if the man is old and is in control of himself and sure that she also is in control of herself. [In that case] there is no harm if he shakes her hand. But if he is not sure that she will not desire [him] he is not allowed to shake hands with her and thus expose her to *fitna*, much as he would not be allowed to do that if he were afraid for himself. But to look at her covetously is in no case permitted–except in case of necessity.[106]

Hanafi authors, since the eighth century, hold that womens' congregational prayers under a woman who serves as Imam "have been abrogated because of the *fitna that resides in their assembling*."[107] If they pray congregational prayers they have to renounce on singing out the *adhān* and the call to begin the prayer *(iqāma)* because their voice is *fitna*. A woman should not serve as Muezzin, because the Muezzin sings out the *adhan* from the highest spot. "For fear of *fitna* the woman is prohibited from doing this." If a woman Muezzin calls other women to prayer "their prayer is licit in spite of its being morally reprehensible as it *contradicts the Sunna and exposes to fitna.*"[108]

A seventeenth-century Hanafi mufti from Damascus, Ḥaṣkafī, states–contrary to classical Hanafi doctrine–that young women have to veil their face. He states: "This is not because the face is part of the shame zone but because the fear of *fitna*, much as in its touching, even if [the man who touches it] is immune against lustful desire."[109]

This development is by no means restricted to the Hanafi school of law. The sixteenth-century Egyptian Shāfiʿi jurist Shirbīnī refers to a debate among Shāfiʿī and Mālikī jurists about the question whether the political authorities should forbid unveiled free women to leave their houses and to enter into the public space. This debate may have originated already in the eleventh century. According to Shirbīnī the thirteenth-century Shāfiʿi Damascene scholar al-Nawawī was of the opinion that the majority of the legal scholars did not forbid unveiled women to leave their houses. The rationale for the requested intervention of the political authorities in imposing the veiling on women is the female gaze that seduces men and leads to their developing an untamed carnal appetite (*shahwa*). As the law orders Muslims to close the door of all possible causes of unrest and disorder (*sadd al-bāb*) Muslims and Muslim authorities have to act in the face of this danger. This opinion is criticized by qāḍī ʿIyāḍ, a Spanish scholar of the twelfth century, it must therefore have circulated in many regions of the Muslim world before Nawawī's time. Qaḍī ʿIyāḍ holds that facing the seductive power of women's eyes is a matter of self discipline for men and does neither call for the imposition of

---

106 Sarakhsī, *Mabsut, op. cit.*, vol. X, p. 154.

107 Shaybānī, *al-Aṣl, op. cit.*, vol. III, p. 132; see also Sarakhsī, *ADD*, vol. I, p. 133.

108 Sarakhsi, *Mabsūṭ, op. cit.*, vol. I, p. 133.

109 Ḥaṣkafī, *Durr al-Multaqa, op. cit.*, vol. I, p. 298.

the veil on free Muslim women nor on waiting for the intervention of the state. Nawawī transmits this opinion of Qaḍī ʿIyāḍ and supports it. Some of the later jurists (*muta'akhkhirūn)* insist that veiling is a legal obligation under the sacred law for free Muslim women and that not to perform this obligation may very well violate the public interest (*maṣlaḥa ʿāmma*). Not to react to this violation of public interest may constitute a violation of the rules of honor and morality (*ikhlāl al-murūʾa*).

Shirbīnī holds that Nawawī shares the opinion according to which veiling is a legal obligation for free women and that qāḍī ʿIyāḍ's opinion is "weak". Many Shāfiʿī scholars of the fourteenth century hold that hands and face should be considered as part of the shame zone of the free women. But at this period, this opinion is still contested in the Shāfiʿī school. Shirbīnī apparently favors the opinion according to which it is a legal obligation for the free women and he wants the political authorities to guarantee its application. It is important to see that this veiling obligation is claimed only for the profane social sphere. That a woman's face ought not to be veiled during prayer and not before unrelated men (*ajānib*) is taught by Māwardī in the eleventh century. In the fourteenth century the important Shāfiʿī scholar al-Subkī upholds this doctrine as far as the prayer is concerned, but requests that all free women veil her face in the presence of unrelated men. This kind of debate and the comments quoted by Shirbīnī illustrate a development of legal norm production between the thirteenth and the sixteenth century in which the legal arguments built on social qualities ascribed to men and women by the religious tradition are increasingly supplemented by a call for state intervention against women who refuse to follow this normative development. [110]

The notion of *fitna* also becomes increasingly important in the Shāfiʿī school of law during that period. In fourteenth century Aleppo, the Shāfiʿī scholar al-Adhraʿī states that any man's gaze on anybody–with the exception of his wife and his slave women–is absolutely forbidden if it may lead to temptation and sedition (*fiṭna*), even if that temptation and sedition may just be a probability. Whenever a sufficient reason (ḥikma) to fear *fitna* is found through the contemplation (*ta'ammul*)[111] of the risks implied in a situation, the gaze on all other women has to be avoided.[112]

The Mālikī school follows a similar development. The eighteenth-century scholar Al-ʿAdawī holds that the rules for a woman's uncovering her body cannot be explained only by the shame zone rules. As an example he cites the case of a free Muslim woman who finds herself in the presence of a free Non-Muslim woman. While the same gender (*mujānasa*) rules for women allow them to reduce their shame zone to the part of the body between navel and knee in the presence

110 Shirbīnī, *Mughnī al-muḥtā ilā maʿrifat maʿānī alfāẓ al-minhāj, op. cit.*, vol. III, p. 129.

111 Baber Johansen, "Dissent and Uncertainty in the Process of Legal Norm Construction in Muslim Sunni Law," in *Law and Tradition in Classical Islamic Thought. Studies in Honor of Professor Hossein Modarressi*, edited by Michael Cook, Najam Haider, Intisar Rabb, and Asma Sayeed (New York: Palgrave, 2013), pp. 127-144.

112 Shirbīnī, *op. cit.*, vol. III, p. 129.

of other women, this does not apply, according to Al-ʿAdawī, to a free Muslim woman in the presence of a free Non-Muslim woman. In this case the free Muslim woman has to cover her whole body except the face and the hands. The difference in religious affiliation finds its expression in the dress code. The unity of the gender has to give way before the difference of religion.[113] This rule no longer applies if the Non-Muslim woman is the slave of the free Muslim woman. The dress code of the first case should be read as a sign of distance and ranking that is not needed in the second case where the ranking is obvious. Al-ʿAdawī explains: "Her shame zone with the Non-Muslim woman is the same as her shame zone with the Muslim woman except that it is forbidden for her to uncover in her presence more than her face and her palms, because it does not follow from the prohibition to uncover [a part of her body] that [this part of the body] is shame zone."[114] In other words, the shame zone rules explain a part only of the obligations of free Muslim women to cover themselves.

The same argument is developed by the Shāfiʿī jurists, latest since the thirteenth century, except that they do not differentiate between Non-Muslim women who are free or slaves. The thirteenth-century Damascene scholar Nawawi teaches "the most correct opinion holds that the protected Non-Muslim woman is not allowed to look at the Muslim woman."[115] His sixteenth-century commentator, Al-ʿAdawī, translates this into the following sentence: "The most correct opinion holds that it is forbidden for a [free] Non-Muslim woman, be she a protected Non-Muslim under Muslim rule or not, to look at a Muslim woman. The Muslim woman has to veil in her presence", because in Sura 24;31 God has listed "their women-servants" as persons before whom a free Muslim woman does not have to veil. He did not mention free Non-Muslim women. If she [the free Non-Muslim woman] was allowed to look [at the Muslim woman] then the specification [of Sura 24;31] would not make sense. It is correctly transmitted from [the second caliph after the Prophet] ʿUmar, may God be satisfied with him, that he forbade the women of the non-Islamic book religions to enter the public baths together with the Muslim women, because they would probably spread the information on the Muslim women's [bodies]. The second opinion holds that it is allowed taking into consideration the unity of the gender, much as the men [are allowed to enter the same public baths]. Concerning men, they make no difference between the gaze of the Non-Muslim on the Muslim and the Muslim on the Muslim. Yes, according to the first opinion it is admissible that she sees from her what appears from her in her working dress, according to what the Rawḍa[116] says [...] and that is what one relies on. It is also said she can see only the face and the palms [of the Muslim woman].

---

113 Al-ʿAdawī, *op. cit.*, vol. I, p. 246.

114 Ibid., p. 247.

115 Nawawī, Minhāj, *op. cit.*, vol. III, p. 131.

116 Rawḍat al-Ṭālibīn, a book written by al-Nawawī, see Carl Brockelmann, *Geschichte der Arabischen Literatur*, 2nd edition (Leiden: Brill, 1943), vol. II, p. 396.

Bulqīnī[117] said that she has the same relation to her as an unrelated man. This has also been accepted by the qadi and others.[118]

A fourteenth-century text from Cairo, written by a prominent Mālikī jurist, Ibn al-Ḥājj, shows *fitna* as the product of Cairo's markets: its principal authors are women who enter a shop in the market accompanied by their husband and whose husband then leaves them, thus exposing the shop owner to the tribulations of *fitna* by the woman's voice, her flirting mockeries and her sheer unaccompanied presence. Ibn al-Hājj recommends that such a shop owner abandon his shop and find a different way of living or accept poverty as the price of his salvation from *fitna*.[119]

Another danger lurks in the arrogance of the wives of powerful husbands or the daughters of powerful fathers.

> Others wear thin cloths that mark [the body] or are transparent or both together. Others may wear a short dress without trousers and other things more that are known as the habits of women in our time. And in addition they pretend that this is permissible. They create their own rules such as saying that the flax seller or the water carrier and their likes do not belong to those men in front of whom they have to be shy and diffident. [...] An example of this is that some highborn women (*baʿḍu l-ashrāf mina l-nisā'*) pretend that they only have to be shy and diffident in front of a highborn man (*sharīf*) but not with others. And some highborn women in some places do not, in principle, veil from an unrelated man and they talk to him for an extended time and amuse themselves with him pretending that he does not belong to the men in front of whom they have to be shy and diffident.[120]

When women, trusting their social ranking and the power of their families, see class and power of husbands and families as sufficient reason for not veiling in front of men of lower classes and for not shying back from talking to them uncontrolled by third persons, social standing seems to indicate a limit for the efficiency of the modesty rules for women. This, according to Ibn al-Hajj, is the most important form of *fitna*.

Is the protocol of the gaze concerning gender relations built on the assumption that women embody a power that if unveiled would be harmful for them, for men and for the public order? If so, what kind of power is meant? Reading the jurists on *fitna* one is tempted to think in terms of seduction. Women and men clearly have the power to seduce each other and if no precaution is taken that may bring about dishonor to them and create a major factor of public disorder. If this were the reason adduced for the veiling rules, the public display of female charms

---

117 Bulqīnī, Shāfiʿī jurist and qadi in Egypt and Damascus second half fourteenth and beginning of fifteenth century.

118 Shirbīnī, *op. cit.*, vol.III, pp. 131-132.

119 Muḥammad ibn al-Ḥājj al-Fāsī al-ʿAbdarī, Mudkhal al-sharʿ al-sharīf (Dār al-Fikr wa l-nashr wa l-tawzīʿ, no date), vol. IV, p. 33. On Ibn al-Ḥājj see André Raymond and G.Wiet, *Les Marches du Caire. Traduction annotée du texte de Maqrīzī*, Institut Français d'Archéologie Orientale Du Caire, 1979, pp. 78-80.

120 Ibn al-Ḥājj, *op.cit.* vol. IV, p. 103 (see also p. 104).

would be one of the factors that the protocol of the gaze is meant to control and to prevent. A second one, the power of women to give life, might also need to be controlled, to preserve intact descent, lineages and the honor of free men.

But there are important reasons to doubt that this type of power is the main rationale for the protocol of the gaze and its transformation into a justification for the state control over the modesty of women. The rules of veiling and segregation apply only to free women. Many jurists of different schools draw attention to the fact that the *Qur'ān* in Sura 24 (*al-Nur*), verse 31, speaks of women but that the rules of veiling and segregation that it reveals concern free women only.[121]

The *fiqh* has always recognized another role for another type of women: the slave women. Slave women are not allowed to veil. They are not protected, or at least not to the same degree as free women, against tactile harassment. Thus, slave women are forbidden to veil, they are held to display their charms, they have no right to social distance and little protection from tactile harassment because the law entitles all men to touch them as if they were close relatives. Their body is, as the jurists never tire of telling their readers, like the male body: contrary to the shame zone of the free woman that changes with her transition from the private realm of the household into the public sphere of prayers, streets and public places, the slave woman's shame zone rests the same whether in the household or in the streets and public places: it is always restricted to the zone between navel and knee.[122] Basing the call for increased veiling and segregation of the free woman on the notion of *fitna* is in clear contradiction with the prohibition of veiling and segregation of the slave women. This contradiction between the *fitna*-reasoning and the norms covering the visibility of the slave has not escaped important Muslim jurists.

The Hanbali scholar Ibn Qayyim al-Jawziyya (d. 1351), the prominent student of Ibn Taymiyya, comments upon it in the following words:

> To forbid the gaze on the old disfigured and ugly free woman and declare it licit on the slave woman of radiant beauty is a calumny of the *sharīʿa*. Where did God forbid this and allowed that? God, be He exalted, only said: Say to the believers that they cast down their eyes (Sura 24, *al-Nur*, 30). God and His Prophet did not set free for the eyes the gaze on the slave woman of radiant beauty. If [the man] fears temptation *(fitna)* if he gazes at the slave woman, it is, no doubt, forbidden to him [to look at her]. The suspicion *(shubha)* [concerning the permissibility of that gaze results from the fact] that the lawgiver ordered free women to cover their faces from [adult] strangers while he did not impose the same on the slave women. But that [norm applies] only to slave women who do menial services and are put to use. Now, as far as the concubines are concerned, the custom is that they are protected and preserved and secluded. Where did God and His Prophet grant them permission to uncover their faces in the markets

---

121 Sarakhsī, *Mabsut, op. cit.*, vol. X, pp. 157, 161; see also Ibn Qudāma, *Mughnī, op. cit.*, vol. I, pp. 639-40; Shirbīnī, *Mughnī al-muḥtāj, op. cit.*, vol. I, p. 185; Muḥyī al-Dīn ibn Sharaf al-Nawawī, *al-Majmūʿ sharḥ al-Muhadhdhab*, ed. Zakariyyāʾ ʿAlī Yūsuf (Cairo: Maṭbaʿat al-ʿĀṣima, n.d.), vol. I, p. 185.

122 Sarakhsī, *Mabsut, op. cit.*, vol. X, pp. 157; Ibn Qudāma, *Mughnī, op. cit.*, vol. I, pp. 639-40; Shirbīnī, *Mughnī al-muḥtāj, op. cit.*, vol. I, p. 131.

> and streets and the places where people assemble? And where did He allow men to savor the pleasure to look at them? This is a blatantly incorrect statement on the sacred law. This blatantly incorrect statement has been given more strength by the fact that some jurisprudents (*fuqahā'*) were heard saying: The free woman is entirely a shame zone except her face and her two palms, the shame zone of the slave woman is not normally visible such as her belly and her back and her legs and so [people] thought that what becomes visible regularly has the same status as the face of the man. That is only true in prayer, not as far as the [rules of] the gaze are concerned. In fact, the shame zone is two shame zones: one shame zone concerning the [licit] gaze, the other concerning the prayer. The free woman is entitled to pray with uncovered face and palms but she is not entitled to go out in the markets and the places where people assemble in the same way. And God knows best.[123]

The *fitna* argument for increased veiling and segregation of the free woman stands in blatant contradiction to the legal norms concerning the slave woman. The power of women that requires their veiling has, therefore, to be searched for, not in the protection of men from their *fitna*, but in the qualities and capacities that distinguish free women from slave women. In fact, both types of woman share the power to give life to children and to seduce men or being seduced by men, but they are equipped, through the rules of the classical *fiqh* with different capacities and qualities. For the free woman, these capacities and qualities consist, in particular according to the *Hanafi fiqh*, of the following:

a) she guarantees the freedom of her legitimate children (that is not automatically guaranteed by Hanafi jurists for the children of concubines);

b) she guarantees the family cohesion and the husband's authority. This authority is strongly reduced in the marriage of a slave woman (the married slave woman has to continue to serve her master and she is entitled to spend time with her husband only when her master does not need her services; her husband is the father of their children, but the master of the slave woman is the owner of these children. The husband's fatherly authority over his children is thus strongly reduced);

c) finally, the strongest reason for the veiling of the free woman may well be that the veiled and secluded free woman embodies one of two licit role models for women: the virtuous, free house wife who when leaving the house is covered from head to foot, cannot be confounded with the slave woman, who embodies the second female role model of the *fiqh:* the slave woman is not entitled to veil, has no claim to social distance or protection against tactile harassment, does not come from a family background that is comparable to that of her master or her husband, her marriage does not grant her the seclusion in the home of her husband, and does not guarantee the freedom of her children. The free woman's power that requires her veiling and her seclusion consists thus of the power to guarantee her husband's paternal and marital authority, her children's status, and the reputation of her male family members. All these are endangered if she becomes visible and accessible like a slave woman. Slave women as well as aristocratic women,

---

123 Ibn Qayyim Al-Jawziyya, *Iʿlām al-Muwaqqiʿīn, op. cit.*, vol. II, pp. 46-47.

if we are to believe Ibn al-Ḥājj, limit the validity and efficiency of the modesty rules that require the veiling of the free women: slave women are excluded by law from the application of these rules, aristocratic women tend to neglect modesty rules in order to enhance the protection of their social status: the political and economic power of their families give her a status, according to Ibn al-Ḥājj, that allows her to determine the extent to which she applies the modesty rules to herself.

8. Conclusion

Three models of power expressed through invisibility have thus been characteristic for the history of Islam and the Muslims: God's creative omnipotence expressed in a strict concept of invisibility, the caliph's or Sultan's political power and majesty symbolically expressed through a concept of restricted accessibility and visibility and last but not least the free woman's power to preserve the freedom of her children, as well as the paternal and marital authority of her husband, through her invisibility and inaccessibility, i.e. through veiling and seclusion.

Of these three models the one of the invisible and inaccessible political authority exists no longer. Elected presidents and highly visible kings are constantly engaged in communicating with the citizens of their states through television speeches, public rallies and pictures in newspapers. They have to convey the images of statesmen constantly engaged in communication with their citizens. This communication has become an instrument of government, much as in earlier time invisibility and inaccessibility.

As far as gender relations are concerned, the power distribution between slave women and free women has ceased to exist after the abolition of slavery in the Muslim World. All women are now free women and thus guarantee the freedom of their children. Slavery of the wife can no longer diminish the paternal authority of the husband. All women now share in the power to give life to free children. The veiling distinction between slave women and free women no longer exists. And still, the pressure on unveiled women to veil is growing, because the effort to ascribe to unveiled women the status of women of lower moral and civil status still continues.

As far as political leadership is concerned, a new concept of power and its symbolic representation can no longer be based on the analogy between the ruler and God. As far as gender relations are concerned, the difference between free women and slaves no longer exists. Both changes bring to an end a situation in which the symbolic expression of power could be assured on the level of political power and gender relations by reference to the Qurʾānic model that power finds its symbolic expression in invisibility and inaccessibility. Neither are the rulers invisible nor are veiled women secluded. The model of God's invisibility no longer serves as a model that humans can imitate in order to express the religious character of political and female power. The public conversation between governments and citizens, men and women brings about visibility as a necessary condition for interaction. This is an important change in the religious and political culture and it will require a thoughtful and careful mode of practice and thought.

In the Image of the Invisible

Kathryn Tanner

Classical Christian theologians often maintain that God is incomprehensible, beyond human powers of positive explication through concepts and speech, because God is without limits or bounds. God is without limits of time, being framed by no beginning or end. Existing in perfect simplicity, God is without internal limits or boundaries dividing the divine nature into manageable component parts or aspects for our comprehension. The absolute fullness of being and goodness, God transcends all divisions between kinds and exceeds all bounds of a particular nature or mode of being that might allow God to be set alongside others or encompassed by anything it is not. The divine, in short, cannot be comprehended or contained in any respect; it is simply not anything that we can get our heads around. Classical and contemporary Christian theologians, following Genesis verses to this effect, also commonly claim that human beings are created in God's image. Putting the two ideas together one might expect them therefore to develop just as commonly the way in which human nature reflects divine incomprehensibility. Classical theological discussion of what it is about humans that makes them the image of God frequently moves, however, in the opposite direction: such discussion often simply amounts to the effort to find some clearly bounded human nature of quite definite character that both reflects the divine nature and sets humans off from all other creatures. Humans are created in the image of God because, unlike other creatures, they have reason or free will or the ability to rule over others as God does.

Given this interest in well-defined and well-bounded characteristics that are ours by nature, theological anthropology runs afoul of a number of contemporary intellectual trends. Bio-technologies, particularly interspecies gene transfers, call into question the fixed boundaries of natural kinds. Violence bred of ethnic and religious division in our world familiarizes us all too well with the bellicose potential of narrowly drawn, closely guarded identities. Feminists remind us of the way appeals to fixed and given natures help solidify unjust social arrangements and disguise their contingency. Postmodernists of various stripes caution against the insistence on a self-identical, coherent character, rigidly predicated on the exclusion of others so as to promote protective postures that degrade and sever human connection with them. And they lead us to question the ethical priority of self-discovery, as if the truth about oneself–an already established nature or identity–could determine all by itself what one might become, one's place within the world and the character of one's responsibilities, in sovereign independence of any unpredictable entanglements with human and non-human others beyond one's control.

The intent of this chapter is to move theological anthropology away from this sort of fixation on a fixed human nature, this preoccupation with established capacities and given identities, by diagnosing its theological underpinnings and developing an alternative account of the way humans image God in conversation with trends in early Christian thought that cut against other classical positions. I'll try to show, thereby, how an apophatic anthropology is the consequence of an apophatic theology. If humans are the image of God they are, as Gregory of Nyssa affirmed, an incomprehensible image of the incomprehensible: "If, while the archetype transcends comprehension, the nature of the image were comprehended, the contrary character of the attributes ... would prove the defect of the image ... [S]ince the nature of our mind ... evades our knowledge, it has an accurate resemblance to the superior nature, figuring by its unknowableness the incomprehensible Nature."[1]

At least in part, preoccupation with a well-bounded and clearly defined human nature seems fomented by theological anthropology's isolated attention to humans in and of themselves, as if the image of God could be located *in* them, in abstraction from their relations with others, particularly the God they are to image. The underlying problem is simply the presumption that human beings have a definite nature to begin that could be considered in itself and perfectly well specified in its own terms. What Augustine attempts in Books 8-11 of his *De Trinitate* would be a prime illustration of such a problem—at least if one considers the influence those particular books have had on theological anthropology in the West. Augustine tries to support the intelligibility of rules for trinitarian speech—e.g., the rule that persons of the trinity are really distinct in virtue of their relations with one another but one and equal in their divinity—by finding analogues for those rules in the more familiar character and dynamics of the human mind and heart. The effect of this, however, is often in these books to turn attention away from human consciousness in relation to God—indeed, to turn attention away from its relations with anything not itself, whether above the human (God) or below it (sense objects). Only the internal dynamics of human consciousness—the self's relations with itself—can mimic, for example, the perfect equality and union of distinct things which is the rule for the trinity; in relations with anything else there is, if not distance or disunity, then at the very least a marked lack of equivalence among the things related. For these reasons, Augustine goes so far as to suggest that the mind is a *better* image of God when knowing itself rather than God.[2] The strong impression from such discussion is that human consciousness is the image of God all by itself, in an ideally self-enclosed self-sufficiency—e.g., when knowing, loving, or remembering only its own pure productions.

The alternative would be to consider human nature an essentially relational affair, indistinct apart from and clearly definable only in terms of its determina-

[1] Gregory of Nyssa, "On the Making of Man," trans. H. A. Wilson, in *Nicene and Post-Nicene Fathers, vol. 5,* edited by Philip Schaff and Henry Wace (Peabody, Massachusetts: Hendrickson, 1994), chapter 11, section 4, p. 396; sections 2-3 are also relevant.

[2] In Augustine, *De Trinitate*, Book IX, Ch. 11, section 16.

tion by what it is related to. Human beings would therefore become the image of God only in an actual relationship with God bringing with it the only real correspondence with divine life and action to be found in human existence. Humans would be the image of God, properly speaking, only, say, when actually contemplating God face to face in heaven, as Augustine himself avers in the culminating books of *De Trinitate*. Considered apart from such a relationship, there would be nothing much to say about the reflection of God in human nature per se. Humans would at most be only in a secondary, less proper sense the image of God in virtue of whatever it is about them that is a prerequisite for such a relationship (e.g., in virtue of the cognitive capacities that when suitably expanded by God's grace enable them to see God in that fashion). Were one to read Books 8-11 of Augustine's *De Trinitate* through the lens of what he says in later books about the true or proper image of God in knowledge of God face to face–something that the West typically fails to do–then this simply becomes Augustine's considered opinion to begin with.

A more radical deflection, however, of concern for a well-bounded and well-defined human nature comes about in theologies for which human beings are not the primary image at all. If one reads the Genesis passages through New Testament, mostly Pauline ones, it is possible for the image of God to take on a primarily intra-trinitarian sense.[3] The image most properly speaking–the express or perfect image of God (following Hebrews 1:3)–is the second person of the trinity. And what that image is to mean for us is then most properly demonstrated in the human life of the Word Incarnate. If we are to image God, we have to be formed according to God's own image–the second person of the trinity–in something like the way Jesus was.[4]

The Genesis discussion of human beings' creation in the image of God can be viewed then in christologically focussed trinitarian terms. Humans are not simply the image but 'in' or 'after' it, as the verses say (Gen 1.27), because the image referred to here is itself divine–either the second person of the trinity or the Word incarnate. Which one makes little difference since in the latter case the primary image is still the second person of the trinity and the second person of the trinity only becomes applicable to us in becoming incarnate. Since the Holy Spirit is thought to unite us to Christ and allows us thereby to be made over in his image, often a great deal of interest is directed, moreover, to Genesis passages that could be taken to refer to the Holy Spirit–the spirit hovering over the waters (Gen 1.2), or the living soul breathed into Adam (Gen 2.7). The Holy Spirit itself was given to humans when they were created, in order to form them according to the image of God that is the second person of the trinity; they thereby became a human image of that divine image like (but not exactly like) the Word incarnate to come, Jesus Christ. The theology of Cyril of Alexandria sees the full and explicit development of such a view: "in the beginning ... the Creator of all, taking dust of the ground and having formed man, breathed upon his face the breath of life. And what is the

---

3 See, for example, Romans 8:29; 2 Corinthians 4:4; and Colossians 1:15.

4 See, for example, Galatians 4:19; Ephesians 4:24; and Colossians 3:10.

breath of life, save surely the Spirit of Christ ... ? But since He, [the Spirit which is able to gather us and form us unto the Divine Impress] fled away from the human nature ... the Savior gives us this anew bringing us again into that ancient Dignity and reforming us unto His own Image."[5]

With this more radical loss of a primary preoccupation with human nature per se as the image of God comes an odd refocusing of what's of interest about human beings, both when they actually image God in Christ and when considering their 'capacities' for it. In theologies that deny the possibly subordinationalist import of talking about the second person of the trinity as the image of the first–i.e., 'image' does not mean any lesser degree of divinity–the second person of the trinity is not comprehensible while the first is incomprehensible, but images it in its very incomprehensibility. And this holds for the incarnation of the second person of the trinity too. The second person of the trinity–whether the first born of creation by being the one through and for whom the world was created, or the first born of the dead by becoming incarnate for our salvation to everlasting life–remains in a strong sense an 'image of the invisible.'[6] Jesus is not the comprehensible stand in or substitute for an incomprehensible divinity but the very exhibition of the incomprehensible divinity of the Word in a human form or medium.[7] Jesus displays in his life what it means to be an incomprehensible image in the flesh of an incomprehensible God.

There would then be something incomprehensible about human nature as it is shaped by a relationship with God that makes it like God, and, secondarily, even something incomprehensible about it from the very start, one might say, which renders it capable of being worked over into a divine form. Like God who is incomprehensible because unlimited, humans might have a nature that imitates God only by not having a clearly delimited nature. Every other creature imitates God by expressing the goodness that God is in a limited form; they are good by being a definite something–a pig or a rock–indeed the best pig or rock they can be. Humans are a definite sort of creature distinct from others and in that sense of course still have a particular nature; they are not God who alone is different from others by not being a kind of thing. But humans can still stand out by their failure to be clearly limited by a particular nature as other creatures are. Failure of definition by remaining ill defined is not so much the point; what's primarily at issue here is a failure of definition through excessive love. Humans seem to have an underlying concern for what is absolutely good per se–for God–for what is not merely good in certain respects but fully good in a perfectly unlimited way. They want in some sense to *be* that absolute good rather than any particular sort of thing, rather than the specific sort of creature they are, by being formed in

---

5 Cyril of Alexandria, *Commentary on John*, trans. E B. Pusey (London: Walter Smith, 1885), Book 5, chapter 7.39, p. 550.

6 See Colossians 1:15.

7 Even in a theology like that of Athanasius, where the stress is on the pedagogical function of the Word's incarnation in a visible form, *what* is revealed in the contest with idolatry is the incomprehensible character of divinity.

and through a relationship with the absolute good—for example, by knowing the absolute truth that is God, the absolute good for human cognition, that comes by way of God's very presence to the mind. The weirdly unlimited character of human nature and drives would then be the fundamental reason for traditional theological preoccupation with human intelligence and will when discussing the way humans are the image of God. These 'faculties' are of interest because of their excessive openness, one might say, because of their attraction to formation through what exceeds their own or any limited nature.

Otherwise expressed, if humans are to be made over in God's image—so radically reworked as to be deified in the way Jesus' humanity is—then what is of interest about human nature is its plasticity, its openness to formation through outside influences and the unusually wide range of possible effects of such a process of formation in the human case. For humans to come to be in the image of God is an extreme case of coming to be oneself in relation to what one is not—God, what is most unlike creatures generally. All creatures are formed in relation to what they are not but humans do this in an exaggerated way that opens them to a radical sort of reformation from without in the divine image. Irenaeus expresses this essential malleability to divine formation well: "Offer to Him thy heart in a soft and tractable state, and preserve the form in which the Creator has fashioned thee, having moisture in thyself, lest, by becoming hardened, thou lose the impressions of his fingers. But by preserving the framework thou shalt ascend to that which is perfect, for the moist clay which is in thee is hidden [there] by the workmanship of God. His hand fashioned thy substance; He will cover thee over [too] within and without with pure gold and silver, and He will adorn thee to such a degree, that even 'the King Himself shall take pleasure in thy beauty (Ps xiv.11).'"[8]

All living creatures become themselves by taking in things from outside themselves; seeds, for example, require food from without in order to germinate. Humans, because they are made to be in the image of God, require God for their nourishment. In heaven, indeed, God will be our only food and drink, as Gregory of Nyssa maintains: "while our present life is active amongst a variety of multiform conditions, and the things which we have relations with are numerous, for instance, time, air, locality, food and drink, clothing, sunlight, lamplight, and other necessities of life, none of which, many though they be, are God—that blessed state which we hope for is in need of none of these things, but the Divine Being will become all [1 Cor 15.28], and instead of all, to us, distributing Himself proportionately to every need of that existence ... . God [will] become ... locality, and home, and clothing, and food, and drink, and light, and riches, and dominion, and everything thinkable and nameable that goes to make our life happy."[9]

---

8 Irenaeus, "Against Heresies," trans. Alexander Roberts and James Donaldson, in *Ante-Nicene Fathers*, vol. 1, ed. Alexander Roberts and James Donaldson (Grand Rapids, Michigan: Eerdmans, 1989), Book 4, chapter 39.2, p.523.

9 Gregory of Nyssa, "On the Soul and the Resurrection," trans. W. Moore, in *Nicene and Post-Nicene Fathers*, vol. 5, p. 452.

In the case of all other livings things, whatever they take in is formed according to the limits of their pre-established natures. For example, the natural resources assimilated by a plant for its nourishment–light, water, nutrients from the soil, and so on–are transformed to conform to the plant's nature. The plant remains itself, becoming merely a bigger and better version of itself, where there was genuine nourishment for the plant's good. When human beings take in God as their proper nourishment, they come out, to the contrary, as God. They are turned thereby into the matter, so to speak, for a new divine organization of what they are. They become God's image, rather than God's becoming theirs; humans are reworked according to God's pattern of living, rather than God being reworked according to a human one. Humans when they are formed in the image of God take on Christ's identity, in short. Like what happens to light, water, and soil–but now with a peculiar reversal of consequences from the usual scenario–men, women, children, Greek and Jew, free and slave–all go into the process of reformation and come out as Christ. "This is the purpose for us of God ... to raise our flesh and recover his image and remodel man, that we might all be made one in Christ ... that we might no longer be male and female, barbarian, Scythian, bond or free (which are badges of the flesh), but might bear in ourselves only the stamp of God, by Whom and for Whom we were made, and [having] so far received our form and model from Him, that we are recognized by it alone."[10]

To generalize from this, one might say human beings are unusually impressionable, in a way that the language of image often unpacks in a quite concrete way: they are like soft wax that a vast variety of seals might indent to their image; they are the mirror of whatever it is upon which they gaze. They take their identities from the uses to which they put themselves, like vessels that gain their character from whatever they are made to carry. Earthen ware or pure gold, what goes into them for certain purposes establishes what they are; whatever their fundamental constitution as vessels, when full of shit (for example), they can only be shit pots.[11] Less graphically speaking (and in a more contemporary idiom), one could say that human life takes a variety of forms depending on what it is that people care about.[12] "Such is the strength of love, that the mind draws in with itself those things which it has long thought of with love, and has grown into them

10 Gregory of Nazianzen, "Orations," trans. Charles Gordon Browne and James Edward Swallow, *Nicene and Post-Nicene Fathers*, vol. 7, ed. Philip Schaff and Henry Wace (Grand Rapids, Michigan: Eerdmans, 1983), 7.28, p. 237. I don't take this quotation (and others like it) to mean that what made you a man or a woman before is simply wiped out, along with your previous identities, but that those differences remain to be distinctively refashioned according to the same form of Christ; they become like diverse matters for a new fundamental reorganization that takes the same Christ-like shape each time. You are no longer identified as a man, say, rather than a woman, but what made you a man is still there as the material for the new organization of you that makes you Christ.

11 See Basil the Great, *On the Human Condition*, trans. and intro. Nonna Verna Harrison (Crestwood, New York: St Vladimir's Seminary Press, 2005), p. 72.

12 See Harry G. Frankfurt, *The Reasons of Love* (Princeton, New Jersey: Princeton University Press, 2006).

by the close adherence."[13] Human beings exercise self-reflective powers; they are able to make an object of themselves in projects of self-fashioning and re-fashioning, following changeable judgments about what it is that is most important to them–fancy cars, the respect of their peers, wisdom, and so on. They attach themselves to these objects of desire and draw them into themselves, so to speak, as variable organizing principles of their lives. "Human nature adapts itself to the direction of thought and it changes according to whatever form it is inclined to by the impulse of free choice."[14] This means–to return to a previous metaphor–that "[h]uman nature is in fact like a mirror, and it takes on different appearances according to the impressions of free will. If gold is held up to the mirror, the mirror assumes the appearance of gold and reflects the splendor of gold's substance. If anything abominable is held up, its ugliness is impressed in the mirror–for example, a frog, toad, centipede, or anything unpleasant to behold."[15]

Reflective capacities of self-judgment mean humans can try to reshape in a selfcritical fashion even those desires they cannot help having by nature. One may have the natural desire to eat but one need not shape one's life around the importance of food– asceticism is a case in point. Humans have the capacity to use the passions of their animal natures (as Nyssa would term them)–their natural attraction, for example, to what benefits them–as instruments of either virtue or vice.[16] That attraction may be the energy propelling them towards, say, profligacy–or God. Humans have the power to cultivate or discourage those natural drives and tendencies that they start out with whether they like it or not, making efforts, for example, to alter their intensities through stimulation or neglect, or efforts to rework the way they figure in one's life as a whole. Indeed, these self-reflexive powers account for why human lives can become so horrible, much more horrible than those of other animals; the anger, for example, that an animal might fleetingly feel when faced with an opponent can be husbanded by the human mind–dwelt upon–so as to pervade all one's dealings with others, in a host of variable forms–envy, malice, conspiracy, deceit–with the result that one's whole nature is traced anew after that design.[17]

Human beings have plastic powers, self-formative capacities, and it is the fact that those capacities are not determined to one thing as natural desires are–the fact that those capacities need not incline in a predetermined direction according to the givens of one's nature or essential definition (following a Thomistic understanding, for example, of natural desires)–that accounts for the heightened variability of their effects in operation. People turn out in wildly different ways, for

---

13 Augustine, "On the Holy Trinity," trans. A. W. Haddan, *Nicene and Post-Nicene Fathers*, vol. 3, ed. Philip Schaff (Grand Rapids, Michigan: Eerdmans, 1956), Book X, chapter 5, section 7, p.138.

14 Gregory of Nyssa, "Fourth Homily," in *Commentary on the Song of Songs*, trans. and intro. Casimir McCambley (Brookline, Massachusetts: Hellenic College Press, 1987), p. 92.

15 Ibid.

16 Gregory of Nyssa, "On the Soul and Resurrection," p. 442.

17 Gregory of Nyssa, "On the Making of Man," chapter 18.3-4, p. 408.

better or for worse. Or, one might say the self-formative capacities of humans do have a nature but the particular nature of rational volition is just to have no definite nature to be true to, in the way that animals are true to their natures when acting properly, for their own good. Humans can think of a variety of things that it would be good to do in certain respects or for certain purposes, and what they decide about what is most important to them in the course of such deliberations decides in great part the character of their lives, the identity they come to exhibit in their acts–*that* is just their nature.

The early eastern church's stress on free will as the image–or often secondarily, rule in the sense of self-rule–could now be taken in a new light, not as the promotion of some vaunted power in a positive sense, an imitation of divine omnipotence, but as an interest in the unusual plasticity of human lives absent any predetermined direction by nature. Free will is an indication of variability. Their unusual powers of selfdetermination mean humans can become anything along the continuum of ontological ranks, from the bottom to the top. Humans, it is true, are determined to God–being formed in the image of God is their good, by nature. But that is just *not* to be determined in any particular direction as other things are, since God is the absolute good and not a limited one.

All the qualities of humans typically highlighted by the theologians I'm interested in here have something to do with their rational capacities, and there is probably a good reason for this even from a more modern point of view (as I have implied) if indefinite plasticity, the nature that is no nature, is what these theologians are trying to get at. Especially in the early church figures I'm drawing upon, however, such a focus often dovetails with a marked matter-versus-spirit dualism and with an exaggerated disjunction between human and non-human which such a dualism often enforces. It is therefore important to see the way that plastic or non-natured *bodies* are the ultimate issue even for these early church theologians–at the end of the day it is our bodies that are to be remade into Christ's body.

Mitigating any matter-spirit dualism for all these figures (who generally hold a hylomorphic anthropology in any case) is the fact that souls are influenced as bodies are (e.g., through the incorporation of outside factors and influences) and the fact that the object of self-formation includes the body. It is very easy therefore to express what they are getting at in a more contemporary idiom not, so obviously at least, bound up with any need to distinguish spiritual from material: Human beings form themselves with reference to a whole host of outside influences–people, places, animate and inanimate influences, what have you–and what is formed is their whole lives, irrespective of any division between the material and the spiritual. When our minds are therefore formed according to the divine image, so are our bodies: when the mind is "adorned by the likeness of the archetypal beauty ... the nature which is governed by it [i.e., the body] ... is adorned by the beauty that the mind gives, being, so to say, a mirror of the mirror."[18]

[18] Ibid, chapter 12.9, p. 399; the discussion continues into sections 10-11.

When it is the plasticity of human lives before the divine that is at issue, blurring the boundary between spirit and matter is often, indeed, a primary gambit. See, for example, the use of the oxymoronic notion of 'spiritual matter' in Augustine's treatment of Genesis: rational creatures have an essential character like unformed matter (the abyss)–i.e., they exhibit matter's lack of form per se–when considered apart from the well being–that knowing well–that results from their being informed by God's own image.[19] They are fluid wax in need of sealing; otherwise empty mirrors to be made light by light.

Moreover, human materiality is essential to the image of God so as to take the whole of existence, irrespective of any division between spirit and matter, to God. (This is why angels or disembodied pure intelligences are not the image.) Only in virtue of the fact that they have bodies can the whole world hope in humans. Humans demonstrate that, appearances to the contrary (especially in the cultural and philosophical milieu of the early church), the material world itself is plastic by extension just as plastic to divine influence, one might hope, as human lives. God formed humans out of the dust of the earth so that when formed in the image of God humans might show that the earth too can be made over in God's image: both matter and mind are made for a single grace.[20]

Understanding the image of God as the second person of the trinity deflects attention from the character of human nature for a final reason: because there is a sense in which humans, considered in and of themselves, never become a proper image of God at all even when formed according to it. The image of God in a proper sense is just God, the second person of the trinity. Not being God, humans can therefore never simply become that image in and of themselves through any process of transformation. Since there is no ontological continuum spanning the difference between God and creatures, one cannot hope to become the divine image, this perfect or proper image, by approximating divine qualities–for example, by improving one's mental capacities in some gradual approach to God's own perfect rationality.

And yet, without abolishing or mitigating the difference between God and humans, humans do become the divine image–by attaching themselves to it. It is by being identified with what they are not that the divine image becomes their own. Humans become the image of God in the strongest sense (not imaging the image but simply identified with it) when they are not trying to *be* it at all, not trying to image the divine image in a human way, but are brought near to it, so near as to become one with it. Humans, one might say, are never sufficiently fluid or flexible simply to be the image in and of themselves, to be made over into some good approximation of it; they cannot hope, therefore, to achieve a simple reproduction of the divine image in some perfect human imitation considered on its own terms. Humans, instead, have the image of God only by clinging to what

19 See Hilary Armstrong, "Spiritual or Intelligible Matter in Plotinus and St. Augustine," *Etudes Augustiniennes* (September 1954), pp. 277-283.

20 Gregory of Nyssa, "An Address on Religious Instruction," trans. Cyril C. Richardson, in *Christology of the Later Fathers*, ed. Edward Hardy (Philadelphia: Westminster Press, 1954).

they are not–that divine image itself–in love. There is only one perfect or express image of God–the second person of the trinity–and that perfect image becomes humans' own only through their exceedingly close relationship with it–e.g., by its own actual presence within them, made their own by the first person of the trinity through the power of the Holy Spirit on the basis of second person's incarnation in human flesh. Humans show off, so to speak, the light that is the divine image itself–and are in that sense good images of God themselves–by exterior illumination, by glowing with a light that remains another's and not by some phosphorescent assimilation of that light into their own natures as some now human property.

All creatures can do this same showing off or shining back of the divine glory. Plasticity is not a prerequisite for it. Even now creatures can glorify God, glow with a kind of divine penumbra by pointing to, and in that sense making manifest, the goodness of the God who made them: the wonders of the world speak of the wonders of God. In the reformation of the world to come, when, for example, death will be no more, all creatures and not just humans can image the divine in the way we have just been talking about by living off, for example, the very eternal life of God, by drawing themselves on powers that remain divine, in virtue of a close relationship or oneness with God, that makes those powers their own. Because of its fluid character, the character or identity of human nature itself is remolded in the process–that is its peculiarity. Something, in other words, happens to human nature itself when it reflects the image of God. To switch metaphors, human nature is not like iron that simply glows when the divine flame is applied to it without any fundamental change in its character; were the iron to cool it would show its usual properties. It is more the nature of non-human things to be inflexibly themselves like that, even when feeling the divine heat. Human nature is not made for resistance and therefore humans are more like wood set ablaze by God in that their character will never be the same–their defects purged, let's say, of everything short of the good in the process. Human nature is itself reworked in the image of God so as to become humanly perfect–e.g., perfectly virtuous or perfectly pious.

This refashioning is not the divine image per se but specifically human perfection, and as such forms only a dim, distant analogue of divinity. Human perfection, which follows from union with the divine image, is always an image of an image (Christ) of an image (the second person of the trinity), in a radically inferior medium–indeed, before the eschaton in which perfection is achieved, an image of an image of an image in a thoroughly corrupted medium (e.g., one hard and unimpressionable to divine imprint). The image of God remains, properly speaking, a divine image and before that image any difference between humans and non-humans pales in significance.

The perfect form of imaging found in the second person of the trinity is beyond anything achievable in human life. The divine image is perfect because it is not an image by participation, by sharing, that is, in something that it is not in some imperfect fashion. The second person of the trinity is like an image in that it both has a relation of origin with the first person of the trinity (it comes from the first person, begotten by it) and reproduces in itself what makes the first person divine. But this is a perfect imaging—everything that is divine about the first person is found again in the second—and therefore not an imaging by participation: an image by participation is not its archetype but a mere image of it in virtue of some inferiority. Unlike things that become images by participating in what they are not, the second person of the trinity simply *is* what it images and therefore does not become an image by participating in what it is not. Unlike other images, it does not acquire the capacity to image something by, say, being impressed by it. Being an image cannot be an accidental acquired characteristic of that sort in the divine case since in divinity accidents are identical with essence—that is, divinity simply is everything that is said about it. The second person of the trinity does not in any sense borrow from the first what it does not itself have; one cannot say that the second person of the trinity "is made illustrious by the mere addition to Himself of features that were not originally His own, so that He shines as it were by reflected light from glories bestowed upon him, and not by his own natural luster."[21] Instead, whatever the second person gets from the first is properly its own by nature; the second person of the trinity is divine in and of itself and not simply in virtue of being the image of the first person. What is "the very Image and Likeness and Effulgence" of the Father must be "bearing innate within Himself the proper characteristics of His Father's essence, and possessing in all their beauty the attributes that are naturally the Father's."[22] Finally, unlike things that participate in what they are not, the second person of the trinity does not participate in the divinity of the first in any variable degree (more or less is not applicable to its imaging of the first, being a perfect image) and whatever it images of the first person of the trinity it does not stand in danger of losing (like, say, dry sand that is in danger of losing the imprint of one's foot when one walks away). The relation between the second and first persons of the trinity is for these reasons analogous to an imaging relationship that comes about in virtue of a shared nature. The second person, in other words, is something like a natural image of the first in the way a son might be the spitting image of his father (this is taken to be the point of 'son' language in the Bible), and nothing like an image produced in a medium foreign to the original—say, the way a flesh and blood person might be reproduced with paint on a canvas.

Contrary to all that has just been said for the second person of the trinity, human beings are mere images of God by participating in God. They are fashioned by God so that they image what they are not—God—in an imperfect fashion. They receive what is not their own and therefore they do not have it in the way God does, in a perfect or divine fashion—fully, unchangeably, and without susceptibility of loss.

---

21 Cyril of Alexandria, *Commentary on John*, Book 9, chapter 14.9, p. 255.

22 Ibid, chapter 14.7, p. 246, where Cyril is discussing Christ, but the point remains the same.

Human beings are images of God by participation, moreover, in two major ways. At the very lowest level, human nature itself is an image of God–not just our rationality, free will or plastic capacities–but everything about us that is given to us by our Creator. And the same holds for every other creature. Everything that creatures are or have for their good is received from God, and constitutes a kind of image of God in a created form if what God is always trying to give to others in creating them is the goodness of God's own life. Creatures form created versions or approximations of God's own goodness, following (for example) the principle that a cause contains its effects in a superior fashion: creatures image God in that God as their cause contains in a super-eminent divine fashion what they are.

Participating in God is just what it means, indeed, to be a creature. God is (for example) life itself, life through itself, while everything else receives its life from God, without simply being it, in and of itself. Any creature therefore has life in some degree or fashion and can lose it. Expressing much the same thing in a Thomistic way, God does not participate in being but *is* it: to be *God* just is to *be*; in God there is no distinction between what God is (essence) and the fact that God is (existence). To participate in being is, by definition, not to be it, if participation means participating in what one is not; and therefore with participation arises a distinction between essence and existence, the very constitution of created things.[23]

Although we image God in and through what we are as creatures we do not do so independently of God. That is indeed one of the points of saying that we image God through participation. This is not an accidental mirroring of God, by chance or happenstance in virtue of what have become independently of God, on our own steam apart from any relation to God, the way a pumpkin might by chance or happenstance have grown of itself into the image of a human face. We image God because we have been fashioned by God. Indeed, we are the image of God only by participating in God, by continuing to receive what we are from God. To be a creature just means to lead an insufficient life of oneself, to lead a kind of borrowed life.

Creatures can be more or less the image of God in virtue of their particular created characteristics. We have seen this in the case of human beings–the way they are more the image of God than animals, and more the image of God in certain respects than others–in virtue primarily of the peculiar plastic capabilities that open them to reformation according to an absolute rather than merely partial or relative good. But this is still participation at the lowest level–participation in virtue of the character of created qualities themselves, participation by way of imitation in an ontologically inferior, because non-divine, medium.

Even what we are to become by being formed in Christ's image is a low-level image of God of this sort–in so far as the end product, so to speak, is a human state–a most excellent state indeed, but still a human one. The reflection of God in humans, when the Spirit conforms them to Christ, is in this sense like the re-

---

23 See Cornelio Fabro, *Participation et Causalité selon S. Thomas D'Aquin* (Paris: Beatrice-Nauwelaerts, 1961), pp. 468, 610.

flection of the sun in a mirror: the reflection is not at all like the sun itself in most respects–e.g., its extremely small, relatively cool, quite dim so that we can look at it without being blinded, and so on.

Indeed, the difference between God and creatures is the primary problem for this first sort of image through participation. The difference in media, so to speak, between the human image and its divine archetype makes too big a difference here; the divine simply cannot be imitated, strictly speaking, in what is not divine. Because God is their source, creatures must be imitating God in what they have of the good, as we have said; but the difference between God and creatures–the fact that they do not both figure within the same ontological continuum–nonetheless forbids the idea of any real approximation to the divine on the creature's part. There is nothing in between God and creatures, as the idea of imitation, particularly when used to discriminate between one sort of creature and another, might suggest. One is either one or the other. There is only one true image, then–the divine image–which perfectly reflects its archetype. Anything short of that is hardly an image at all.

In a second, much stronger sense of being an image by participating in what we are not, what we are not itself becomes part of us, an ingredient of our constitution. We are the image of God not by way of a human imitation of God, not by way of what we are ourselves, but in virtue of some sort of incorporation of what remains alien to us, the very perfection of God that we are not. God becomes part of us, an ingredient in our faculties, as a prerequisite for the excellent exercise of human operations. Cyril, for example, and Augustine, too, distinguish between our existence and our wellbeing and claim that the latter is a function of God's own entrance within us. We are rational creatures, say, and that is a sort of image of God–the low-flying kind–but when we know well, then we are the image of God in a stronger sense in virtue of the fact that the truth itself, God, has entered within us to give us the truth. The excellent functioning of our native capacities is not a self-sufficient operation, then, in the sense of simply unrolling from our own capabilities, but requires a strong dependence on the very powers of God which have become ours for the taking–in some extraordinary gift of God to us of what is not ours by nature. The perfection of human living that is Christ's and (to a lesser degree) ours in him would be the supreme case of this sort of thing–of human powers elevated through the entrance of God's own powers, through the gift of the Holy Spirit itself forming humanity according to the image of the second person of the trinity.

Here we image God by living off God, so to speak, in the way a foetus lives off the life of its mother, living in and through or with her very life. This is the mirror that is bright not by anything that is its own but only through the presence of the sun's own light. This–to use the more common biblical imagery perhaps–is the branch that lives on the alien sap of the vine to which it has been engrafted.

These two senses of image by participation–the weaker and stronger–are obviously bound up with one another. The first sense of image by participation is, for example, the presupposition for the second: one cannot participate in God in the strong sense, have God within you, unless there is something to you apart from God—unless one is an image of God in the weak sense by having an existence and nature of one's own as a creature. Those created capacities that image God (in a weak sense) more than others provide the openings, moreover, through which one becomes an image in the strong sense. Those capacities one might even say are the prerequisites for being an image in the very strongest sense. All things can come to live off the eternal life of God, when, say, that is the only life left to them. But God's gift of God's own self can become a true constituent of only certain sorts of created natures—ones whose functions are not limited by nature, those that inherently have room for God internal to them. The strong sense of image by participation is, finally, what enables the strongest version of the weak way human acts can be the image of God: by having the one whom we are not, Christ, the very incarnation of God, for our own, we should one day be able to live a human life that imitates God's own in the most perfect way possible for mere humans.

To conclude, we are then—body and soul—an incomprehensible image of the incomprehensible both in our natural capacities and in what we become in relation to the true image, the Word incarnate. Human capacities imitate God's incomprehensibility in only a negative and prospective way in virtue of their not being limited by a predetermined nature. Rather than being unlimited through inclusiveness, through unbounded fullness, as God's perfection is, we are unlimited in our powers through lack, through a failure of pre-determination, by not being anything in particular to start.

We might one day come to imitate in our humanity the inclusiveness of the absolute being and goodness of God but only when aided by God to become what we are not. Formed by the Word when that day comes, humans may imitate the incomprehensibility of God in a positive sense, e.g., by becoming incomprehensibly good as God is good. Like what happened in Christ's own human life, the new pattern of human lives will then be ultimately comprehensible according to an archetype that cannot be understood—according to the incomprehensible pattern of the Word's own relations with the other members of the trinity. Because he is the Word incarnate, Jesus' life follows the pattern of the Word's own relations with the other members of the trinity and ours will too, united with him.

Incomprehensible in its own fullness of goodness, this archetypal divine pattern will remain, moreover, invisible in its divinity even as it surfaces as the organizing principle of human life. The divinity of Jesus' life is an inference, hidden behind the fact of human acts that save; all one sees is a human life with unusual saving effects, unimaginable apart from divine powers, which one consequently must affirm by faith rather than sight. In much the same fashion, what is responsible for making our lives this way will not appear *as* itself or per se, in any part of them, but will appear invisibly, only in and through the unusual character of a human life otherwise inexplicable in merely human terms.

We will come to be more than an imitation of the incomprehensible only by assuming or taking on the identity of what we are not, the alien identity qua divine of the Word incarnate itself. By attaching ourselves to the incomprehensible that has attached itself to us (in becoming incarnate for this very purpose—so that we might attach ourselves to it), we become in the strongest sense incomprehensible ourselves. One with Christ, incomprehensible in his divinity, we take on the very incomprehensibility of the divine rather than simply running after it, working to reproduce it in human terms. This is the hidden incomprehensibility behind, indeed, the visible incomprehensibility of a new human pattern of living. Christ's own life provides, not just the pattern of a new human way of life for our imitation, but the cause of that pattern in us, by our assimilation within it. The second person of the trinity not only shows forth the true image in human form by becoming incarnate but makes us like that image by uniting human nature thereby with the very incomprehensibility of the divine life. It is by being bound to the incomprehensible in and through Christ–and thereby gaining a new identity in him apart from anything one is oneself–that one comes to live a boundlessly full and good life.

Is Seeing Believing?

'Visibility' and 'Self Concealment' of God in Jewish Theology after the Holocaust

Alfred Bodenheimer

I.

In her study on the description of Jewish martyrdom during the first crusade of the year 1096 and its presentation in the Hebrew chronicles, Swedish scholar Lena Roos describes a change of paradigm in the perception of anti-Jewish violence from antiquity to the Middle Ages. Antique sources, i.e. II Maccabees use the formula "a decree was made" (הרזג הרזגנ) to talk about the measures that the king of an enemy took to oppress Jews or suppress the teaching of Torah. Even though God was seen as the Lord of history, He was tolerating rather than directly causing inimical acts and cruelties of foreign rulers. In the Hebrew Crusade Chronicles that talk about Jews being killed and killing themselves and their children in the face of forced baptism, the word "decree" (which has finally become prominent as circumscription of the whole event as תרזג ונתת (the decree of 4856)) has got a new meaning. As Roos writes: "the decree is issued by God. (...) It can be seen as a response to the question that is so frequently asked in the Hebrew Crusade Chronicles: Why did God allow this to happen? The answer is: God caused this to happen."[1]

900 years later, looking back on the Holocaust, it seems very doubtful, whether and how we can bring God into contact with the gas chambers and chimneys of Auschwitz, let alone how and why we could and should describe him bluntly as the agent of horror. Quite different from the writers and recipients of the Hebrew Crusade Chronicles in the twelfth century, who might have seen themselves in a kind of concurrence with Christendom on holiness and the readiness to stand divine tests, most Jews of the twentieth and twenty-first century object to such ideas. If we read reactions of Jewish thinkers made on the eve of catastrophy, in the midst of its duration and in the aftermath, we can observe a certain move from the will to see God within the events happening to a tendency of stating his self-concealment. In more radical cases, we find a denial of God's existence, or at least of his being involved in the world. Altogether they confirm a tendency that

---

1 Lena Roos, *'God Wants It!' The Ideology of Martyrdom of the Hebrew Crusade Chronicles and Its Jewish and Christian Background* (Turnhout: Brepols, 2006), pp. 200f.

according to my lecture of Jewish Holocaust theology is evident: Talking about God in relationship to the event of the Holocaust means, for Jews after the Holocaust, talking about Jewish politics for the present and the future, including, of course, the state of Israel. Jewish Holocaust Theology transforms God to a national good (or, by denying his presence, transforms Judaism to a pagan form of living). If Yehoyada Amir has asked the question, how modern Judaism can still see Jewish history from the perspective of a history governed by God that emanates in the fate of this one and only small people,[2] then the Holocaust has become the answer for a consequent rejudaisation of history in the eyes of many Jews. Even if Jewish history is not seen as the center of world history, it is still seen by them as a special case, a history with an intrinsic mission.

There were quite some representatives of the Ultra-Orthodox community who saw the sanctions of Nazi Germany against Jews in the time shortly before systematic murdering began as a sign of God's reaction in a classical way. Shlomoh Zalman Unsdorfer, a rabbinic scholar from the school of the Pressburg Yeshiva founded by the famous and radidal Chatam Sofer and by then led by his great-grandson, wrote a text in January 1942, where he tried to explain the situation of Jews, submitted to many discriminations by the means of godly sanctions:

> They ordered us to wear gele Tsaykhen (yellow insignia) [to announce] that we are Jews. Because of our many sins, how ashamed we were of our Jewish garments and names, of our fringes and of the mezuzah on our doorposts, when it was our obligation to have everyone who saw us recognize that we were the seed of the blessed God, when it was our obligation not to transgress, heaven forbid, the strict sin of shaving the beard with a razor! Out of shame before the gentiles, we did not want to be recognized at all by the sidelocks of the head. Now, as over-against this, the evil ones have decreed that everyone should recognize that we are Jews.[3]

Here, the very classical idea of *mipnei Chataeinu* (because of our sins) is intertwined with the (also classical) principle of *mida keneged mida* (measure for measure) as a means of God's sanctioning and giving merit. Of course, this is before the mass murder has begun–still it shows the urge of 'reading' reality as a sign how to improve one's deeds and especially of strengthening one's faith rather than losing it. Tragically, Rabbi Unsdorfer himself was killed in the war.

In 1941, the then active Rabbi of Lubavitch Yosef Yitzhak Schneerson took the events in Europe as a cause to call for a *Machane Israel* (Camp of Israel), a mass movement that was to stand for bringing "immediate redemption."[4] Warn-

---

2 Yehoyada Amir, "The Concept of Exile as a Model for Dealing with the Holocaust," in *Wrestling with God: Jewish Theological Responses during and after the Holocaust*, ed. Steven T. Katz, Shlomo Biderman, Gershon Greenberg (Oxford: Oxford, 2007), pp. 305-317, see 307-309.

3 See Shlomoh Zalman Unsdorfer, "Texts to different Torah portions 1942 and 1943," in *Wrestling with God*, pp. 52-60, see 55.

4 See Yosef Yitshak Schneersohn, "Proclamations and different Essays 1941-1943," in *Wrestling with God*, pp. 173-190, see 175.

ing American Jews in a prophetically inspired manner that ignoring his words and following the American Way of Life would bring them destruction as it was to be seen in Europe, and promising them redemption by following his call, he lay the basis for today's Habad movement, one of the most influential and the most global Jewish movements whatsoever.

One of the most interesting orthodox writers during the war was the "Esh Kodesh" (holy fire), Rabbi Kalonymos Kalman Shapira, deported in 1943 from the Warsaw Ghetto, where he wrote his famous work, to Treblinka. What strikes most in reading parts of his writings is that he came back on what he wrote on earlier occasions in order to correct it according to later experiences. His claim of 1941 that people should rather learn Tora than using their spare time to learn or recite psalms was amended in the following year by a bitter remark:

> The above was said and written in 1941. Then–however bitter were the troubles and suffering, as is apparent from the text above–it was at least possible to lament, to find words to describe a handful of events, to worry about the survivors, and to grieve for the future–how will they rebuild the schools and yeshivas etc.? We still had the wherewithal to admonish and inspire those who remained, with the desire for Torah and worship. This is no longer the case, now at the end of 1942, in a radical excision. Those individuals who survive, pitiful and few, are broken in slavery and Egyptian bondage, downtrodden and terrified for their lives. There exist no words with which to lament our woes. There is no one to admonish, and there is no heart to awaken to worship and to Torah. How many trials must one undergo as the price of a prayer, and how many tests must be withstood, just to observe Sabbath, even for those who genuinely long to observe it? There is certainly no spirit or heart left to grieve for what the future holds, or to plan reconstruction on the destroyed edifices at such time as God will have mercy on us and save us. Only God, He will have mercy and save us in the blink of an eye. As for the rebuilding of all that has been destroyed, that will only happen with the final redemption and the resurrection of the dead. God, alone, can build and heal. Please, O God, have mercy; please do not delay rescuing us.[5]

Dan Garner has called Shapira's approach atheodicetic. No explanation for suffering, no talk of punishment, but a shift to a pure cry for redemption. God has become invisible, only the formula of "Egyptian bondage," remembering the time before the miraculous exodus, gives a hint of His presence even in the most desperate of situations. But visibility, as it exists in some way for Unsdorfer or Schneerson, this isn't. No more project, no more concept can be bound to God in this situation.

Many years after the war, Eliezer Berkovits has tried to show that "Faith after the Holocaust" was dependent precisely on recognizing God's hiddenness during the Holocaust. Only as a witness of a sometimes hidden God, seeing its own history as one of thousands of years rather than focussed on the destruction of Auschwitz, the Jewish people was to obtain its faith for the future. Berkovits was especially concentrated on disputing the position of Emil Fackenheim who, after

---

5 See Kalonymos Kalman Shapira, "Holy Fire," in *Wrestling with God*, pp. 40-50, see 43, note 1.

all, saw the future of the Jewish people in gaining normality. Normality, Berkovits claims, would be the end of Judaism. Insofar, God's temporary invisibility becomes the condition for testifying him in history, in fighting a human autonomy gone wild by the pure decision to cling on to Him. The consequence may not be, according to Berkovits, therefore, to make Israel a state like all states. Judaism has to pick up the chance to remain a "holy nation."[6]

Regarding the grippling of more than one generation of scholars for descriptions of God's concealment during the Holocaust, it is fascinating to see that in the twenty-first century, feminist theology is fighting for a new kind of visiblity of God. Melissa Raphael describes the hidden face of God in a different way: It is God's female face hidden by a male paradigm of imagining God as awesome, mighty and omnipotent and ignoring his suffering, solidary, loving, "female" face. Raphael sees women themselves and their striving for easening the suffering as a part of God's face that was very well visible in Auschwitz—against the male face of cruelty and might.[7]

Of course, this latter approach is highly political, too, in breaking a male dominance of Holocaust theology. After all, as this short overwiew might clarify, Holocaust theology does not so much believe, what it sees, but it sees, what it believes. The cultural transformations of the images of the divine in this seminal field of Jewish self understanding are and will remain important, yet complex and politically as well as socially and not at least highly ethnocentric modes of talking and explaining the unexplainable. Because since it *is* unexplainable, almost everything can be said about it. On the background of this epistemological approach, I now want to watch a little closer on one very influential work of the twentieth century, which has become so important partly because of the fact that it starts from the point of a visibility of God in the historical present, continuing it to a social and political position.

II.

If, as I have claimed in the above chapter, Jews have been going on since the Holocaust in searching (or locating) God exactly within his "hiding" during the time of the extermination of six million European Jews, at the same time, the practical historical coincidence of Holocaust and the Founding of the State have caused an urge to view the two closely intertwined, not only historically, but also theologically. One of the most imminent and famous examples for the trial of a combined view of both historical events is Rabbi Joseph Soloveitchik's famous essay "Fate and Destiny", also appeared (in English) under the (Hebrew) title "Kol Dodi dofek"

---

6 See Eliezer Berkovits, "Faith after the Holocaust," in *Wrestling with God*, pp. 463-484.

7 See Melissa Raphael, "The Female Face of God in Auschwitz," in *Wrestling with God*, pp. 649-662.

(The voice of my Beloved is Knocking).[8] Rabbi Soloveitchik, who lived from 1903-1993, was for many years the uncontested spiritual leader of modern orthodox Judaism in America and maybe even the world, named by his students and admirers in all simplicity "the Rav". Having been born into of one of Lithuania's most prominent rabbinical dynasties, he made his PhD in Philosophy at Berlin University shortly before Jews were driven out from German Universities, and then went on to the US, where he lived and tought in Boston, while at the same time he became the spiritus rector of Yeshiva University in New York.

His first famous philosophical work "Halakhic Man" was written during the second world war, and it tries to place man, as far as he lives according to the Jewish law, within a system of references between man and God, insofar as life as such, by being bound within the structures of Halakha is in constant relation to the divine.

We might draw the conclusion, then, that for Soloveitchik it is exactly the option of God's hiding that is strictly impossible. We might turn the question whether seeing is believing into the answer that only believing is seeing. This point, which–as has to be stressed–is entirely free of all mystical or irrational orientations, but actually regards itself as an antidot to them, is crucial for any understanding of Rabbi Soloveitchik's thinking. Man who is immersed in a life confronted with God's presence uttering itself in his constant halakhic duties, sees God's presence in the world as an ongoing challenge.

As for the suffering of the people of Israel, which is dominating the whole complex of Holocaust theology and also is the point of departure of "Kol Dodi Dofek," the approach of halakha in some way also elevates the status of hester panim, the hiding of God's face. This is so, because God's presence in halakha has reached a quality that can be objectivated and separated from the actual status of wellbeing. In fact, halakha creates a new form of challenge regarding suffering. As opposed to what Soloveitchik calls the "child of fate," a person who is seeing herself passively delivered to what she and the collective she belongs to have to endure, the "child of destiny," seeing his own obligation to put himself and the people around him into close contact with God (i.e. the man of Halakha), develops an entirely different approach to suffering:

> When the "Child of Destiny" suffers, he says in his heart, "There is evil, I do not deny it, and I will not conceal it with fruitless casuistry. I am, however, interested in it from a halakhic point of view; and as a person who wants to know what action to take. I ask a single question: What should the sufferer do to live with his suffering?"[9]

What is entirely new in "Kol Dodi Dofek," a lecture that Soloveitchik gave on the occasion of the Israeli day of independence in 1956, is his application of this idea of Halakhic man to an understanding of Jewish history, or, to be more precise, to

---

8 Rabbi Joseph B. Soloveitchik, *Kol Dodi Dofek: Listen–My Beloved Knocks,* translated and annotated by David Z. Gordon, edited by Jeffrey R. Woolf (New York: KTAV, 2006).

9 Ibid., 6.

the experiences of the Holocaust on the one hand and the foundation of the state of Israel on the other. Because here it is not an existing system of coordinates referring quasi automatically to all kinds of duties of a man in his steady encounter with God. It is rather a reading of historical and political events of the time. In them, God has not simply the character of an all-embracing power, but rather shows himself through the acting of humans in a way that uncompromisingly demands understanding and interpretation. God becomes visible in history, and, as always in Soloveitchik's thinking, God's visibility is linked to duties of man, respectively of the Jew.

The metaphor of the voice of the knocking lover is taken from the beginning of the fifth chapter of the Song of Songs. The lover is knocking at his girlfriend's door, but she does not feel herself ready at first to open him and tarries to get up. Finally, when she does, he has gone and can not be found anymore, causing a never ending, unsuccessful search and yearning for him.

Reading the song of songs allegorically, as it is done by a broad classical-rabbinical consensus, Soloveitchik tries to name the knocks of the lover (i.e. God) that have lately called for the people of Israel and about which he fears that they might not be heard or understood in the appropriate way—meaning that Israel could miss a one time chance that has historically been opened to him during a short period of time. By this—and this is one crucial "iconic" point I want to make here—Soloveitchik retransforms the rabbinic allegorization of the song of songs, namely that the relationship of lover and beloved is to be read as a relationship between God and Israel—into a theo-historical interpretation of events taking place at the very time being. In significant difference from many rabbinical scholars of his time, who tried to master catastrophes or extraordinary experiences such as the Holocaust by referring to biblical or midrashic analogies in order to draw theological consequences, Rabbi Soloveitchik, in a nearly prophetic manner, reads signs on the wall—or rather knocks at the door—in order to take steps to fulfill the conditions of Gods ruling of history. The very revolutionary line of his thinking is that he reads various signs that all go in the direction of the Jews becoming masters of their own history as knocks of God. As opposed to the relinquished "child of fate," the "child of destiny" should rather become master of his (historical) bearing. Jews, as Soloveitchik perceives, might miss their chance, because they are not up to realizing that the image of the divine has changed dramatically, from one historical moment to the other. His striking claim that religious Zionism (and only religious Zionism) has the theological tools to read God's historical turn in His messages sent to Israel (accompanied by the warning that even religious Zionists, especially in America, might fail to fulfill their duties) can be read as a turning point in Jewish political theology. The character of Halakhic man has changed from life in the constant presence of God to an autonomous competence of interpretation, what Judaism as "destiny" (as opposed to "fate") demands. By this, of course, political decisions are dichotomically split in acts due to or radically against God's will.

Of course, Rabbi Soloveitchik's words cannot be read without considering their immediate context. Two years after Rabbi Soloveitchik's speech, the Head of the Satmar Hassidic group in America, Rabbi Joel Teitelbaum, published his work "Vayoel Moshe," where he lashed Zionism and argued that it was bearing responsibility for the extermination of European Jews in the Holocaust. It is clear that the way of thinking of Rabbi Teitelbaum and those like him was already known by the time of Soloveitchik's speech.

In order to clarify Soloveitchik's approach, which basically describes the development before and after the founding of the state of Israel as a challenge comparable to the biblical Exodus, I shortly want to list in detail the "Six knocks" he extrapolizes from world politics in the late forties and early fifties.

1. The UN resolution of November 29th, where Russia and the Western states in an unpreceded act unanimously voted for the founding of a Jewish state as part of the land between Jordan and Mediterrean: "I do not know who the representatives of the press, whit their human eyes, saw to be the chairman in that fateful session of the General Assembly in which the creation of the State of Israel was decided, but he who looked carefully with his spiritual eye saw the true Chairman who conducted the proceedings–the Beloved. He knocked with his gavel on the lectern."[10]

2. Israel's victory in the War of Independence, in fact not only the victory of this small army against united Arab armies, but the happening of the war altogether: "Had the Arabs not declared war on Israel and instead supported the Partition Plan, the State of Israel would have remained without Jerusalem, without a major portion of the Galilee, and without some areas of the Negev. If thousands of years ago Pharaoh had allowed the children of Israel to leave immediately, as Moses had originally requested, Moses would have been bound by his word to return in three days. Pharaoh, however, hardened his heart and did not listen to Moses. "The Holy One then took Israel out with a mighty hand and by an outstretched arm" (Deut 4:34). Consequently, the force of the promise [that the children of Israel would return to Egypt] was vitiated. No contract that is based upon mutuality of promise binds one side if the other party refuses to fulfill its obligations: Listen! My Beloved Knocks."[11]

3. The forced acceptance of a Jewish state by Christian theology–against the deepest conviction of Christians that all rights on the Promised Land as mentioned in the Hebrew Bible referred in an allegorical sense to Christianity, as Soloveitchik explains. "I find satisfaction in reading about the State of Israel in the Catholic and Protestant newspapers. Despite themselves they must mention the name of Israel when they report the news of Zion and Jerusalem, which we possess."[12]

4. The cohesive power of the Jewish state in relating even assimilationists anew to their Judaism: "Many who were once alienated are now bound to the Jewish State with ties of pride in its mighty accomplishments. Many American Jews who were partially assimilated find themselves beset by hidden fear and concern

---

10 Ibid., 32.

11 Ibid., 33.

12 Ibid., 35.

for any crisis that the State of Israel is at the time passing through, and they pray fo its well-being and welfare even though they are far from being totally committed to it. Even Jews who are hostile to the State of Israel must defend themselves from the strange charge of dual-loyalty and proclaim daily and declare that they have no stake in the Holy land. It is good for a Jew when he cannot ignore his Jewishness and is obliged to perpetually answer the questions 'Who are you?' and 'What is your occupation?' (Jonah 1:8), even when extraodinary fear grips him and he does not have the strength or fortitude to answer with true pride, 'I am a Jew, and I fear the Lord, the God of heaven' (Jonah 1:9). The unrelenting question of 'Who are you?' ties him to the Jewish people."[13]

5. The realization for the peoples of the world that Jewish blood is not cheap, that Jews for the first time in the annals of Jewish exile, are able to defend themselves. "If the antisemites describe this phenomenon as being 'an eye for an eye,' we will agree with them. If we want to courageously defend our continued national and historical existence, we must, from time to time, interpret the verse of an 'eye for an eye' literally. So many 'eyes' were lost in the course of our bitter exile because we did *not* repay hurt for hurt. The time has come for us to fulfill the simple meaning of 'an eye for an eye' (Ex 21:24). Of course, I am sure everyone recognizes that I am an adherent of the Oral Law, and from my perspective there is no doubt that the verse refers to monetary restitution, as defined by halakhah. However, with respect to the Mufti and Nasser, I would demand that we interpret the verse in accordance with its literal meaning. (...) Revenge is forbidden when it is pointless, but if one is aroused thereby to self-defense, it is the most elementary right of man to take his revenge."[14]

6. The fact, that, as opposed to the time of the Holocaust, when persecuted Jews found no place to escape, there will now always be a safe haven, where the gates are open fo them to escape, survive and build up new lives.

Of course, in its ideological aim, Rabbi Soloveitchik's text is an appeal to "his" public, the religious Zionists of America, to open their hearts and their purses for the construction of Israel (and definitely not only its religious institutions), or to immigrate to the land and settle especially its empty areas as the Negev, in order to create facts against its enemies who might want to reconquer and destroy it. Soloveitchik, full of the deepest reproach to American Jews, including himself, to have failed in front of the task to do more for Europe's Jews during the Holocaust, feels the vocation to call on them not to fail again.

But there remain two consequences of the way he has chosen that cannot be taken lightly: From a purely philosophical view, it remains unclear, what the halakhic interpretation of the state of a "Child of Fate", respectively a "Child of Destiny" exactly has to do with his interpretation of political and historical events. If we would say that halakhah is exactly the power enabling the Jew to stand beyond history, then the historical task of the Jew regarding his historic challenge (which shall not even been denied here) is more of an aporetic question confronting his

13 Ibid., 36.

14 Ibid., 37-39.

halakhic worldview of "destiny" than it is its true fulfilment. Secondly, on a political level, the religious basis of his argument, as it is in fact documented by the title "Kol Dodi Dofek," has had an enormous impact on religious Zionism by itself. If it is not the *image*, it is the *sound* of the divine, His knock, that becomes the basis for an era of a kind of New Prophetism, arguing with the claim of immediate action and understanding of what God asks Jews to do–not as individuals, but as a collective, in fact as a power with military and political means at its hands.

It may, for example, be true to regard self defense as an ultima ratio in the situation of fight; the abrogation of the monetary interpretation of Talionic law, interpreting "an eye for an eye" as to be taken literally in certain cases–and expressively so by a scholar who declares and also lives absolute loyalty to the principle of the Oral Law–can have the most dramatic consequences that I don't have to elaborate here.

Rabbi Soloveitchik himself (concerning the "fourth knock", related to the assimilationists) refers to the "Hiding of the Face" of God (Hester Panim). I think, in his text "Kol Dodi Dofek" we see a very decisive reaction on this trial to get along theologically with the devastation of the Holocaust: The unseen, hidden God is to become a visible God, his knocks loud and not to be overheard, his message clear and not to be misunderstood. Similarly, American Jews who have failed to during the Holocaust, are, according to Soloveitchik, in a situation where they cannot afford to fail again concerning their support for Israel, so their ears and eyes are wide open in order not to miss any 'message'. In some way, orthodox Judaism in its want to hear God's voice and see His deeds in unparalleled clarity is, until present, trying to compensate for the Holocaust. The wrestling for "destiny" in what can hardly be called other than "fate" has led to an understandable, yet problematic need to act. A culture that has grown in endless dispute on and casuistic deconstruction of the "truth" of texts, finds itself drawn back to the call to take history into its own hands according to a truth, which has to be put as an absolute one in order not to endanger the righteousness of the actors.

Part II

Spiritual Transformation and the Divine

Images of the Divine and Spiritual Transformation in Judaism

Michael Fishbane

1. Introduction

Our consultations on 'Images of the Divine and Cultural Orientations' encourage the broadest factual and phenomenological focus–given the potential dialectics of the two poles of this topic. A double delimitation would therefore seem advisable, in my view, and make for the most productive comparative discourse. The first delimitation narrows the cultural scope to the personal and its sphere of action to individual praxis. I shall therefore re-frame the broad scope of our topic in terms of 'Images of the Divine and Spiritual Transformation'. This will permit an examination of the relationship between certain images of the divine in culture and the ways they are used for human spiritual development. The second delimitation further narrows the scope to Jewish thought and spirituality (with a special emphasis on the Jewish mystical tradition). Even so, the topic exceeds the contours of our forum. I shall therefore highlight selected examples or types for consideration. In this context, I intend my contribution to be an essay in historical and constructive theology–in a manner I shall hope to make clear throughout.

Judaism (in both its life and thought) is a complex and dense exegetical culture, founded upon the Hebrew Scriptures. Consequently, the diverse images of God in this canonical source constitute its normative base. This pertains initially both to the range of such images (historical and literary) within Scripture itself, as well as to the various reinterpretations or reception of this material preserved therein. That is to say, the primary ground for this exegetical culture is found already in the Bible–from earliest ancient Israelite antiquity. Just think, for example, of the classic formulation of the human image-divine found in Genesis 1: 26, where the human person is said to be created *be-tzalmeinu ki-demuteinu*, that is: "in our image, according to our likeness" (where the reference apparently includes God and the divine pantheon).[1] The anthropomorphism of this statement is palpable, and reformulated with no hesitation in this regard in Genesis 5:1, where the narrator introduces an archival genealogy of ante-diluvian ancestors with the comment: "This is the book of the generations of Adam: When God created Adam, he made him in the image of God, *bi-demut elohim*" (and then adds, like the first source, that this Adam figure was created "male and female"–presumably meaning either a primal androgyn or a primal human pair). This depiction is

[1] All translations are authors, unless otherwise noted.

subsequently valorized (with all due circumspection) in the great ecstatic vision of the late priest Ezekiel, who portrays a divine figure upon the heavenly throne seemingly shaped as a *demut ke-mar'eh adam*, "a likeness like the appearance of a human" (Ezekiel 1:26). But such a bold view did not comport with all theological sensibilities in late biblical antiquity, as we can confirm from the fairly contemporary theology of Deutero-Isaiah, who sharply rejected such imagery through a prophetic voice which asks, only slightly rhetorically, and with palpable inner-textual resonance, *el miy tedamyun el u-mah demut ta'arkhu lo*, "to whom will you liken Me (God) and what likeness will you estimate for Him?" (Isaiah 40:18).[2]

We needn't extend examples, for it is quite evident, from even this limited instance, that the normativity of an image of God is both diverse and dynamic within the Hebrew Bible itself: diverse, insofar as positive and negative values may accrue to it; and dynamic, insofar as ongoing theology counterpoints older language for its own ends. Obviously, these two exegetical poles have starkly divergent implications for what it means to 'speak of God' (in terms of a positive theology), and also to 'have God in mind' (in one's personal spiritual orientation; be this in terms of interior images or their mental focalization).

But the issue only begins here. For Judaism is also founded upon a vast assortment of scriptural interpretations, and thus, necessarily of its inherent images of God. All these extend 'biblical historical theology' and reconstruct it for Jewish religious culture in numerous ways. The monumental midrashic collections of late antiquity and the early middle ages comprise one witness to this phenomenon (also with positive and negative anthropomorphic ascriptions); as do various other streams of rabbinic exegetical tradition. For example, medieval Jewish philosophy repeatedly sought to purify these biblical images of God and construe them as abstract concepts or ideas through one or another mode of allegorical reformulation. Indeed, the very process of such allegorization—of focusing on the deeper ideational form or intent of the content—is itself a process of purification of one's mind and focusing on the divine intellectual ideal, rather than the external 'imagery'. Thus for a rational philosopher like Maimonides (in *The Guide for the Perplexed*), the biblical phrase *be-tzalmeinu ki-demuteinu* (Genesis 1: 26) most properly refers to a certain comparable structure of mind and reason that link God (through the angelic agent intellect) and the human being (in their fullest intellectual capacity); and indeed, in his view, it is precisely by honing the mind and purifying it of all gross (surface) images that one may undergo a spiritual transformation and become a true 'person' (not just a rational animal).[3] The process of negative theology, or the intellectual exercise of divesting the mind of all positive images, is thus a spiritual practice (of philosophy), whose goal is an interior 'service (or worship) in the heart'. By contrast, different currents of Jew-

---

2 See my comments in Michael Fishbane, *Biblical Interpretation in Ancient Israel* (Oxford: Clarendon Press, 1985), 325. The doubled clause seem to suggest a divine voice followed by a human one.

3 I. 2; see *The Guide for the Perplexed*, translated by S. Pines (Chicago: University of Chicago Press, 1960), 21-3.

ish mysticism project bold images of the Divine Image onto the supernal realms; and although these mystics never hesitate to stress the super-sensual aspect of these constructions, they nevertheless valorize these shapes and their symbolic potential. Thus for a kabbalist like R. Joseph Gikatilla, whose work, *Sha'arei 'Orah*, derives from the same time as Maimonides' *Guide* (thirteenth century), the supernal Divine Anthropos, in whose 'image' humankind is formed, is a transcendent configuration homologous with our human bodies. This bold correlation between the human and Divine Image enabled mystics to contemplate Divinity in and through the structures of the human being; thereby exemplifying the words of Job, "I shall see (envision and contemplate) God through (the structure of) my flesh (body)" (Job. 19:26).[4]

And so, let it be stated from the outset: although such cases of construction are certainly historical, in the diachronic sense of constituting something of the after-life of biblical images, they are synchronic as well—being our latter-day construction and reformulation of these various constructions. Hence we must always recognize that historical theology is *itself* a constructivist enterprise at its very core. We ever stand within the constraints of our hermeneutic horizon; and this being so, these various constructions reveal our own historical standpoint in the very process of their reconstruction. Or to state this point somewhat differently: images of the divine and *our* cultural orientations (to restate the theme of our consultation) are always complexly intertwined. We may realize this entwinement at various levels of methodological self-awareness, but never so much as when we attempt to appropriate older images for our own spiritual benefit. We shall thus spiral along this circuit, in various evidential loops, until the end, when I shall offer my own personal interpretation. Along the way, we shall be guided by several Jewish examples as we think about the relationship between divine images and human spirituality.

2. Conceptual Turn # 1: Thinking About Images and Self-Transformation

Conceived broadly, Jewish theology swings between two extremes: between the pole of positive images of God, drawn primarily from Scripture, and that of their negation, by means of various kinds of re-conceptualization; between the pole of dynamic, living characterizations of God, conceived of as a personality of sorts, and more static, conceptual characterizations of this reality; between traditions of the sayability and visualization of God, variously drawn from older resources, and others cautioning silence before the unimaginable infinite of unknowable Divinity. But these poles are also variously brought into correlation or alignment. At one extreme, there is an attempt to mark off the relationship between the diverse approaches to images as two types of cultural orientation. Maimonides'

4 This trope became standard fare in kabbalistic and hasidic writings over the centuries.

approach is paradigmatic. For him, the bold anthropomorphic images in the scriptural and cultural canon of Judaism are for individuals of a common bent, with no philosophical inclination or training; whereas their negation (or transcendence) is the higher methodological path, meant for intellectuals who strive to serve God with their reason and a pure heart. But the Law intervenes. How does one fulfill the divine will, and the many injunctions to pray and bless God for all worldly beneficence? Is not this language filled with the boldest of anthropomorphic images (referring to a God who brings forth bread from the earth; who causes rain and dew; and who hears prayer)? This is undoubtedly the case; and so the philosopher (who remains observant) must employ the Law in service of the transcending standards of philosophy—and use the concrete language of prayer and blessings (and many other theological figures) as a means for training the mind towards inner purity, and the performance of the commandments as focusing devices for mindfulness of God at all times.[5] In this way, the daily and obligatory tasks of religious life are philosophically recast as functional means for individual self-transformation. Ultimately, the images must be transcended; for the more one becomes "like" God, the more one becomes a pure and refined intellect (albeit in the sub-lunar realm). Such a "likeness" is an inconceivable "image;" for the divine image becomes hereby an ultimate intellectual abstraction. To refine one's ideas and thoughts into a purified mind is the only proper philosophical-spiritual orientation—and, ultimately, this cognitive achievement is world transcending.

Mystics had other goals and took the task of accommodating oneself to the Image of God in other directions. This required a quite different set of spiritual pyrotechnics, and a different correlation between the human image and its divine archetype. Let us return to Gikatilla's great *Sha'arei 'Orah*, just mentioned. At the very outset, this kabbalist tells us that: "The true essence of God cannot be grasped by anyone but God! ... So what do all those depictions that we read in the Torah—concerning God's hand, foot, ear, and eye—mean? Know and believe that although those descriptions indicate God's true being, no creature can know or contemplate the (ultimate) essence of what is (there) called 'hand', 'foot', 'eye', and so on. [So d] o not (ever) imagine that the divine eye is actually in the form of an 'eye' (etc.); ... (for) these (depictions) are (in truth) but inner—innermost—aspects of the Divine Reality ... (Indeed,) there is (absolutely) no similarity in (either) substance or structure between God and us .. (Hence) our (bodily) organs ... (are merely) symbols of most recondite, supernal realities. The mind cannot know these realities directly; and can (at best) only be reminded of (or referred to) them—as when one writes (the words) 'Reuben son of Jacob'. (Certainly) the form of these letters is not the form, structure, and essence of the real Reuben son of Jacob, but is merely a mnemonic device; .. (that is,) a symbol of the particular entity called by that name".[6]

And if all this is true with respect to the more explicit scriptural references to God's body or mind or will, it is similarly so with respect to the numerous

5 For overall considerations, masterfully presented, see I. Twersky, *Introduction to the Code of Maimonides* (Mishneh Torah) (New Haven: Yale University Press, 1980), 371-97.

6 R. Joseph Gikatilla, *Sha'ar I* (Warsaw: Ergelbrenner, 1883), 2a.

implicit or indirect epithets of God that Gikatilla details in this opus—all of which are intended to provide a full lexicography of the spiritual hints of Scripture with respect to the supernal realms encoded there. That is, each term or epithet of divine reference marks a recondite dimension of the divine dynamic, a coursing of spiritual and creative energies that takes on the imaginal form of a Divine Anthropos—moving downward from the supreme gradation called Supernal Crown (*Keter 'Elyon*) through the several modes of Intellect (*Hokhmah* and *Binah*), Emotion (*Hesed* and *Din*), and Creative Vigor (*Tiferet* and *Yesod*), coalescing (in the lowest gradation) in the Queen of Heaven (*Malkhut* or *Shekhinah*).[7] Reading Scripture is thus a (carefully guided, hermeneutic) procedure, a spiritual entry into the very verbal images of Scripture—which are not solely symbolic tropes of the supernal Pleroma, but actual 'energy fields' for contemplating these transcendent networks of divine power and creativity. Thereby, the language of Scripture becomes modalities for mindfulness and spiritual ascendence and purification of an entirely different order than that proposed by philosophers like Maimonides. One may suppose that Gikatilla's mystical dictionary of scriptural terminology (and divine Names) provides a conceptual (if not intentional) counterpoint to Maimonides's bold philosophical dictionary (nouns, verbs and divine Names), which comprises major portions of the opening 70 chapters of his *Guide*. In both cases, images are 'means' for their transformation and transcendence. Allegory shifts the mind from content to form, and thereby directs it to the purity of Thought; whereas symbolism provides vectors for the mind to inhabit, as it ascends towards the nullity of human thought in the mystery of Ineffable Unknowing.

3. A Conceptual Interlude

I wish to consider this mystical project a bit further. When absorbing such Neo-platonic philosophical traditions, early and later medieval Jewish mysticism did not simply see itself as valorizing the divine images of Scripture in terms of esoteric archetypes or ontological realities. It also turned the horizontal (or polar) contrasts suggested earlier (i.e., between an imaginal and imageless God) into vertical structures. Highest in spiritual value, and transcending the hierarchy itself, was the quintessentially imageless infinite of Divine Unendingness—the so-called *Ein Sof*, or Illimitable. On the one hand, this 'reality' was beyond conception and imagination, devoid of every depiction and mental trace (and thus a valid heir

---

7 *Hokhmah* and *Binah* refer to Wisdom and Understanding, respectively, and designate the upper Male and Female (transcendent intellectual forms that symbolize the 'insemination' of ideas and their being 'conceived' by the mind); *Hesed* and *Din* refer to Mercy and Judgment, respectively, and also designate Grace and Rigor; *Tiferet* and *Yesod* refer to the Male Splendor and its Principle of Creative Generation, respectively; and *Malkhut* refers to Lady Sovereignty, the queen of Divine Immanence, also known as *Shekhinah*. *Tiferet* and *Malkhut* denoted the lower Male and Female principle, the main spiritual focus of attention of the mystic in worship.

of abstract philosophy); but it also yielded modalities of emanation, not solely the ontological reality of mystical metaphysics (called the *sefirot*, or supernal gradations), but also the ontic structures of imaginable images of God such as we know them in Scripture and use them in our human world. In this way, a conjunction was effected between the conceivable mystical valences of Divinity, comprised of biblical images, and the philosophical negation of these very images, and indeed anything sayable or knowable about Divinity–with the result that the latter now served as the ultimate, imageless font or pre-condition of the various theological images found in Scripture.

Conceived in such hierarchical terms, the task of the adept could take at least two forms. One was to reverse the primordial process of origination and spiritually to ascend from the lower to the higher realities–from the sensual to the super-sensual orders, and from the images to their negation. In this process, the self would ideally undergo a corresponding spiritual transformation–moving from the natural and tactile features of worldly images of God, and of oneself as an earthly configuration thereof, to their transcendent referent: the illimitable Nothing–beyond all Being, as it were; perhaps even to the Origin of all origins (if you will forgive this foundational locution). Another form proceeds differently, and attempts to perceive the higher realities in the lower ones in a meditative apperception; or, to state this matter otherwise, to realize that these lower realities are merely sensate (symbolic) modalities of the higher ones, so that the task of the self would now be to participate in both realities simultaneously–i.e., live them in their concrete worldly reality, thick with concrete imagery, while simultaneously thinking them in terms of their ultimate, spiritual truth, beyond all imaginative presumption.

This leads us to wonder how one might proceed in the process of reversal, if we follow the first route, or live the double reality, if we follow the second. Related to such matters is the issue of how one might keep both realities in dialectical tension, so that the images of God do not become (through inadvertence or thoughtlessness) reified figures or mental idols, but may serve as a trellis for one's spiritual ascent; or also (if we now think this dialectic from the other side) of just how the image-less Divine Reality might be 'imagined' to enter the human imaginary for the sake of religious praxis (especially prayer), while retaining its ultimate, transcendental character.

These questions are essential for any Jewish historical and constructive theology which tries to take the images of God seriously but not falsely; and which tries to take them as functions for the spiritual life–helping to guide the self to a higher personal truth, beyond all metaphor. Thinking about these matters takes us beyond the theological polarities noted above, to more dynamic hybrids of thought or practice. This integration involves another turn of the conceptual wheel.

4. Conceptual Turn # 2: The Role of Images for Spiritual Ascendence

The intricate weave between historical and constructive theology is exemplified in a most remarkable passage in the *Zohar*, the classic of Jewish medieval mysticism that began to emerge in thirteenth century Spain. It offers a meta-statement of the issue and its textual dramatization. The passage (I. 103a/b) is a meditative commentary on Genesis 18:1, "He (Abraham) was sitting in the opening of the tent." This historical tableau is transformed into a mystical figure (or event) via the citation of Proverbs 31:23 (which serves as its homiletic proem), "Her husband is known in the gates, when he sits among the elders of the land." What does this text 'truly mean' beyond its reference to a man who is the husband of a "woman of valor"? And further: just what is the correlation between the two passages that will serve to constitute the hermeneutic revision of the first one? The interpretative shift is precipitous. From two (perceivable and conceivable) earthly scenes, the text abruptly introduces a dogmatic theological locution about (an unperceivable and inconceivable) divine transcendence. The text states: "The Holy, Blessed One, has ascended in glory. He is hidden, concealed, and wholly other. There is no person in the world, nor has there ever been such, who could understand His wisdom or withstand Him;–for He is wholly hidden, concealed, transcendent, (and) other." The speaker goes on to say that this holds for all creatures–above and below: for neither the divine beings nor the human ones could ever conceive of any 'Where?' that He might be;–for He is Every-where and No-where, when it comes to knowing Him or His Whereabouts. If so, how could one say "Her husband is known in the gates?–since (in Jewish mystical symbology) 'her husband' is (in truth) the Holy Blessed One" (i.e., *Tiferet*, the Supernal Glory of Divinity in the Pleroma, and spiritual consort of the Heavenly Bride, His wife of Valor, the *Shekhinah*). How could the Unknown be "known"?

This theological query is answered in a remarkable way. "Truly! He *is* known 'in the gates (*she'arim*)', since He may be known and cleaved to according to the way one opens one's imagination (*de-mesha'er be-libbeih*)–each person according to their capacity to cleave to the spirit of Wisdom. Hence, one knows (God) in one's mind (heart) in proportion to the nature of one's imagination: hence 'He is known' by these 'gates' (i.e , imaginal forms)–but no one could even know or cleave to Him as He truly is!" The teacher thus indicates that God, who transcends all knowledge, may be known through the imagination and its forms; and he goes on to say, via a citation of Psalm 24:7, that these gates are the "openings (*pithei*) of eternity", or the entry points within the world and the heart whereby one may ascend ("openings within opening") towards the truly unknowable mystery of God. Hence Abraham, who sits at the "opening (*petah*) of the tent" is symbolic of all persons who sit at the entry point to the unknown, supernal realms in this world–this entry point being (symbolically) the *Shekhinah* herself. Whoever is able to perceive these portals (in the world and the soul) may enter the succeeding levels and ascend towards God. But this discernment and enactment is particularly difficult in these days, when Israel is in exile–for mind and spirit are alienated (the soul is in exile) and the entrances to the mysteries obfuscated by human misprision. All this will change with the return from exile, the teacher adds, for then one will see in clarity what is now obscured in a glass darkly. As Scripture says: "I shall return to you when life is due" (Genesis 18:10).

All this is remarkable. The *Zohar* text offers a meditation on images and the imagination, by means of scriptural passages that are interpreted in terms of the imagination of God through the images of the world and heart. The images of Scripture become 'means' of thinking with and through images towards the transcendent and unknowable Other, as much as possible. And these images teach the truth of the necessity of images for the religious spirit, and that one's religious life depends on the quality and cultivation of these images. Moreover, and just as remarkably, the teacher says that these images are the openings towards transcendence (the husband or divine Glory) that may be perceived through the portals of divine immanence (the wife or *Shekhinah*) located in and throughout the world (in and through all the images that guide our outer vision and human insight). The way to God is through every "opening of the tent" in tangible and imaginal existence; each moment may orient the heart towards God through the entry points of perception, when refined by the imagination as a symbolic carrier of the questing spirit for Divinity. But images will always remain as 'The Palm at the End of the Mind' (in the poetic image of Wallace Stevens). There is no *ke-deqa' ye'ot*, "as It truly is," for the seeking religious spirit. The human imaginary is not mindless. To the contrary: in our present situation, spiritual ascendence is only and necessarily through the purification of the worldly and existentially real.

5. Conceptual Turn # 3: Imaginal Images and their Human Enactment

In addition to the divine figures in Scripture, Jewish religious thought addressed itself intensely to the meaning and purpose of the commandments. I referred earlier to the fact that the philosopher Maimonides taught that a key purpose of the commandments for the philosophical adept was to cultivate a focused mindfulness of God in and through their enaction. That is, they had a particularly spiritual-rational utility for the human worshiper, and absolutely no theurgical effect whatsoever. This stated, Maimonides also remarks, in works designated for the common (non-philosophical) person (the worshiper as such), that when performing the commandments one should divest oneself of all disruptive (worldly) "thoughts" and "imagine" that the *Shekhinah* (or divine presence, in rabbinic parlance) is "*as if* before one always".[8] Here again is a focus on mindfulness; and

---

8 *Mishneh Torah, Hilkhot Tefillah,* IV. 16 (*halakha* 15 specifies the central importance of *kavvanah*, or "directed intention", in prayer; # 16 discusses its performance); in the edition of S. Fraenkel (Jerusalem-Bnei Brak, 2006), II, 60 (with commentaries). On this phrase, and the duty to perform prayer with a focused mind, see Y. Tversky, "'Ve-Yera'eh 'Atzmo Ke-'ilu Hu' 'Omed Li-Fnai Ha-shekhinah': Kavvanat Ha-Lev Ba-Tefillah Be-Mishnato shel

although this imaginal presence has no form or image, it is still a configural consciousness (or mode of awareness) in the worshiper's mind–a filling of the mind, as it were, with a total sense of divine presence, something a philosopher would strive to achieve through modes of rational intellectualization.[9] Nevertheless, even in this case one can detect a concern to stress the importance of emptying the mind of all worldliness and purify one's act of worship by a spiritual focalization of the religious mind.

The kabbalistic tradition moves in a entirely different direction. Since its diversity and complexity is beyond the scope of these reflections, we can best serve our goal by focusing on one key typology; namely, the correlation of the commandments with an imaginal portrayal of the supernal Torah in anthropomorphic form. To fully appreciate this, we must first note how two notions from ancient rabbinic theology were totally transformed. The first is an old notion (classically expressed by R. Simlai in babylonian Talmud *Makkot* 23b) that there was a totality of 613 commandments in the Torah, this being composed of 248 positive commandments ("thou shallt") and 365 negative commandments ("thou shallt not")–the former group being the 'total' of the limbs of the body, the latter the sum of the days of the year. Hence on this view, which gained wide currency and was frequently cited and justified, the commandments collectively serve to regulate the entirety of the human person (body) at all times (daily). The teaching is thus an inchoate expression of a profound intuition of the integral nature of the commandments with human existence–a kind of mystical *theogoumenon* regarding the human meaning of the divine commandments. Such a view comported well with a sense of a revealed Torah, and could be kept separate from simultaneous notions of a primordial Torah that anteceded the creation by two millennia–and even served, according to a classic formulation, as the ideal blueprint for that very creation (*Genesis Rabba* I. 4; III. 5).[10]

But suddenly, with various subtle precursors, there burst into view the mystic ideal that this cosmic Torah was a supernal configuration in humanoid form, and that the commandments were correlated with the limbs of this Figure. A classic formulation occurs in *Zohar* II. 165b:

> All the commandments are limbs through which the Mystery of Faith is perceived. One who does not contemplate and gaze at the mysteries of the commandments of the Torah does not understand how the limbs are mysteriously arrayed. The limbs of the body are all arrayed according to the mystery of the commandments. Thus: just

---

Ha-Rambam," in *Kenesset 'Ezra ... Mehqarim ... le-Ezra Fleisher* (Jerusalem: Yad Ben-Tzvi, 1994), 47-67.

9 Maimonides frequently mentions the importance of "remembering" God "always" (of having God continuously in mind) in his various writings. Cf. *Guide* III. 44; *Hil. Berakhot* I. 3.

10 In the first citation, God "looked (*hibit*) into the Torah and created the world"; in the second, God "studied (*nit'aseq*)" the book of Genesis and "created His world". See in *Midrash Bereshit Rabba*, edited by J. Theodor and Ch. Albeck (Jerusalem: Wahrman, 1965), 2, 20.

> as there are great and exalted limbs (in the human body), and if even one of them is removed (be it small or great) that person is blemished, so all the more so is it so that if one removes even one of the commandments of the Torah causes a blemish where there should be none.

Though couched in mystical formulations, the overall intent is clear: there is a profound spiritual correspondence between the supernal Divine Form ('the Mystery of Faith') and the human body, such the human performance of the commandments decisively affects this transcendental array in ways large and small. This is the theurgical effect; and it means, mystically, that human actions on earth, in and through the body, affect the purity and perfection of the supernal archetype. But there is a corresponding contemplative aspect, and it is that a meditation on the commandments puts one in mind of their transcendental dimension and thus of the profound parallelism between the divine and human. That is, though the Torah is narrative and commandment, and a structure of divine will in language, the mystic will perceive just how it mediates between the ontology on High and its ontic realization on earth.

This also means that the human person is perfected by enacting the ideal divine structure. One properly begins by contemplating the higher imaginal truth (the Mystery of Faith), and then turns to its faithful performance. The two realities are reciprocally affected: just as human beings purify their limbs through the performance of the commandments, and become a spiritual whole; so, correspondingly, is the divine Whole strengthened and unified thereby and able to conjoin in new creative forms and configurations. A striking reading of an ancient rabbinic teaching brings this out. According to an old homiletic comment on Leviticus 25:3, "And you shall observe My commandments and do them", R. Hanina bar Pappa wondered why Scripture has repeated the exhortation–for what does "and you shall do them (*va-'asitem 'otam*)" add? And he answered, with exegetical ingenuity, that the listeners are told that if they observe the commandments they would "make themselves!"–a revolutionary reading based on an implied re-vocalization of the object pronoun (not: do *'otam*, "them", but as if: make *'atem*, "yourself").[11] Yet, for all its force, this exegesis reflects the classic rabbinic sense of the transforming effect of the commandments upon the human performer. But the *Zohar* (III. 113a), and many commentators who followed in its wake, turned this reading on its head, and went so far as to say that when one performs the commandments: "It is as if he has *made Me*! ... (For) since they (the Holy One and the Shekhinah, the main male and female gradations of the pleroma) are (thus) aroused (through the commandments) ... you have indeed *made them*!" With deft legerdemain, the mystic teacher first transfers the older exegesis from the person to God ("made Me"), and then justifies it by a daring hyperliteral reading of the original scriptural passage, insofar as the plural "them" *now* refers to the Supernal Pair of the Pleroma! Hence, in this case, the exegetical comment serves

---

11 See *Leviticus Rabba* 35.2; in the edition of M. Margulies, *Midrash Wayyikra Rabbah* (Jerusalem: Wahrmann, 1962), IV, 825 f.

to direct the human mind to the divine image that is affected thereby! Put differently: human exteriority influences divine interiority, since the human image is a concrete embodiment of a transcendental imaginal configuration. The earthly Torah is a crossing point of the two–for those who understand.

If this example demonstrates the root of the commandments in the divine configuration as a whole, another thirteenth century source derives them from a primary duality within this pattern and gives another perspective on the transforming effect of the divine commands on the human soul and body. This source is embedded in the commentary on the Song of Songs of R. Ezra of Gerona; for at a certain point, this kabbalist, interrupts his mystical exegesis and presents a long rationale for the commandments, fully infused with esoteric dynamics and considerations. Like R. Moses de León (a principal composer of the *Zohar*), in his key work on the rationales of the commandments (*Sefer Ha-Rimmon*), R. Ezra also locates the source of the positive and negative commandments in the primary commands to "remember" (*zachor*) and "observe" (*shamor*) the Sabbath day, respectively.[12] Now these two earthly injunctions flow out of the divine aspects of love and fear and have, in turn, their transcendental source in the supernal gradations of *Hesed* and *Din*, the divine attributes of Mercy and Judgment. This homology deploys further, insofar as the religious aspects of love and fear of God (which regulate the human desire to obey God and fear sin, through positive performance or negative restraint, respectively), depend on the human emotional regulation of the primary psychological dyad (the "good" and "evil inclination"; *yetzer tov* and *yetzer ha-ra'*). Hence the positive and negative commandments, emerge out of the divine gradations of Love and Judgment to help a person perfect and regulate the inner balance of their inclinations, and thus enact their proper proportion in the world, so that not only will the person (body and soul) be regulated, but so too will all the ethical and social and religious realms of life. Thus the imaginal projection of the divine emotions into the supernal spheres (as meditative and mystical constructs) provide an esoteric rationale for their enactment for the adept, even as their regulative effects work inherently on every obedient person (in this sense there is a parallel with Maimonides' distinction between the intentional or inherent effect of the commandments for the philosopher and commoner, respectively). With this as prelude, listen to R. Ezra's own words.

> You must know that all the commandments depend on two principles, the positive and negative commandments: the positive ones derive from the attribute of *zachor* and the negative from the attribute of *shamor*–which correspond, as is known, to two of God's attributes. Thus one who does the commandments of his Master and fulfills it, derives from the attribute of love ... which correspond to the positive commandments; and one who refrains from doing something out of fear of his Master derives from the attribute of fear, which is lower than the attribute of fear ... And you must (further) know that the human being is comprised and infixed by these two attributes ... the good inclination on the right ... and the evil inclination on the left ... And since these two attributes, the good and evil inclinations, which correspond to the positive and nega-

12 See in the edition of E. Wolfson, *The Book of the Pomegranate: Moses de Leon's Sefer Ha-Rimmon* (Atlanta, Georgia: Scholar's Press, 1988), 14, lines 10-14.

> tive commandments, are infixed in the person, and the Torah was given with positive and negative commandments, one should train oneself to follow the way of the good qualities, so that the negative ones be drawn after them and nullified thereby ... For this reason were the commandments ... given, so that the evil inclination be subdued and subordinate to the good one.[13]

In this significant portrayal of the supernal roots and esoteric rationale for observance of the commandments, one may observe that their purpose is explicitly oriented to the human being and their spiritual transformation (their reciprocal theurgical effects notwithstanding); and thus their imaginal depiction is, reciprocally, a source of spiritual orientation and contemplation to guide the perfection of the divine image in the self. And it is through such interior reflections of the self that there derive diverse exterior effects upon the social world. The proper alignment and realization of these multiple correspondences is the ideal.

6. Conceptual Turn # 4: Channeling Divine Mercy Through Oneself

The divine attributes of love and fear located in the supernal gradations of Grace and Judgment constitute a root structure for the positive and negative commandments of the Torah, as we have just seen (and R. Ezra's formulation has numerous subsequent correlates). These all refer to obligatory behaviors. However, speculative schemes were developed that took matters to another level, even to the highest supernal gradation called *Keter* (or Crown). This gradation is even beyond the highest intellectual spheres of Wisdom and Understanding (below which are the ethical gradations grounded in Grace and Judgment), and therefore transcends even these mind-transcending orders. For if the human mind can neither conceive nor ever know the formations of thought and meaning in the supernal ideational realms, so much less can it fathom this most recondite and supernal of dimensions–the Crown, which is imagined at the crossing between Absolute Transcendent Infinitude (the so-called *Ein Sof*) and the formations of the Supernal Pleroma. But all this notwithstanding, mystics repeatedly sought to portray something of that realm, and in a scheme of interest to us here, even imagined it as constituted by a recondite arch-hierarchy of pure mercy. In this way, the divine Tetragram (located in the center of the pleroma, and called *Tiferet* or Splendor), which was (divinely) said to be composed of thirteen attributes of mercy in Exodus 34: 6-7,[14] was traced back to its supernal archetype within *Keter*. The result of this is that the imaginal hierarchy of that form is wholly arrayed in dynamics of mercy, with the consequence that all of the lower gradations have this dimension

---

13 R. Ezra, "Peirush 'al Shir Ha-Shirim," in *Kitvei Ha-Ramban*, edited by Ch. D. Chavel (Jerusalem: Mosad Ha-Rav Kook, 1962), II, 496 f. R. Ezra's authorship is critically accepted.

14 For this formulary, and its reuses in Scripture, see Fishbane, *Biblical Interpretation*, 335-50.

as their deepest structure. One worldly implication of this is that for a person to truly imitate God, they must do much more than activate the divine gradations which encode the obligatory commandments (rooted in the ethical spheres), and channel the dimensions of mercy that emanate throughout the supernal hierarchy. Hence the human being, formed in the image of this esoteric imaginary, must not only enact the commandments with all their limbs, but also, through them, do deeds of kindness in the world.

R. Moses Cordovero's (sixteenth century) theological-ethical tract called *Tomer Devorah* spells all this out in a most remarkable way.[15] Compassionate Mercy flows out of *Keter* in all its recondite patterns, and discharges its energies throughout the Divine Pleroma–moving through the two attributes of *Hesed* and *Din*, downward through the Male Principle of *Tiferet*, and thence, through all of its procreative powers, into the receptive Female Principle called *Shekhinah*, which gathers them as a Mother, and delivers them (as a beneficent overflow) into the world as created entities, all formed in the image of her Manifold Unity (She being a composite microform of all the supernal gradations). Human beings, formed in the image of the Whole, and composed with the energies of this great World Mother, thus have a special role in channeling the flow of divine creativity, and especially compassion and loving kindness into social existence. And this they do by actions that are fundamentally informed by the divine principles of pure mercy. All this gave a special valence to an old rabbinic dictum about *imitatio dei*. Reading the strong exhortation in Scripture to "keep" the divine commandments and "walk in God's ways" (Deuteronomy 11: 22), one midrashic comment asks how it is possible for a human to walk in God's ways (taken to be an act of emulation, not of obedience!), and answers (with the old attribute formulary in mind),[16] "Just as He is called merciful (*rahum*) so be ye merciful; and just as He is called *hanun* so be ye compassionate" (*Sifre Deuteronomy* 49).[17] And if one should further wonder, as did R. Hama bar Hanina (third century) just how these attributes could be enacted (that one be "like" God), consider his own response, which annotates the general injunction with specific supererogatory behaviors–like burying the dead, clothing the naked, visiting the sick, and feeding the hungry (babylonian Talmud *Sotah* 14a). All these acts are assembled from divine models derived from Scripture, and serve as examples of how humans could be godlike on earth.

But Cordovero goes further, since for him the issue is not merely the imitation of a figural model but of actualizing the Divine Image through its human exemplars. For this one has to train oneself in the ways of mercy and compassion, thereby to become a pure channel for its enactment on earth. Thus: just a mercy streams out of the Supernal Hierarchy, through the Visage and Body of the Divine Pleroma, and through the *Shekhinah* as providential grace for the world–

---

15 First published Venice 1588, and frequently thereafter; most recently Bnei Brak: Daat Kedoshim, 2003.

16 See note 14.

17 See in *Sifre ad Deuteronomoium*, edited by L. Finkelstein (N.Y: Jewish Theological Seminary, 1969), 114.

expressed as the light of the Countenance for giving joy and grace, the Word of speech for proper guidance and support, or the outstretched Arm for beneficent giving and care–so should mercy similarly flow through the person towards their neighbor. In human terms this means (as he stresses) the cultivation of a kindly eye and brow and mein, which express kindness and not anger; a gentle and wise word which express compassionate care and instruction; and open hands and an alert body to give gifts and render aid as needed. Mercy is therefore not a spiritual abstraction; but has concrete earthly expressions, and their flow through humans is one way that divine providence is beneficently extended by those created in the divine Image–to others whose image is in need of support or repair. All this requires work and habitude (Cordovero uses the expression *le-hargil ha-'adam 'atzmo*, "one should train oneself", which he derives from Maimonides),[18] so that the human being may realize their divine archetype and become a pure channel for the realization of God's Mercy on earth. Thus, insofar as the source of beneficence transcends duty and obligation, supererogatory love is at its human core. And ultimately, the source is God–for Compassionate Mercy is the Transcendent Truth of God, according to this religious vision. Nothing higher is imaginable; and in a sense, nothing more is necessary. The ancient word of the psalmist, "The world is founded upon *hesed* (gracious mercy)" (Psalm 89:3),[19] is hereby raised to its supernal apex in the Divine Heights. And when oriented towards the world and human culture, the realization of this Image is nothing other than the Kingdom of God, on earth as in heaven.

Cordovero's teaching is a spiritual challenge. Before turning to a personal reformulation of this matter, let me first restate an earlier point with the benefit of our preceding inquiry.

Jewish historical theology reconstructs from Scripture and rabbinic tradition the image of the imageless God in terms of various archetypes of divine providence. These structures are in different ways transcendent and immanent, impersonal and personal, abstract and embodied. Each construct is a creative exemplar of living theology at specific historical moments; and they are only perceived as 'historical' and 'constructed' images when they are alienated from the real and living spiritual imaginary of the spectator. From within, these productions are dynamic flow and reformulation; whereas from without they may seem artificial exegetical ploys or projections. One's standpoint is crucial. So viewed, religion is a practice of divine embodiment, fulfillment, and transformation; and human constructions of its reality *are their realized forms* in history.

Having said this, we may now ask: what might be the contemporary tenor or import of such constructions of Jewish historical theology? I pose this question in a personal sense. To be sure, there are aspects of Cordovero's theological ethics that have a modern appeal; and there is also no doubt that the very formulation of the material, for all the concern to represent it in and through its own terms, is a contemporary construct (in the language of modern religious studies). This

18 Cf. in *Mishneh Torah, Hilkhot De'ot*, I. 7 (*yargil 'atzmo*).

19 *Hesed* has the further sense of 'unrequited love' or 'care'.

conceded, I should also readily concede that my theological concerns are not Neo-Platonic, or at least not in any simple sense, and I would thus not readily subscribe to its esoteric ontology (onto-theology in excess). So then, with all this stated, I again ask: is it possible to reconstruct this construction for ourselves, in a way that might take this mystical theology of divine ethics seriously, but not succumb to a false consciousness (that is, ignore or disguise the fact that I/we are not neo-Platonists or esoteric believers)? Is it possible to accede to an image of a cosmic flow (in lieu of emanation) that has theological and ethics demands or implications? Or more vitally, can something of this be salvaged which doesn't fill our hearts with empty metaphors, but still has the power and force of ontological truth?

7. Conceptual Turn # 5: A Personal Statement

Having posed the question, I cannot avoid the challenge. And insofar as I feel called to take Cordovero's teachings seriously, particularly his notion of an image of a Transcendent God with compelling ethical and spiritual valences,–what might be said?

Perhaps this: I would suggest that what Genesis 1:26 may teach is that humankind is *en toto* a form of embodiment (via our minds and bodies) of the divine gift of creation, ever flowing and emergent from Divinity, itself supernally Other and even Otherwise than Being. This is not a statement of foundations, but the imagination of an ultimate height, passing over every beyond, and even an opening of the mind to the mindless, as it were, and the reaching of thoughtless thought towards ultimacy. And having suggested something of 'emergence' as a master trope, we may now go on to say that we humans may be deemed nodal points of divine realization, at various modalities of actualization–such that it is our human task to keep the life of the universe flowing in ways that may enhance and sustain existence in all its varieties. Just these factors impose responsibilities and restraint, as well as duties and tasks–both in conjunction with our religious traditions, and in view of their ideals of human transformation (or world transfiguration).

God's reality flows through human eyes and words and deeds, and humankind sees and touches and engages with other beings (sententious or otherwise) in this experienced universe. God ever exceeds all these images; but God is also their most ultimate expression, so to speak.

Hence we may imagine ourselves, duly grounded in Scripture, as images of the imageless God–and just as in prayer we use images to direct our mind and ascend beyond their shapes, so too in action might we use the image of ourselves to bespeak deep divine structures in search of realization through humankind. For some seventeenth century English metaphysical poets, the images of God (and the prayer-poems constructed with them) were perhaps something like self-consuming artifacts–used-up, so to say, in the various recitations of the mouth and meditations of the mind.[20] Perhaps we can similarly suggest that our seeing and doing and saying, all our modes of embodiment, are equally (or in some correlative sense) self-consuming artefacts: human images of God's actuality on earth, but also figures to be transcended through human action. The images keep us aware of the ultimate dimensions of our sacred task, even its role as a divine service–without limiting our human works or grace. We humans bring matters to pass, and the images that guide us (divine and otherwise) may pass on as well. To think less is to demean ourselves and theology; but to think more is to demean both of them in the other direction.[21] It is a high-wire act.

So there it is–a possibility and a suggestion. And in conclusion, let me add this as well. Theology dares to construct God, even out of the resources of tradition. So let me now push this point to an imaginable extreme. Might we perhaps even say, and not with tongue in cheek, that our lives are also, somehow, constructs of Divinity–living images and realizations of the Source of Life and Being, formed and reformed daily, and in this great sense we are, so to speak, human facets of the kingdom of God, which is even now both here and becoming?
I leave the question open.

---

[20] See S. Fish, *Self-Consuming Artifacts; The Experience of Seventeenth-Century Literature* (Berkeley CA: University of California Press, 1972).

[21] I have developed some of the thoughts in this section in my *Sacred Attunement. A Jewish Theology* (Chicago: University of Chicago Press, 2008).

Between Sensual and Heavenly Love

Franz Rosenzweig's Reading of the Song of Songs

Paul Mendes-Flohr

> Sensual love blinds us to heavenly love; by itself it could not do so, but since it has the element of heavenly love unconsciously within it, it can.
>
> - Franz Kafka[1]

Jewish and Christian theologians alike tend to distinguish human *eros* from divine love, a distinction captured by Augustine's transformative translation of the Greek *eros* by *agape*, or by the Latin *caritas.*[2] Accordingly, the unabashed erotic imagery of The Song of Songs has recurrently occasioned theological perplexity.[3] But it is precisely the 'sensuality' of *The Song of Songs* that renders it in Rosenzweig's view the most eloquent statement in the Hebrew Bible on the meaning of revelation, of the divine-relation. Indeed, he refers to this love song as the

---

[1] Franz Kafka, *The Collected Aphorisms*, trans. by Malcolm Pasley (London: Syrens [Penguin], 1994), p 18. These aphorisms were composed between October 1917 and February 1918, that is at least two years before the publication of *The Star of Redemption.*

[2] See Jean-Luc Marion, *The Erotic Phenomenon*, trans. by Stephen E. Lewis (Chacago: The University of Chicago Press, 2005); see also Shadi Bartsch and Thomas Bartscherer, eds., *Erotikon. Essays on Eros, Ancient and Modern* (Chicago: The University of Chicago Press, 2003).

[3] One hermeneutic strategy to explain the eroticism of the Song of Songs is presented in Pope Benedict XVI's inaugural encyclical, *Deus Caritas Est* (God is Love) of January 2006. The Holy See notes that the Song has two words for love, *dodim*, 'a plural form suggesting a love that is still insecure, indeterminate and searching.' This love he identifies with human *eros*, which 'comes to be replaced by the word *ahaba* (sic),' or in Christian parlance, *agape.* As 'the typical expression of biblical notion of love,' *agape* is to be contrasted 'with an indeterminate, "searching" love.' *Agape* 'expresses the experience of a love which involves a real discovery of the other, moving beyond the selfish character that prevailed earlier' with *eros*. 'Love now becomes concern and care for the other. No longer is it a self-seeking, a sinking in the intoxication of happiness; instead it seeks the good of the beloved: it becomes renunciation and it is ready, and willing, for sacrifice.' In a word, according to this reading, the Song of Songs projects a trajectory from 'erotic love (*eros*)' to a 'self-donating love (*agape*),' *which* Pope Benedict XVI characterizes as a 'path of ascent and purification.' In a word, according to this reading of the Song of Songs, the erotic must be overcome and transcended. Rosenzweig would demur. For him, as we shall argue, *eros* is the existential grammar of both human and divine love.

"*Kernbuch der Offenbarung*,"[4] the focal-book of revelation. Yet God is not once mentioned, nor even alluded to in this dialogue between a man and a woman, testifying to the physical delights and anguish of their mutual love. The Song's vivid imagery, expressing sexual affection and erotic desire would even be considered bold in our liberated culture:

In an exchange of lavish, indeed, hyperbolic praise of each other's physical features, the male lover exclaims, 'How beautiful are thy feet in sandals, O' prince's daughter! Thy rounded thighs are like jewels, the work of the hand of an artist. Thy navel is like a round goblet that never lacks of wine; thy belly is like a heap of wheat set with lilies. Thy two breast like two fawns, the twins of a gazelle' (7.2-4).[5] And the female's response to her lover's ecstatic paean to her beauty and erotic appeal, is a laconic but exultant acknowledgment that his adoration and desire are reciprocal: 'I am my beloved's, and his desire is toward me. Let's go forth into the field ... ' (7.11).

Somehow these passionate love songs found their way into the Hebrew Bible. Any debate among the rabbis responsible for establishing the canon regarding the appropriateness of their inclusion was brought to a close when Rabbi Akiva, declared 'For all the ages are not worth the day on which the Song of Songs were given to Israel, for all the *Ketuvim* (Writings) are holy, but the Song of Songs is the Holy of Holies' (Mishnah *Yadayim* 3.5). There was a proviso, however. The Song of Songs was to be read as an allegory and its sexual imagery ignored. Hence, Jewish tradition understood the book as an allegorical testimony to the mutual love of God and the Children of Israel.[6] Refracted through this interpretative lens, the Song of Songs also gained a firm footing in Israel's liturgy, where it is recited during the morning service on the intermediate Sabbath of Passover. Under the influence of the Kabbalah, the custom arose, especially among the Hasidism and Sephardim, of reciting the Song of Songs on the eve of the Sabbath.

Christians also read the Song of Songs as an allegory. Starting with Origen, it has been read as bespeaking the relationship abiding between Christ and the Church, or between Christ and the individual believer. From the Renaissance on, there was a major hermeneutic shift and the Song of Sons was increasingly read literally as secular love song *pur et simple*. This trend, led by the Hebrew humanists Grotius and Clericus came to a head with Herder and Goethe, who expunged all remnants of an allegorical reading of the book.[7] As Rosenzweig observed:

---

4 Franz Rosenzweig, *Der Stern der Erlösung*, 2nd. ed. (Berlin: Schocken Verlag, 1930), vol. 2, p. 147.

5 Translations by the author.

6 Isaac B. Gottlieb, "The Jewish Allegory of Love: Change and Constancy" in *The Journal of Jewish Thought and Philosophy*, vol. 2 (1992): 1-17. Cf. "Allegorical explanations are rare in Jewish exegesis, except for this [the Song of Songs]." Ibid., p. 2.

7 For a detailed and perceptive review of the history of Christian interpretations of the Song of Songs, especially as pertinent to Rosenzweig's understanding of that history, see Samuel Moyn, "Divine and Human Love. Franz Rosenzweig's History of the Song of Songs," in *Jewish Studies Quarterly*, 12 (2005): 194-212.

> Unfortunately, Herder and Goethe had at least preserved this much of the traditional conception: they regarded the Song of Songs only as a collection of love lyrics, thus leaving it its subjective, lyrical soul-revealing character. But thereafter the same road was followed further. Once the Song of Songs was understood as "purely human," the step from "purely human" to "purely worldly" was also possible. Thus it was delyricized with a will. From every side, the effort was made to read dramatic action and epic content into it. ... Such comprehensive rearrangements or rather convulsions of the traditional text have been undertaken by biblical criticism on no other biblical book. ... The language of the revelation of the soul seemed somehow uncanny for the spirit of the century that recreated everything in its image, as objective and worldly.[8]

Read literally, the sensuality of the Song of Songs now preoccupied its commentators, and obliged them to ask rhetorically, 'what strange error allowed these pages to slip into God's word?' [9] But Rosenzweig would regard the uncovering of the book's sensuality to be of great dialectical significance. Similarly, the questioning of the validity of reading it as an allegory brought into relief the meaning of the Song's putative analogy (*Gleichnis*) of human to divine love.

At this dialectical juncture of the modern interpretation of the Song of Songs, Rosenzweig notes, one is 'confronted by the choice either to accept the "purely human," [the] purely sensual sense" of the book "or to acknowledge that the deeper meaning lodges here, precisely in the purely sensual sense, directly and "merely" in analogy.'[10] Rosenzweig puts it paradoxically. The Song of Songs, because 'it is indeed purely human, purely sensual,' it is 'more than [an] analogy.'[11] The paradox is to be explained by Rosenzweig's understanding of anthropomorphic language that abounds in the Hebrew Scripture and, indeed, the religious imagination in general. For Rosenzweig, anthropomorphic imagery is not to be deemed, as many medieval philosophers and modern students of religion would say, an inevitable concession to human imagination; it is rather a theological necessity.[12] The human and the divine do not inhabit two separate realities. There is thus, certainly with respect to love, an intrinsic or rather an ontological homology between human, dialogical love and divine love. Rosenzweig would, therefore, argue that love, human as well as divine, is sensual, and must be so.[13]

---

8 Rosenzweig, *The Star of Redemption*, trans. William Hallo (New York: Holt, Rinehart and Winston, 1970), p. 199f.

9 Ibid., p. 199.

10 Ibid.

11 Ibid.

12 Rosenzweig, "Zur Encyclopedia Judaica," in *Der Mensch und sein Werk. Gesammelte Schriften*, vol 3: *Zweistromland. Kleinere Schriften zu Glauben und Denken*, eds., Reinhold and Annmarie Mayer (Dordrecht: Martinus Nijhoff Publishers, 1984), pp. 731-746; Barbara Galli, "Rosenzweig Speaking of Meetings and Monotheism in Biblical Anthropomorphisms," in *The Journal of Jewish Thought and Philosophy*, 2/2 (1993): 219-243.

13 The ontological homology between divine and human eros does not imply that they are identical. For one, as Kierkegaard noted, human love is preferential, whereas God loves in principle everyone. As Rosenzweig puts it, "man loves because God loves *and* as God loves." *The Star of Redemption*, p. 199 (italics added). Further, because it is preferential

The recently published correspondence between Rosenzweig and Margret Rosenstock, the wife of a close friend with whom he had a passionate affair, indicates that there was a strong autobiographical moment to this thesis.[14] In fact, he wrote a draft of his commentary on the Song the Songs, while stretched out on his lover's bed waiting for her to appear for an appointed tryst.[15] This perhaps explains the enigmatic prologue to the passages introducing his commentary. He opens the prologue with a citation from the Song of Songs, 'love is strong as death' (*Stark wie Tode ist Liebe*. The Song of Songs, 8.6), and continues to ask, 'Strong in the same way as death? But against whom, does love display its strength?' And he proceeds to answer his own question:

> Against him whom it seizes. And love, of course, seizes both the lover as well as the beloved, but the beloved otherwise than the lover. It originates in the lover. The beloved is seized, her love is already a response to being seized: Anteros is the younger brother of Eros. [Anteros, one will recall is the god of passion, the god of mutual love and tenderness.] Initially it is for the beloved that love is strong as death, even as nature has decreed that woman alone, not man, may die of love. What has been said of the twofold encounter of man and his self applies strictly and universally only to the male. As for woman, and precisely the most feminine woman above all, even Thanatos can approach her in the sweet guise of Eros. Her life is simpler than that of man by reason of this missing contradiction [between Eros and Thanatos]. Already in the tremors of love her heart has become firm. It [her heart] no longer needs the tremor of death. A young woman can be ready for eternity as a man only becomes when his threshold is crossed by Thanatos. No man would die the death of an Alcestis [who

---

human love is unreliable; subject to mercurial emotions it is liable to collapse. In contrast, divine love is universal and unfailing, or as Shakespeare would be it, 'marble-constant.' But, Rosenzweig emphasizes, it would be mistaken to conceive of love as an attribute: 'Love is not an attribute but an event.' Ibid., p. 164. As an inter-subjective event *(Ereignis)* it is temporally bound (to the present) and as such must be constantly renewed. Rosenzweig's argument, of course, is phenomenological, not theological. Upon expounding upon the phenomenological meaning of revelation as the experience of divine love, he explores the experiential texture of Jewish and Christian liturgical prayer as a prolepsis of the revelatory experience that is accessible to all the congregants. Liturgical prayer engenders the temporal space of the universal experience of divine love, an experience that is paradoxically both present and eternal. 'Nothing in the miracle of revelation is novel. Thus revelation is at all times new [*allzeit neu*] only because it is primordially old [*uralt*].' *The Star of Redemption*, p. 111; *Der Stern der Erlösung*, vol. 2, p. 30.

[14] See Rosenzweig's letter on Margrit Rosenstock, 15 November 1918: 'Liebe, II 2 [that is, the section of *The Star of Redemption* dealing with the Song of Songs] ist so schön. Ich freue mich auf die Stunden in grünen Zimmer [Margrit's bedroom], wo ich dir Hauptstücke vorlesen werde. Diesmal zuerst nur mit dir allein. [...] Eigentlich kennst du es freilich schon, es steht wohl ebensoviel von dir drin wie von mir.' Rosenzweig, *Die 'Grittli'-Briefe: Briefe an margrit Rosenstock-Huessy*, ed. Inken Ruhle and Reinhard Mayer (Tübingen:Bilam, 2002), p. 190.

[15] See Bernard Casper, "Von Einheit und Ewigkeit. Ein Gespräch zwischen Leib und Seele: ein unveröffentlichter Text Franz Rosenzweigs," in *Bulletin des Leo Baecks Instituts*, 74 (1986): 65-71.

> volunteered to die for her husband, on Appolo's promise that her husband would never die if someone were found to die in his stead.] Once touched by Eros, a woman is what a man only becomes at the Faustian age of a hundred: ready for the final encounter–strong as death.[16]

Rosenzweig's oft-criticized sexist language is at least partially explained when one realizes that he wrote these words for his lover, Gritli as he affectionately called her.[17] Further, he would undoubtedly concede, the roles of lover and beloved–of Eros and Anteros–can alternate. But his words, addressed to Gritli as a love-letter, also had a theological message. Alluding to the closing sentence of Part Two of Goethe's Faust, he asserts, 'Like all earthy love, this is only an analogy'[18]–an analogy that is also an homology. Human *eros* and divine *eros* coincide. In a recent study, Samuel Moyn, in my judgment, rightly questions the view of some commentators that for Rosenzweig human love is a mere metaphor for divine revelation, and perceptively notes that 'Rosenzweig's theory of revelation is a *theory of eros*.'[19] But Moyn continues to state it is a theory 'that presents love as an alternative to death.'[20] Love, however, is not an alternative to death; it is rather a counter-weight to death, for after all it is not stronger than death; it is as strong as death. Being strong as death love neutralizes death's sting.

Death remains, but when one is in the embrace of love, the existential anxieties attendant to our singularity, crowned as it is by our inexorable death, are cauterized and suspended.

Despite the edifying appeal of such a statement, it would be a mere apodictic assertion without an explication of the philosophical presuppositions of Rosenzweig's conception of revelation, or rather *Offenbarungsglaube*–his affirmation of divine revelation as a historical and existential fact. This faith was born of a long and difficult gestation. And if I may extend the metaphor, the birth of Rosenzweig's faith was facilitated by many midwives, representing various cultural and philosophical schools. In the end, the process focused on one overarching question: Can the concept of revelation address a reality that philosophy is inherently incapable of acknowledging? Although it took several years to crystallize, the answer was, at least as formulated, rather simple and straightforward. Since philosophy understands its mandate to illuminate necessary and universal truths, it excludes from its purview contingent or accidental phenomena, such as, the genetic, cultural and circumstantial details that determine the biography of each and every human being. By its very nature philosophy does not concern itself with the life story of an individual; the questions attendant to the existential

---

16 *The Star of Redempton*, p. 156.

17 Cf. 'Das Buch II 2 [...] gehört dir. [...] Es ist nich "Dir" aber–dein. Dein–wie ich.' Rosenzweig to Margrit Rosenstock, 2 November 1918. *Grili-Briefe*, p. 177. Cf. fn. 12, above.

18 *The Star of Redemption*, p. 156.

19 Samuel Moyn, *Origins of the Other. Emmanuel Levinas between Revelation and Ethics* (Ithaca, New York: Cornell University Press, 2005), p. 146 (italics in original).

20 Ibid.

singularity of an individual are beyond the ken and interest of philosophy. Focusing on universal necessary truths, philosophy is interested neither in the date of my birth nor that of one's death, nor in date of birth of one's children and their prospective, inevitable death–the contingent realities that engage one's deepest, most personal concerns. Or as Rosenzweig put it with disarming simplicity: Philosophy does address itself to a single living individual who has a first and last name. Yet one's being, one's individual existence is determined by the fact that each person has a first and last name. Viewed from this perspective, 'The human being in the utter singularity of his individuality, in his being as determined by a first and last name (*in seinem durch Vor- und Zuname festgelegten Sein*), stepped out of the world which knew itself as the [rationally] conceivable world, out of the All of philosophy.' [21]

Death is but the ultimate signature of one's singularity. One's death is experienced by anticipation, by the realization that one dies utterly alone, even if blessed with friends and family. It is in the light of this brute existential fact that we must live our lives as single, finite beings. And it is precisely in light of this existential fact that Rosenzweig concludes the *Star of Redemption* with the buoyant declaration 'Into life' (*ins Leben*). Fully cognizant of our finitude, we are to journey into life. Philosophy may help survey the path, to chart the terrain and topography we are to encounter along the way, but, alas, it cannot relieve of us the existential anxieties engendered by our singularity. Since time immemorial philosophy, east and west, has recommended that we transcend these concerns by splitting our selves into two, a body and a soul; one should focus on the soul as the true center of one's being, one's *ontos,* which bears the imprint and thus promise of eternity, and our transitory bodies that indeed are destined to perish. Modern, post-Enlightenment philosophers have offered a twist to this division by suggesting that one transcend one's finite self by identifying with humanity. Rosenzweig regard Kant's formula as most representative of this view. One gains a glimpse of immortality, to be sure, as but a postulate of practical reason, when one transcends one's self–ignores the promptings of one's own inclinations and concerns – and heeds the categorical imperative and therefore acts on behalf of rational humanity and the universal ideal of an ethical community. Within these equations, ancient and modern, the particularities of the em-bodied self are left out, are abstracted. With reference to the Kantian discourse, Rosenzweig speaks of the meta-ethical self, the self not comprehended by the universal compass of the practical reason.[22] But the self invariably protests. Enjoining an ontological distinction between the body and soul, expressed with various terms, philosophy denies 'the fears of the earth.'[23] Philosophy 'bears us over the grave which yawns at our feet with every step. It lets the body be prey to the abyss, but the free soul flutters away over it. Why should philosophy be concerned if the fear of death [which bespeaks the self's consciousness of its singularity] knows nothing

21 *Stern der Erlösung*, vol. 1, p. 16; *The Star of Redemption*, p. 10 (translation emended).

22 Ibid., p. 10f., 63-82.

23 Ibid., p. 3.

of such a dichotomy between body and soul, if it roars Me! Me! Me!, if it wants nothing to do with relegating fear onto a mere "body"?'[24]

In contrast to philosophy, the *Offenbarungsglaube* that determines the existential ground of biblical faith cannot concede a division of body and soul, of a self abstracted from the particularities of one's lived life. Divine revelation, Rosenzweig maintains, addresses one's earthly anxieties, one's meta-ethical self enmeshed in the existential, often petty and banal, but nonetheless ever pressing realities of one's utterly singular, em-bodied life. In revelation God addresses each and everyone of us by our first and last name, acknowledges the particularities of our finitude, our finite, em-bodied existence in particular, distinctive bodies, bracketed by particular, distinctive biographies. Addressing the singularity of a particular existence, revelation must perforce be sensuous. It does not address the universal *ontos* one happens to inhabit or share in, but it addresses one with a first and last name, as one who has a particular date of birth and as yet determined day of death, it addresses one who dwells in a particular body, and whose heart palpitates with distinctive earthly fears and hopes. It this respect, revelation is love, and as such is analogous and homologous with mundane love, of the love of one human being for another. We love one another as em-bodied in our particularities, and when that love is erotic it *includes* the shape of the other's face, the aroma of the other's skin, the quality of her or his voice. Love is perforce sensuous–and *ergo* as strong as death. Love does not conquer death or eliminate it. Indeed, as a Midrash alluded to by Rosenzweig notes, death is the crown of creation (Breshit Raba, 31A).[25] But while death is 'the ineradicable stamp of [our] creatureliness'[26] it also marks the *dénouement* of life; in contrast to other creatures, we humans are conscious of the prospect of our inevitable death. As the Psalmist notes, we walk in the shadow of death, of our of own and of others who are dear to us. The dark shadows of death denote the anticipated 'has been' or past perfect of human existence.

In contrast to death, love is utterly in the present. Hence, 'Love which knows solely the present, which lives on the present, pines for the present–it challenges death'[27]–not death in general as an abstract concept but the death that is the supreme emblem of our singularity and that will consummate our existential finitude, Hence, Rosenzweig concludes, 'the keystone of the somber arch of creation [that is, our death, the pinnacle of our singularity] becomes the cornerstone of the bright house of revelation. For the soul, revelation means the experience of a present (*Erlebnis einer Gegenwart*)...'[28] So it is for divine and human love.

Love lives in the present tense, death points to the past perfect. Love signals an undivided attentiveness to the present and the presence of an Other, in love one beholds the Other un-deflected by considerations of time, of past or future; in

---

24 Ibid.

25 *The Star of Redemption,* p. 155.

26 Ibid., p. 156.

27 Ibid., p. 156f.

28 Ibid., p. 157; *Der Stern der Erlösung,* vol. 2, p. 89.

love one draws the Other out of the undifferentiated multitude of humanity, and celebrates the Other's particularity. Love is perforce sensuous and thus neutralizes the existential sting of our finitude. That is why love–human and divine–is, indeed, the crowd of creation. Thus Rosenzweig comments:

> The created death of the creature portends the revelation of a life which is above the creaturely level. For each created thing, death is the very consummator of its entire materiality. It removes creation imperceptibly into the past, and thus turns it into the tacit, permanent prediction of the miracle of its renewal [through love]. That is why, on the sixth day, it was not said that it was "good," but rather "behold, very good!" "Very," so our sages teach, "very"–that is death.[29]

Echoing the 'very good' of creation, the Song of Songs exclaims, 'Love is strong as death.'

[29] *The Star of Redemption*, p. 155.

God Sharing in the Conditio Humana

Reflections on the Potential of Christian Imagery from a Lutheran Perspective

Friederike Nüssel

1. The Impulse of Jürgen Habermas

The capacity of religious ideas and imagery to provide cultural orientation has been emphasized by a philosopher who in the last decades of the twentieth century contributed significantly to the intellectual foundation and social acceptance of a secular conception of society in the public sphere in Germany and to some extent in Western Europe–Jürgen Habermas. A few weeks after September 11th, 2001, when he was awarded the Peace Prize of the German Book Trade, Habermas included in his acceptance speech a critical look at the consequences of the 'derailing' process of secularization. In the last few years, Habermas has been travelling around the world and purposefully feeding his diagnosis of contemporary society into the global discourse. According to this diagnosis, the intellectual tenor of the age is marked by two basic trends. On the one side, there is a trend of "the spread of naturalistic world views"[1], as found for example in the materialistic interpretation of neurobiological research or in debates on genetic research. On the other side, Habermas observes a trend "of an unexpected revitalization of religious communities and traditions and their politicization across the world"[2]. Thus, we find ourselves positioned between naturalism and religion–which is the title of Habermas' collection of philosophical essays published in 2005.

Habermas explores the trends mentioned above not only from a descriptive, sociological viewpoint. He is alarmed by them, because he considers them a threat to the democratic constitutional state and therefore to the essential preconditions for peaceful co-existence in society. In order to defend its own prerequisites against these attacks, the democratic constitutional state in Habermas' view needs to "defend its religious and nonreligious citizens from each other."[3] However, this is only possible if the citizens in "their civic interactions are not based on a mere *modus vivendi*; their existence within a democratic system must also

1 Jürgen Habermas, *Between Naturalism and Religion: Philosophical Essays* (Cambridge: Polity Press, 2008), 1.

2 Ibid., 1.

3 Ibid., 3.

be founded on conviction"[4]. The democratic state depends on its citizens respecting each other "as free and equal members of their political community"[5]. This form of solidarity among citizens, however, cannot be enforced by law. Rather, the democratic, liberal and secular state "depends in the long run on mentalities that it cannot produce from its own resources"[6]. Accordingly, "it is also in the interest of the constitutional state to conserve all cultural sources that nurture citizens' solidarity and their normative awareness"[7]. This is the crucial point of Habermas' diagnosis–a diagnosis that clearly reveals the positions put forward by the new atheism to be naïve, if not irresponsible in relationship to society.

In his Peace Prize Acceptance Speech Habermas puts his exhortation to be protective of cultural sources in more concrete terms by suggesting that secular society should "not cut itself off from the resources of spiritual explanations, if only the secular side were to retain a feeling for the articulative power of religious discourse"[8]. Conversely, however, he expects religious citizens to be able to consider their "religious convictions reflexively from the outside"[9] and to translate them into generally accessible language, thus implementing them into secular contexts. Habermas does not present a way of how such a translation of religious beliefs should be done or how it could succeed. This is up to the religions themselves. Instead, he reconstructs Kant's philosophy of religion as a model of such a translation process. This clearly shows what precisely it is that Habermas thinks religious convictions have to offer. At the same time, his interpretation indirectly offers an opportunity to pinpoint the potential of the Christian religion to provide cultural orientation, and to put it in more concrete terms.

2. Against Defeatism–or, On the Relevance of Religious Imagery in Post-Secular Societies

According to Habermas, Kant "does not reduce the philosophy of religion to the critique of religion,"[10] but "wants to rescue the contents of faith and the religious commitments that can be justified within the bounds of reason alone."[11] Kant already foresaw the dark depths of an enlightenment which reason would fall into, if it regards its purpose entirely to be the realization of its morality. Against the "despair over the pitiable effects of moral action that has its end only

4 Ibid., 3.

5 Ibid., 3.

6 Ibid., 3.

7 Ibid., 111.

8 See the English translation of Habermas' Peace Prize speech: http://www.nettime.org/Lists-Archives/nettime-l-0111/msg00100.html.

9 Habermas, *Between Naturalism and Religion*, 130.

10 Ibid., 215.

11 Ibid., 211.

in itself,"[12] moral thought needs to be reinforced in its confidence in itself, and preserved from defeatism.[13] At this point, Kant–according to Habermas' interpretation–accepted an inconsistency in his moral theory. He not only declared that the promotion of the highest good is everyone's duty, but he furthermore equated the vague, intelligible idea of a kingdom of ends with the biblical notion of the kingdom of God, and thus transposed it into an inner-worldly utopia[14]. By "discreetly anticipating the world-disclosing power of religious semantics"[15], Kant successfully protected his moral theory against the danger of defeatism. For in Habermas' view, Kant's theory gives human beings "the assurance that, by acting morally, they can contribute to realizing the 'ethical community'"[16], which is the philosophical term Kant presented as a translation of the metaphor of God's Kingdom on earth.

In his late work *Religion within the Bounds of Bare Reason*[17] Kant interprets the Christian "statuary faith of the church" as a 'vehicle' for "the pure religious faith"[18]. Here he does not only employ the semantic potential included in the idea of the Kingdom of God, but also conceives Jesus Christ as the personified ideal of moral perfection. To his understanding "the ideal of humanity pleasing God (hence of such moral perfection as is possible in a world being who is dependent on needs and inclinations) cannot be thought by us except under the idea of a human being who would not only be willing to perform any human duty himself, and at the same time also to spread the good about him in the widest possible range through teaching and example, but who also, although tempted by the greatest enticements, would nonetheless be willing to take upon himself all sufferings even to the most ignominious death, for the sake of the world's greatest good, and even for his enemies."[19] While for Kant there is no example needed from experience "to make the idea of a human being morally pleasing to God a prototype for us"[20], because "the idea resides in our morally legislative reason"[21], the imagery

---

12 Ibid., 221.

13 Ibid., 221.

14 Ibid., 222.

15 Ibid., 217.

16 Ibid., 222.

17 Immanuel Kant, *Religion within the Bounds of Bare Reason* (Indianapolis: Hackett Pub. Co, 2009).

18 Ibid., 117.

19 Ibid., 68.

20 Ibid., 69.

21 Ibid., 69. Like in his moral philosophy the capability to follow the moral law is granted in the law itself: "We *ought* to be in conformity to it, and hence we must also be capable thereof. If one had to prove in advance, as is inescapably necessary with concepts of nature (so that we do not run the risk of being delayed by empty concepts), that it is possible to be a human being conforming to this archetype, then we would likewise have to harbor qualms about conceding even to the moral law the authority to be an unconditional and yet sufficient determining basis of our power of choice" (Ibid.). This, however, would imply that we would have to explain "how it is possible for the mere idea of a lawfulness as such to

of Jesus Christ's perfect obedience in his life and suffering may serve as a vehicle. For it "is indeed a limitation of human reason and one which, after all, just cannot be separated from it–that we cannot think of any moral worth of import in the actions of a person without at the same time conceiving this person or his manifestation in the human manner, even though we indeed do not wish to assert thereby that this is also how it is in itself [...]; for in order to make suprasensible characteristics graspable to ourselves, we always need a certain analogy with natural beings."[22]

From the perspective of Christian believers, however, such an explanation of the potential of religious language and imagery may appear rather reductionist. Moreover, for a closer understanding of the Christian semantics and imagery and its potential to promote constitutional democracy and social cohesion in civil societies, it is important to reflect the key ideas that governed the concerted attempt to renew the church in the sixteenth-century reformation movement[23] and in the long run supported the idea of constitutional legality in combination with religious freedom. In the following I will therefore exploit some of the Lutheran impulse and contribution to this process.

3. Re-Orienting towards God's Image in the Gospel of Christ

It is no exaggeration when Martin Marty says in the introduction to his biography of Martin Luther that he "was the most prominent figure in the combined religious and political stirrings of sixteenth-century Europe"[24]. While there is much controversy about what Luther's genuine reformatory insight was, there can be no doubt that the doctrine of justification by faith alone without works can be regarded as the core of his theological thinking. His new understanding of the salvific and freeing message of the Gospel of Jesus Christ allowed Luther to conceive the very nature of God's righteousness as being gracious and forgiving, rather than distributive. Accordingly, in the *Smalcald Articles* (1536) Luther points to the essential role of this article for the true faith of the church in stating: "Of this article nothing can be yielded or surrendered [nor can anything be granted or permitted contrary to the same], even though heaven and earth, and whatever will not abide, should sink to ruin"[25]. In the same year Luther explains in his *Disputation concerning Justification* that while "human nature, corrupt and blinded by the blemish of original sin, is not able to imagine or conceive of any justification

be a mightier incentive for that power than any and all conceivable incentives taken from advantages, this we can neither have insight into by reason nor support by examples from experience" (Ibid.).

22 Kant, Ibid. 71, note 85.

23 Berndt Hamm and Michael Welker, *Die Reformation–Potentiale der Freiheit* (Tübingen: Mohr Siebeck, 2008).

24 Martin E. Marty, *Martin Luther: A Life* (New York: Penguin Books, 2008), xi.

25 The Smalcald Articles, Part II, 1.

above and beyond works"[26], it is nothing but God's grace realized and revealed in Christ's righteousness and "poured into us from hearing about Christ by the Holy Spirit"[27], which allows humans to realize that "man is truly justified by faith in the sight of God"[28]. To comprehend Christ's righteousness implies that this "is outside of us and foreign to us"[29] and "cannot be laid hold of by our works"[30].

Luther's late theological teaching on justification in the 1530s is based on his thorough investigations into the biblical notion of righteousness and justification offered in his early lectures as a professor of biblical studies at Wittenberg since 1512. Through his biblical studies it became evident to Luther that the contemporary practice of penance and indulgences did not conform to the Bible and its teaching on God's grace and righteousness. In 1517 he wrote the *Ninty-five Theses*[31] for a disputation on the power and efficacy of indulgences. Given that they were–without Luther's consent–translated into German and circulated widely in church and academia, Luther's critique of the practice of indulgence and penance his new theological understanding of human sin and divine grace entered the public sphere. Now he had to defend this in disputations with leading thinkers of the time. According to his soteriological insights he argued in the *Heidelberg Disputation*[32] for a theology of the cross over and against a type of scholastic theology that "looks upon the invisible things of God as though they were clearly perceptible in those things which have actually happened"[33]. Luther here declared that only he "deserves to be called a theologian, [...] who comprehends the visible and manifest things of God seen through suffering and the cross"[34].

The capacity to provide cultural orientation of Luther's theology of the cross grew, however, not only from the revolutionary criticism of scholastic theology and his new biblical approach, but is also essentially linked with his deep pastoral concern, his magniloquence, and his acute psychological perception, which allowed him to understand the importance of the Christian imagery for addressing not only intellect and will, but also the senses. One impressive example of his ability to bring the image of Christ close to believers in a consoling way can be found in his *Sermon on Preparing to Die,* which Luther wrote in 1519. Here he advises the readers of the Sermon as they fear death:

---

26 Martin Luther, *Luther's works,* translated and edited by Helmut Lehman and Lewis Spitz (St. Louis: Fortress Press, 1955), vol. 34, thesis 6, p. 151.

27 Ibid., vol. 34, thesis 28, p. 153.

28 Ibid., vol. 34, thesis 4, p. 151. Therefore, justification by faith alone "is a mystery of God, who exalts his saints, because it is not only impossible to comprehend for the godless, but marvelous and hard to believe even for the pious themselves" (Ibid., thesis 5).

29 Ibid., vol. 34, thesis 27, p. 153.

30 Ibid.

31 Luther, *Luther's works,* vol. 31/I, p. 25–33.

32 Luther, *Luther's works,* vol. 31/I, theses 19–25, p. 40f.

33 Ibid., vol. 31/I, theses 19, p. 40.

34 Ibid., vo. 31/I, theses 20, p. 40.

> you must not look at sin in sinners, or in your conscience, or in those who abide in sin to the end and are damned. If you do, you will surely follow them and also be overcome. You must turn your thoughs away from that and look at sin only within the picture of grace. Engrave that picture in yourself with all your power and keep it before your eyes. The picture of grace is nothing else but that of Christ on the cross and of all his dear saints. [...]
>
> (Y)ou must not regard hell and eternal pain in relation to predestination, not in yourself, or in itself, or in those who are damned, nor must you be worried by the many people in the world who are not chosen. If you are not careful, that picture will quickly upset you and be your downfall. You must force yourself to keep your eyes closed tightly to such a view, for it can never help you, even though you were to occupy yourself with it for a thousand years and fret yourself to death. After all, you will have to let God be God and grant that he knows more about you than you do yourself.
>
> So then, gaze at the heavenly picture of Christ, who descended into hell [I Pet. 3:19] for your sake as one eternally forsaken by God when he spoke the words of dereliction at the cross, "Eli, Eli, lama sabachthani!"–"My God, my God, why hast thou forsaken me?" [Matt 27:46]. In that picture your hell is defeated and your uncertain election is made sure. If you concern yourself solely with this and believe that it was done for you, you will surely be preserved in this same faith. Never, therefore, let this [i.e. picture; FN] be erased from your vision. Seek yourself only in Christ and not in yourself and you will find yourself in him eternally.[35]

This passage indicates what lies at the heart of Lutheran theology and spirituality. It is about the assurance of salvation for the individual in the face of death. The thought of dying and death and the fear of eternal damnation and torment in god-forsakenness form the basis for Luther's vehement criticism of the late medieval theology of grace and spiritual practice. Moreover, the passage from the Sermon also shows what Luther considers to be the reason to trust in God's grace. It is the image of Jesus Christ. In our concerns for our own lives, we are to never let this image be erased from our vision. By referring to vision, Luther indicates that he is not employing the notion of the image casually, but with a specific purpose. Since the pictorial image is in Luther's view an important aspect for believe to embrace the senses and memorize the content[36], it is the central task of a sermon

---

35 Luther, *Luther's works*, vol. 42, p. 105f. For a German version of the crucial passage see Martin Luther, *Ausgewählte Schriften: in 6 Bänden*, Insel-Taschenbuch 1284 (Frankfurt am Main: Insel-Verl, 1982), vol. 2, 23: "sieh das himmlische Bild Christus an, der um deinetwillen zur Hölle gefahren und von Gott ist verlassen gewesen als einer, der verdammt sei ewiglich, als er sprach am Kreuz: 'Eli, eli, lama asabthani. O mein Gott, o mein Gott, warum hast du mich verlassen?' (Matth. 27,46) Sieh, in dem Bild ist überwunden deine Hölle und dein ungewisse Erwählung gewiß gemacht. Wenn du allein darum dich bekümmerst und das glaubst als für dich geschehen, so wirst du in diesem Glauben gewiß errettet. Darum laß dir's nur nicht aus den Augen nehmen und suche dich nur in Christus und nicht in dir, so wirst du dich auf ewig in ihm finden".

36 As Johann Anselm Steiger states: "Bilder sind integraler Bestandteil der Lutherischen Mnemotechnik. [...] Bilder prägen sich und damit auch die durch sie bezeichneten *res* der *memoria* besser ein als bloße Worte, die auf Visualisierungen verzichten", see J. A. Steiger, "*Christophorus*–'ein ebenbild aller christen': Ein nicht-biblisches Bild und dessen

to paint a vivid picture of Christ and thereby to nurture religious representational thinking[37]. This is why the Gospel is proclaimed in a way that is perceptible by the senses not only in the celebration of the sacraments, but also in the sermon. In the above quoted passage, the image of Christ is portrayed in a concise way. It is the image of the one who had to experience the utmost godforsakenness on the cross, although he himself had not turned from God in any moment of his life, and precisely by passing through death and hell, he gained eternal communion with God. It is the image of Christ the Gospels paint, and the Christ hymns of the New Testament proclaim as they celebrate the degradation and elevation of the Son of God for the redemption of humankind. Medieval art vividly portrayed this image in all detail for the laity and the educated, and thus transmitted the semantic potential of the Christian tradition, which only few could experience in the preaching of the Word.

For Luther, the image of Christ determines the image of God[38]. Beyond this image, God remains hidden, *deus absconditus*. The hidden God is of no concern to faith, as Luther emphasized quite sharply in his discussion with Erasmus of Rotterdam[39]. Similarly, Philipp Melanchthon argued that theology should focus on God's will and God's grace revealed in Jesus Christ, who could only be recognized through his salvific work. "Christum cognoscere est beneficia eius cognoscere,"[40] therefore, became his principle in his theological *Loci communes* 1521, in which he deliberately omitted the speculative doctrines of incarnation and trinity and only addressed the loci of sin, law and grace. In the debate with Ulrich Zwingli on the right understanding of the Lord's Supper, however, Luther and Melanchthon realized that the basic soteriological concepts could only be explained and defended adequately on the ground of the christological definition of the Chalcedonian Council. In this context it became important to explain, that Jesus Christ as a person was truly God and truly man[41] and that the two natures that are united in his personhood could not be separated again without destroying the integrity of his

Relevanz für die Schrift- und Bildhermeneutik. Aufgezeigt Texten von Martin Luthers und Sigmund von Birkens," in: *Hermeneutica sacra: Studien zur Auslegung der Heiligen Schrift im 16. und 17. Jahrhundert Bengt Hägglund zum 90. Geburtstag ; mit einer Bibliographie der Schriften des Jubilars*, (translated: *Studies of the Interpretation of Holy Scripture in the Sixteenth and Seventeeth centuries for Bengt Hägglund on his ninetieth birthday*), in *Historia Hermeneutica / Series Studia* 9 (Berlin: De Gruyter, 2010), 5–32.

37 For the role of pictures and the relation between painted and verbal images see Jens Wolff, "Ursprung der Bilder: Luthers Rhetorik der (Inter-)Passivitat," in: Ibid., 33–58.

38 Bernhard Lohse, *Martin Luther's Theology: its historical and systematic development*, (Minneapolis, MN: Fortress Press, 1999), 207ff; see also Carl Heinz Ratschow, *Jesus Christus*, Handbuch systematischer Theologie Bd. 5 (Gütersloh: Gütersloher Verlagshaus Mohn, 1982, second edition 1994), 21-37; Notger Slenczka, "Christus," in *Lutherhandbuch*, edited by Albrecht Beutel (Tübingen: Mohr Siebeck, 2005), 381-392.

39 Luther, *Luther's works*, vol. 33, 138–140.

40 Philipp Melanchthon, *Loci communes*, edited by von Horst Georg Pöhlmann, *2.*, durchges. und korr. Aufl. (Gütersloh: Gütersloher Verl.-Haus, 1997), 22f.

41 For the definition of the Council of Chaldecon cf. Heinrich Denzinger and Helmut

personhood[42]. Hence, the relation between divinity and humanity in the person of Jesus Christ cannot be understood the way two planks of wood are glued together. Rather, the unity of the person can only be conceived properly if there is an intimate communion between divinity and humanity, which means communication in the sense of giving and taking. The person of Jesus Christ is thus understood as the place where God's self-communication to the human nature happens in such a way that he does not hold any part of himself back, and that on the other side the human nature in its distinctness from God is not erased, but completed. For the person of the divine Logos, this self-communication means that he shares in the suffering and dying of the humanity accepted in the incarnation so that one can say: 'God suffers and dies on the cross'[43]. In *On the Councils and the Church* (1539) Luther explains the soteriological impact of this in this way:

> We Christians must ascribe all the *idiomata* of the two natures of Christ, both persons, equally to him. Consequently Christ is God and man in one person because whatever is said of him as man must also be said of him as God, namely, Christ has died, and Christ is God; therefore, God died–not the separated God, but God united with humanity. [...] We should always rejoice in true faith, free of dispute and doubt, over such a blessed, comforting doctrine, to sing, praise, and thank God the Father for such expressible mercy that he let his dear Son become like us, a man and our brother! [...] We Christians should know that if God is not in the scale to give it weight, we, on our side, sink to the ground. I mean it this way: if it cannot be said that God died for us, but only a man, we are lost; but if God's death and a dead God lie in the balance, his side goes down and ours goes up like a light and empty scale. Yet he also readily go up again, or leap out of the scale! But he could not sit on the scale unless he has become a man like us, so that it could be called God's dying, God's martyrdom, God's blood, and God's death. For God in his own nature cannot die; but now that God and man are united in one person, it is called God's death when the man dies who is one substance or one person with God.[44]

Hoping, *Enchiridion symbolorum definitionum et declarationum de rebus fidei et morum*, ed. by Peter Hünermann, 43. Edition. (Freiburg ; Basel ; Wien: Herder, 2010), n. 301f.

42 Cf. Oswald Bayer, *Martin Luthers Theologie*, 3., erneut durchges. Aufl. (Tübingen: Mohr Siebeck, 2007), 193-215.

43 For a detailed exploration of Luther's notion of communicatio idiomatum cf. Reinhard Schwarz, "Gott ist Mensch. Zur Lehre von der Person Christi bei den Ockhamisten und bei Luther," *Zeitschrift für Theologie und Kirche* 69 (1966) (Tübingen: Mohr, o. J.): 289-351. For the later christological development and debate in the Lutheran tradition cf. Ulrich Wiedenroth, *Krypsis und Kenosis: Studien zu Thema und Genese der Tübinger Christologie im 17. Jahrhundert*, in series Beiträge zur historischen Theologie 162 (Tübingen: Mohr Siebeck, 2011). For the relation between the doctrine of justification and christology in early Lutheran dogmatics cf. Friederike Nüssel, *Allein aus Glauben: zur Entwicklung der Rechtfertigungslehre in der konkordistischen und frühen nachkonkordistischen Theologie*, in series Forschungen zur systematischen und ökumenischen Theologie Bd. 95 (Göttingen: Vandenhoeck & Ruprecht, 2000).

44 Luther, *On the Councils and the Church* (1539), in *Luther's works*, vol. 41, 103f.

This christological interpretation of the incarnation indicates that God himself shares in the *conditio humana* through the suffering and death of Jesus Christ, and that he completes and elevates the human condition in the resurrection, granting it new life in its human distinctness[45]. Luther's interpretation of the image of Christ thus presents us with the insight of God's true divinity, which is not determined by a punishing type of justice–an image which drove Luther to despair in his first years as a monk–but by God's self-giving love through which he overcomes the power of sin in the death and resurrection of Jesus Christ and grants true righteousness through faith in Jesus Christ. Luther explains this in his sermons, catechisms, and theological writings and at the same time invites Christians to themselves contemplate the image of Christ's death and resurrection over and over again, until this image comes to stay forever. According to Luther, this is what may help to overcome contestations in daily life, but especially when one prepares to die. While Luther in his *theologia crucis* and his understanding of the incarnation and salvific work of Jesus Christ contradicted scholastic incarnation theology, he actually took up some of the semantic potential of medieval Christian art, especially in the portrayal of the *Not Gottes* in medieval *Andachtsbildern*, which symbolize God's empathy as he, as the Father, grieves deeply over the death of his Son whom he carries on is lap[46].

Luther's understanding of the incarnation became highly controversial during the time of the Reformation and in the age of confessionalization[47]. In contrast to Lutheran Christology, Reformed Christology emphasized that there is no real communication between the two natures of Jesus Christ, because this would resolve their distinct character. Hence, it is only the human nature of Jesus Christ that suffers and dies on the cross whereas God in his divinity is impassible and cannot suffer[48]. In this way Reformed theology protected already at its outset *theologia crucis* against the dangers involved in the talk of the death of God, which could be anticipated in Georg W. F. Hegel's speculative interpretation of the incarnation and then became fully visible in the radical critique of religion by Friedrich Nietzsche and others. The productive appropriation of Hegel's connection between Lutheran incarnation christology and the doctrine of the trinity in Karl Barth's revelation theology offered a model for reformed theologians in the twentieth and twenty-first century[49], to overcome this traditional Lutheran-Re-

[45] Cf. Michael Welker, *Gottes Offenbarung: Christologie*, in series Neukirchener Theologie (Neukirchen-Vluyn: Neukirchener Verlagsgesellschaft, 2012), 157ff.

[46] Cf. Colum Hourihane, "Andachtsbild," in *The Grove Encyclopedia of Medieval Art and Architecture* (Oxford University Press, 2012), vol. 2, 64f.

[47] For a survey on research cf. Susan R. Boettcher, "Confessionalization: Reformation, Religion, Absolutism, and Modernity," *History Compass* 2, Nr. 1 (2004), 1-10.

[48] The difference in Christology is fundamental for the distinctive profiles of Lutheran and Reformed teaching, cf. Friederike Nüssel, "Das Konkordienbuch und die Genese einer lutherischen Tradition," Peter Gemeinhardt, editor, "Gebundene Freiheit?," 1. Aufl., *Die Lutherische Kirche, Geschichte und Gestalten* 25 (Gütersloh: Gütersloher Verlagshaus, 2008), 62–83.

[49] Cf. Welker, *Gottes Offenbarung*, part 5, 234ff.

formed conflict. This did, however, not change the corresponding difference in the attitude towards devotional paintings and sculpture as cultural expression of spirituality. Until today, there are no paintings in Reformed churches. This cultural difference still witnesses to what lies at the heart of the christological difference: the concern that by being drawn in a picture, God is drawn into finitude.

Yet, an analogous concern is deeply embedded in Lutheran soteriology. With its central doctrine of justification by faith alone (*sola fide*) without works it focuses entirely on God's sovereign grace in granting salvation without requiring human cooperation. While Luther achieved this reformatory insight in thorough Scripture exegesis, it was also based on his personal experience that it is impossible to rely on human works as a sufficient condition for being worthy of God's justification. For how can a person ever be assured that her works could suffice to please God? By learning to understand the righteousness of God revealed in Christ as the promise of justification by faith alone without works, Luther also realized that it is precisely the attempt to fulfill God's requirements by one's own works which is the apex of unfaith. For in this very attempt one is *ipso facto* denying that God in his creative almightiness has through Christ accomplished everything necessary for reconciliation with mankind and in his revelation of his unconditioned and inexpressible love for humanity has himself proven his trustworthiness. This love of God revealed in the image of Christ deserves nothing but trust. If however human being try to earn God's grace through works and be righteous before God, God is made a liar, as Luther put it. To ignore God's grace is just another way of ignoring God's infinite majesty.

One may see now that for Lutheran spirituality and theology the motivation for morality lies in the semantic potential included in God's gospel and in the imagery of the crucifixion and resurrection of Christ. According to this understanding, human reason acquires motivation for morality not in itself, but in God's love revealed in and through Jesus Christ. In his rational account of the Christian religion, Kant, quite in accord with the Lutheran interpretation, described Jesus as the prototype of a human being, as the *vere homo*. Kant's notion of God is yet different from the Lutheran image of the divine as he sees God as the author of the moral law and the guarantor of convergence between a person's happiness and their worthiness to be happy. Conversely, for Luther God is truly God in precisely his ability and readiness to share and fulfill the *conditio humana* in his Son through the Spirit. This image of the Divine in turn allows for humans to let God be their God, to realize their ultimate dependence of God as the creator and to accept the limitations of human nature. Moreover, in the light of the Gospel humans may realize that they are equal before God[50] and, as God's creatures, should grant one another the respect, empathy and freedom they receive from God in their faith.

50 See Ingolf U. Dalferth, "Bestimmte Unbestimmtheit," *ThLZ* 139 (2014), 3-35.

4. Modern Adaptations in Global Ecumenism

While the reformation movement in the sixteenth century allowed for enormous progress in both public and academic education, it resulted in the separation of the church in the West, followed by religious wars and persecution of those who would not accept the religious orders of their territory. Religious freedom was achieved only through the disaster of the Thirty Years War and violent processes of denominational competition[51], and only in the context of colonialism and the global mission movement in the nineteenth century did the disastrous consequences of church divisions become manifest on a global level. Several Christian youth organizations eventually addressed the common bond between the different Christian denominations in their belief in God's Gospel and became pioneers for ecumenism. In 1910, the approximately twelve hundred participants of the World mission conference held at Edinburgh jointly articulated the desire for unity among the churches in their final communiqué. The ecumenical movement was born and quickly established global institutions to address the various tasks of global Christian formation. Leveraged by the experiences of two World Wars the ecumenical movement sought to build one globally representative organization for member churches to be able to speak to the world with one voice and engage for justice and peace on a global level. Soon after World War II, the World Council of Churches (WCC) was founded for this purpose in Amsterdam 1948.[52] While the Roman-Catholic Church had long been kept its distance to this new global movement and especially its ecclesiological implications, the Second Vatican Council in its Decree on Ecumenism *Unitatis Redintegratio* not only recognized it, but gave a deep theological way:

> Christ the Lord founded one Church and one Church only. However, many Christian communions present themselves to men as the true inheritors of Jesus Christ; all indeed profess to be followers of the Lord but differ in mind and go their different ways, as if Christ Himself were divided. Such division openly contradicts the will of Christ, scandalizes the world, and damages the holy cause of preaching the Gospel to every creature. But the Lord of Ages wisely and patiently follows out the plan of grace on our behalf, sinners that we are. In recent times more than ever before, He has been rousing divided Christians to remorse over their divisions and to a longing for unity. Everywhere large numbers have felt the impulse of this grace, and among our separated brethren also there increases from day to day the movement, fostered by the grace of the Holy Spirit, for the restoration of unity among all Christians.[53]

---

[51] Christoph Kampmann, *Europa und das Reich im Dreißigjährigen Krieg* (Stuttgart: Kohlhammer, 2008).

[52] See for the history Gideon Goosen, *Bringing Churches Together: A Popular Introduction to Ecumenism* (International Specialized Book Service Incorporated, 2001).

[53] See the introduction of the Decree on Ecumenism: http://www.vatican.va/archive/hist_councils/ii_vatican_council/documents/vat-ii_decree_19641121_unitatis-redintegratio_en.html.

As we can see from this passage and also from the basic commitment of WCC,[54] the desire for unity and the reconciliation of divisions between churches is at the heart of the ecumenical twentieth century movement. On this ground the churches assembled in the WCC see their mission in advocating for justice and peace in the world with one voice. This is based on the joint belief in God's true justice and self-giving love revealed in the life, death and resurrection of his Son through the Spirit. In the ecumenical movement the shared belief in God's love and forgiveness without distinction of person assures and fosters human encounter in mutual respect and empathy and the engagement for social cohesion in spite of denominational differences. While the work of WCC is manifold, it reaches the public sphere most effectively through the plenary assemblies. These assemblies serve as a forum for the churches, but their mottos speak to the public sphere in a globally audible way as they narrate the ecumenical journey of churches with the triune God and the community among churches. This journey is motivated and nourished by the eschatological promise and hope in the transforming power of the divine love revealed in Jesus Christ through the Spirit.[55] Hence the ecumenical movement itself can be taken as a witness to the potential of the imagery of God suffering and overcoming death in Jesus Christ that provides cultural orientation in and for today's world. Yet, for believers the promise of God's love and eternal kingdom is not just a vehicle that fosters morality. God is rather conceived as the origin and infinite source of wisdom, love, empathy, and the desire for community.

---

[54] "The World Council of Churches is a fellowship of churches which confess the Lord Jesus Christ as God and Saviour according to the scriptures, and therefore seek to fulfil together their common calling to the glory of the one God, Father, Son and Holy Spirit. It is a community of churches on the way to visible unity in one faith and one eucharistic fellowship, expressed in worship and in common life in Christ. It seeks to advance towards this unity, as Jesus prayed for his followers, 'so that the world may believe.' (John 17:21)." Ibid.

[55] Amsterdam 1948: "Man's Disorder and God's Design"; Evanston 1954: "Christ–The Hope of the World"; New Delhi 1961: "Jesus Christ–The Light of the World"; Uppsala 1968: "Behold, I make all things new"; Nairobi 1975: "Jesus Christ frees and unites"; Vancouver 1983: "Jesus Christ–the Life of the World"; Canberra 1991: "Come Holy Spirit–Renew the Whole Creation"; Harare 1998: "Turn to God–Rejoice in Hope"; Porto Allegre 2006: "God in your grace–transform the World"; Busan 2013: "God of life, lead us to justice and peace".

Image of the Divine and Spiritual Presence

In What Ways Can Christology Provide Cultural Orientations?

Michael Welker

The chapters of this book intend to develop diagnostic proposals of the complex sphere of cultural orientations, by focussing on the religious, symbolic, liturgical, cognitive and normative powers which we see at work in the different faith traditions. They investigate the power of images, icons and metaphors which illuminate religious thinking and moral practices. The following contribution investigates the key Christian "Image of the Divine"–which, as will be shown, has to be translated into "Spiritual Presence of the Divine" in order to decode and to illuminate its cultural orientations.

The anthropological investigation of the *imago Dei* in our faith traditions might be regarded as a common ground of discourse–at least between the Christian and the Jewish traditions. In the Christian perspective, however, it is unavoidable to finally shift from the anthropological notion of the *imago Dei* to the Christological notion and to reflect anthropological patterns and affairs in a Christological light. However, if we merely concentrate on the iconic presence of Jesus Christ in its anthropological shape, we will easily get stuck with the very powerful "frozen" icons of the cradle and the cross, the beginning and the end of Jesus' life with the message of the incarnation and the kenosis. The correlated insistence on a specific nearness of God can easily divide our faith traditions. In contrast to this incarnational and kenotic approach, as valid as it is, it is noteworthy that Paul speaks of a transformation into the "image" of the "Lord who is the Spirit" (2 Cor 3:18). What does this mean?

The standard message of the theologies of the cross used to be that the focus on the condescending and suffering God challenges the self-aggrandization of human beings, and their attempts to dominate the world and other people, and to behave in a god-like manner. In my view, this message has hardly served a subtle cultural analysis and cultural orientation. We gain a very different approach when we reflect the differentiated spiritual presence of the divine, which for the Christian perspective has a Christo-morphic shape in its orientation towards the incarnation, cross and resurrection of Christ. A *threefold spriritual presence* can be and has to bee unfolded in this light.[1]

---

[1] The following draws on insights gained in my book: *God the Revealed: Christology* (Grand Rapids: Eerdmans, 2013).

With the shift from "Images of the Divine" to "a threefold spiritual presence" this chapter replaces conventional dogmatic thinking about "Divine attributes". It also engages the challenge described in the introduction, to speak of the presence of the Divine under earthly conditions while respecting the theological reserve against image and icon making.

1. The "Kingly" Spiritual Presence of Christ and the Cultural Orientations of a Christian Humanism

In light of the pre-Easter life of Jesus, *the kingly rule of Christ* and of "those who belong to him" comes into focus, and send *a clear message of freedom and multidimensional care and love. This spiritual presence revolutionizes hierarchical and monarchical forms of rule and order, both in the churches and (indirectly) in political and civil-societal spheres. For this king is simultaneously brother and friend, indeed he is even poor and ostracized.* With its radically democratic character, this kingly rule appears, on the one hand, uncomfortably confusing. Yet on the other hand, it is exemplary of that freedom-affirming search for orientations that are characteristic for egalitarian orientations, democratic communities and freedom-affirming civil societies. This "kingly" spiritual presence is shaped above all by the praxis of mutual care and support, mercy and love beyond family and tribal realms and the freedom that such love mediates. Loving acceptance, healing, liberating teaching and education, and the push to include as many as possible in it–these all define its praxis.

In continuity and discontinuity with the Torah traditions, love and forgiveness are defined by *free, creative self-withdrawal*[2] for the benefit of others.[3] Free, creative, and (in love) joyful self-withdrawal for the benefit of one's neighbors is incredibly effective at promoting freedom. Love–which *eros, agape* and *philia* can only ever insufficiently define[4]–aims at achieving a state for the beloved where "all things serve the best," where the feet of the beloved are set on "wide places." And yet essential for any understanding of the reign of God is that it is *not primarily a responsibility* for freedom-promoting behavior and action that wins over our hearts and minds, but rather the joyful and thankful *experience of voluntary self-withdrawal by others, performed for our sake.*[5] For this reason it is said that

---

2 Cf. Michael Welker, "The Power of Mercy in Biblical Law", in: *Journal of Law and Religion* 29/2 (2014), 225-235.

3 A particularly illuminating discussion of the connection between the Old Testament images of the kingdom of God, the preaching and work of Jesus, and early Christian life praxis is offered by Christian Grappe, *Le Royaume de Dieu. Avant, avec et après Jésus* (Genf: Labor et Fides, 2001).

4 Michael Welker, "Romantic Love, Covenantal Love, Kenotic Love," in: John Polkinghorne (ed.), *The Work of Love: Creation as Kenosis* (Grand Rapids/London: Eerdmans, 2001), 127–136.

5 Cf. Michael Welker, "The 'Reign' of God," in: *Theology Today* 49 (1992), 500-515;

children are particularly close to the reign of God.[6] Yet an ethos of liberating joy and thankfulness is also fundamental for an ethos of philanthropic welfare and a culture of help.[7] Sadly, many social routines often suppress thankful sensitivity to the enormous potentials of free, creative self-withdrawal in many of our social contexts.

A thankful attentiveness to the great potentials of free, creative self-withdrawal not only among family and friends, but also in education and medical care, in civil and social organizations should sensitize human being to the strongly formative, direct and indirect forces of the kingly spiritual presence of Christ. It is not just from within the shadow of need but also in the light of thankfulness that human beings must examine the enormous challenges of today: challenges in education, therapeutic medicine, the rule of law, and global interculturalism. Through many, often unremarkable acts of love, care and forgiveness, the cultural impacts of this spiritual presence take on form and Gestalt.

William Schweiker–taking up and further developing insights from the Niebuhr brothers[8] and James Gustafson[9]–has made clear that "Christian humanism"[10] also influences other religious and secular forms of practiced love and compassion while also receiving in turn strong impulses from them. The freedom-promoting spiritual presence of Christ is broader than simply all the churches of all times and places. "Just as you did to one of the least of these who are members of my family, you did it to me," regardless whether you recognized my presence in them or not.[11] Conversely, those who limit the image and rule of Christ to "word and sacrament" alone underestimate the breadth of the liberating and culturally orienting presence in the power of the Spirit. And yet it would also be wrong

---

Wilfried Härle, *Dogmatik* (Berlin & New York: de Gruyter, 3rd rev. edn. 2007), 237ff; idem, *Ethik* (Berlin &. New York: de Gruyter, 2011), 328ff, 388ff.

6 Cf. Mt 10:14; Marcia J. Bunge, "Children, the Image of God, and Christology: Theological Anthropology in Solidarity with Children," in: Schuele/Thomas, *Who is Jesus Christ for Us Today?*, 167–181; idem, (ed.), *The Child in Christian Thought* (Grand Rapids & Cambridge, U.K.: Eerdmans, 2001); *idem*, (ed.), *The Child in the Bible* (Grand Rapids & Cambridge/U.K.: Eerdmans), 2008.

7 Cf. J. H. Wichern's emphasis on "thankful love" as a foundational form of communal life in *diakonia* (Johann Hinrich Wichern, *Schriften zur Sozialpädagogik [Rauhes Haus und Johannesstift]*, Sämtliche Werke, vol. IV.1, ed. Peter Meinhold (Berlin, 1958), 119 u. ö.).

8 See e.g. H. Richard Niebuhr, *Christ and Culture* (New York: Harper & Row, 1951); Reinhold Niebuhr, *The Self and the Dramas of History* (New York: Scibner's, 1955), esp. chp. 19.

9 James M. Gustafson, *Christ and the Moral Life* (New York: Harper & Row, 1968).

10 Cf. William Schweiker & David E. Klemm, *Religion and the Human Future: An Essay on Theological Humanism* (Oxford: Blackwell, 2008); William Schweiker, "Flesh and Folly: The Christ of Christian Humanism," in: Schuele/Thomas, *Who is Jesus Christ for Us Today?*, 85–102; Liu Xiaofeng, "Sino-Christian Theology in the Modern Context," in: *Sino-Christian Studies in China*, ed. Huilin Yang and Daniel Yeung (Newcastle: Cambridge Scholars Press, 2006), 70ff.

11 Cf. Mt 25:40 and 25:34ff; John F. Hoffmeyer, "Christology and *Diakonia*," in: *Schuele/Thomas, Who is Jesus Christ for Us Today?*, 150–166.

simply to appropriate an abstract, universal, moral continuum which would be superior to a "merely Christian ethos". Any such value-free moral reign would just be an empty construct.[12]

2. The "Priestly" Spiritual Presence of Christ and the Cultural Orientation of Theological Existence and Liturgical Life

Due to the strengths of the Letter to the Hebrews, discussion of the *priestly dimension* of the Spirit of Christ has often concentrated completely upon the difficult themes of "high priest and sacrificial cult."[13] Jesus Christ is the eternal high priest, chosen by God himself[14], and he presents his sacrifice not in the earthly temple but in heaven, "so that he might be a merciful and faithful high priest in the service of God, to make a sacrifice of atonement for the sins of the people" (Heb 2:17).[15] In this way, Hebrews presents an enormous arc that stretches from heavenly high priest chosen by God and sitting enthroned at his right hand (Heb 1:3; 8:1) to the suffering shepherd who goes to his death for the sake of his sheep (Heb 2:5–18; 13:20). The text does indeed raise a central issue regarding the efficacy of the exalted Christ. And yet it doesn't quite grasp the entire breadth of participation in his life through the power of his Spirit, dealing as it does only with a fragment of his priestly work.

Over against this reduction, one has to appreaciate and to understand the priestly spiritual presence of Christ in all the breadth and multidimensionality apparent in the Christian spiritual life and worship service. Francis Fiorenza has drawn special attention to the way that the appearances of the risen Christ are marked by acts such as the greeting of peace, the breaking of bread, the explanation of scripture, the command to baptize, and the missionary sending of disciples—and these acts are all elementary forms of the worship life and character of the church—from the early church on to most of church-life today.[16]

---

12 See here the instructive discussion between Judith Butler, Jürgen Habermas, Charles Taylor and Cornel West in: Eduardo Mendieta & Jonathan VanAntwerpen (eds.), *The Power of Religion in the Public Sphere* (New York: Columbia Univ. Press, 2011).

13 Heb 2:17; 3:1; 4:14f; 5:1ff; 6:20; 7:26ff; 8:1ff; 9:7ff, 24ff; 10:1ff, 10ff; 13:11ff.

14 "... according to the order of Melchizedek," Heb 5:6, 10; 6:20; 7:1, 10, 11, 15, 17 in reference to a mysterious figure who (following Ps 110:4 and Gen 14:1–24) combined the office of king and priest. Cf. Erich Gräßer, *An die Hebräer (Hebr 1–6)*, EKK XVII/1 and (Heb 7:1–10:18), EKK XVII/2 (Zürich/Braunschweig & Neukirchen-Vluyn: Benziger & Neukirchener, 1990 & 1993), vol. 1: 288ff; vol. 2: 9f.

15 On the theology of sacrifice in Hebrews, Sigrid Brandt, *Opfer als Gedächtnis, Auf dem Weg zu einer befreienden theologischen Rede von Opfer* (Münster/Hamburg/London: Lit, 2004), 174–204.

16 Cf. Francis Fiorenza, "The Resurrection of Jesus and Roman Catholic Fundamental Theology," in *The Resurrection: An Interdisciplinary Symposium on the Resurrection of Jesus* (New York: Paulist Press, 1998), 213–248, 238ff.

The greeting of peace, Communion, baptism, the explanation of scripture, mission–this polyphony of the worship service is bound together with the priestly office, which in turn is then shared through the "priesthood of all believers" and its cultural orientations. Following Luther, Christoph Schwöbel sees this presence as a "dialogue between Christ and community" in the worship service: "In the differing ways in which Christ is spoken of during the worship service–in the gospel narratives, the kerygmatic promises, instructive statements, liturgical formulae and discursive discussions of the epistles–the point of them all is the Gospel, the speech of God in his Word with us, which has its point (even as law) in the Gospel, the promise of the compassionate love of God, that is mediated to us as community with God, to us creatures who are otherwise estranged from God. Conversely, in our own speech to Christ, or through Christ to God the Father in our prayers of thanks, petition, lament and praise, we express our need for lasting community with God, and in doxological speech our aim is participation in God's glory in Christ through the Spirit".[17]

Thus a correctly understood and correctly celebrated worship service will open, solidify and deepen human knowledge of God and salvation. The adequate knowledge of God is always also knowledge of salvation, not just a metaphysical insight or an ultimate idea. A correctly celebrated worship service does not lead simply to an optimized conception of God or an optimized religious sensitivity. Rather it transposes us into a multidimensional relational event in which the spiritual presence of Christ reveals the breadth of God's creative action. The participants are enabled to experience the divine Spirit as the Spirit who lovingly saves and elevates them, and who gives them a share in the life of the resurrected and exalted Christ with many spiritual, educational and ethical repercussions.[18]

3. The "Prophetic" Spiritual Presence of Christ and the Cultural Orientation of Unmasking and Transforming Systemic Distortions in Politics, Law, Religion, and Ethics

For many people, the prophetic spiritual presence of Christ is the most difficult and even offensive of the three dimensions.[19] For those today who seek actively to participate in this prophetic presence, which conflicts do they find themselves

---

[17] Christoph Schwöbel, "'Wer sagt denn ihr, dass ich sei?' (Mt 16,15). Eine systematisch-theologische Skizze zur Lehre von der Person Christi," in: *Marburger Jahrbuch Theologie XXIII: Christologie,* 47; 50ff; regarding the quote from Luther, see *WA 49, 588,* 16–18.

[18] Cf. the excellent ecumenical contribution by Gregor Etzelmüller, *... zu schauen die schönen Gottesdienste des Herrn: Eine biblische Theologie der christlichen Liturgiefamilien* (Frankfurt / Leipzig: Lembeck / EVA, 2010).

[19] This is not yet apparent in the New Testament texts which expressly connect Jesus with the title "prophet" (e.g. Mk 6:4,15; 8:28; Lk 7:16; 13:31ff; Jn 6:14; Acts 3:22; 7:37); the kingly and priestly titles have a far more compelling character in the context of the crucifixion and Letter to the Hebrews respectively.

facing? Naturally they are repeatedly confronted with the moral, social, cultural, communal and political crises and conflicts that arise from their immediate concrete surroundings. But to these are also added the global conflicts in which people are mostly only passively involved: economic, media, scientific and political conflicts. Countless contexts arise in which prophetic knowledge and a prophetic voice are urgently needed, in which people too want bring to bear their warnings and threats, their protests and encouragements, their yes and their no. Yet if we only focus on this overpowering tidal wave of problems before us, then we risk stumbling into resignation and cynicism: We need a new outpouring of the Holy Spirit and entire armies of prophets to tackle this wealth of problems! And yet with such a vague global and religious view, we would hardly grasp the prophetic task involved in the imitation of Jesus Christ.

Prophetic speech in the imitation of Christ is primarily speech that serves God, that allows God to express himself and to take action. "Long ago God spoke to our ancestors in many and various ways by the prophets, but in these last days he has spoken to us by his Son ... the reflection of God's glory and the exact imprint of God's very being" (Heb 1:1–3). Prophetic speech in the presence of Christ seeks *his direction and God's will in the conflicts of the present day.* And for this reason, it also engages in self-critique. According to the biblical traditions, it was only the false prophets, the "lying prophets," who expressed themselves eagerly and quickly and, preferably, in chorus with the politically supported moral majority.[20] The true prophet sought to recognize truth and actualize justice in concrete situations–in the light of God's word. Thus true prophecy carefully tests whether it really is only speaking its own opinions (or current public opinion) or whether it conveys a message oriented toward the Word and Spirit of God. Here we see how, in the imitation of Christ, the prophetic act and the priestly service of proclaiming God's word are closely intertwined, and often connected with difficult self-examination and doubt.[21]

---

20 On the problem of lying spirits and lying prophets, see Michael Welker, *God the Spirit*, translated by John Hoffmeyer, new edition (Eugene: Wipf & Stock 2014), 84-98.

21 A moving testimony is related in David J. Garrow, *Bearing the Cross: Martin Luther King, Jr. and the Southern Christian Leadership Conference* (New York: Viking Penguin, 1986), 58, quoted in Thomas G. Long, *Hebrews, Interpretation* (Louisville: John Knox, 1997), 9: In the middle of the Montgomery bus strike, Martin Luther King's experiences of persecution, hate, threat and suffering reached their darkest point. Over forty telephone callers had threatened violence against him and his family. "Late one night, King returned home from a meeting only to receive yet another call warning him to leave town soon if he wanted to stay alive. Unable to sleep after this disturbing threat, he sat at the kitchen table and worried. In the midst of his anxiety something told him that he could no longer call on anyone for help but God. So he prayed, confessing his weakness and his loss of courage. 'At that moment,' he said later, 'I could hear an inner voice saying to me "Martin Luther, stand up for righteousness. Stand up for justice. Stand up for truth. And lo, I will be with you, even until the end of the world".' It was, realized King, the voice of Jesus speaking a word of promise, a word of reassurance, a timely word of comfort and strength."

Importantly, the prophetic presence is also not to be separated from the welfare work of the kingly spiritual presence. Prophecy in the imitation of Christ consistently acts to serve love and the protection of the weak. It does not promote the spread of hate and violence. Prophecy in the imitation of Jesus Christ consistently holds "those who belong to him" to Christ's Way. Thus true prophecy on the one hand overlaps with the concrete service of welfare and love (the kingly presence), while on the other hand seeking to follow that great line of the worship service in the knowledge of the true and just God and his ways (the priestly presence). Amid this connection, prophecy in the imitation of Christ has the stamina to maintain its eschatological hope: not my will, but rather may God's will be done!

Due to this overlapping and interconnection, the other two offices and their corresponding Gestalten of the reign of God also display aspects of the prophetic character. Those who participate in Christ's royal presence may perhaps be content with a humble and quiet life full of practiced and experienced brotherly and sisterly love. But active engagement for the weak, poor, oppressed, and disadvantaged can also take on a prophetic character even when it is not expressly engaged in public critique of the circumstances that cause poverty and disadvantage. In certain situations, quiet yet determined welfare work both inside and outside the church can penetrate deeper and provoke more strongly than noisy politico-moral posturing. And yet it has to be distinguished from prophetic action. It aims at the concrete alleviation of need and the emergent development of the "work of the reign of God."

In contrast, prophetic witness often proclaims critique and self-critique.[22] This produces tensions and conflicts in communities, churches and societies. These tensions and conflicts become particularly strong when the priestly and prophetic roles clash: We want edifying and devotional worship services, not politico-religious machinations; we want the faith and teachings of the church, not critical social agitation! But from the beginning, most of the world's churches have expressly sought after and approved a close connection between the priestly and prophetic roles, without calling into question the blessings of a peaceful, joyful, and edifying worship service.[23] It is the living, relevant proclamation of the worship service both in preaching and in education, together with the scientifically-critical training of its office-bearers that bind both Gestalten of the spiritual presence together in a regulated way. At the same time, most churches are wary that prophecy not lose its theological content or become disconnected from the word of God and its critique of social, societal, political and economic conditions.

---

[22] See here Walter Rauschenbusch, *A Theology for the Social Gospel* [1917] (Library of Theological Ethics, Louisville: Westminster John Knox, 2010, esp. 118ff, 131ff; Reinhold Niebuhr, *The Nature and Destiny of Man, Vol. II: Human Destiny* [1943], Gifford Lectures (New York: Charles Scribner's, 1964), esp. 23–34 and 244ff; also Milenko Andjelic, *Christlicher Glaube als prophetische Religion. Walter Rauschenbusch und Reinhold Niebuhr*, Internationale Theologie 3 (Frankfurt: Peter Lang, 1998), 55ff, 136ff and 183ff.

[23] The dimensions of proclamation and doxology are emphasized by Thomas Gillespie, *The First Theologians: A Study in Early Christian Prophecy* (Grand Rapids: Eerdmans, 1994).

If only the church's own concerns about religious routines that amplify, or even create, dishonest and befuddling "feel good" atmospheres were as pronounced as their fear of a religiously provoked "moral war of all against all."

One can see more clearly the *prophetic spiritual presence of Christ and its cultural radiation* when realistic perspectives on the cross of Christ are taken into account. To realize this, one cannot reduce the message of the cross simply to the revelation of the suffering and co-suffering God, to God's opposition to death, or similar leading conceptions in many "theologies of the cross", as important as these messages, powerfully elaborated by Luther, Hegel, Bonhoeffer and Moltmann, remain.[24] The nearness of God in the poverty, weakness and powerlessness of the crucified Christ, and God's suffering under the sins of the world should not blind us to God's forceful opposition in the cross and resurrection to the principalities and powers of this world. To recognize this opposition, one must understand the web of real conflicts in which Jesus was caught in the event of his crucifixion. Jesus Christ–who brought humanity the message of the coming reign of God, who mediated to his witnesses the powers of healing, the powers of affection toward children, to the weak, the excluded, the sick, the suffering–it was this Jesus Christ who was condemned by religion, law, global political power, public morality and public opinion, all in a moment of complex unanimity!

Not singular evil figures but rather the "powers of order" (powers that present themselves as "good", and claim to "wonderfully protect" us) all worked together at the cross to oppose Jesus of Nazareth and the presence of God in Jesus Christ. The cross reveals the reality of the world "under the power of sin," it reveals the "night of godforsakenness," not only for Jesus himself but as a continual threatening danger for the world. It reveals the extent to which all public and powerful protective mechanisms–such as the law, politics, religion, morality, and public opinion–can fail us and our societies, and even become a trap.

Against this background, the great challenges and significance of the prophetic spiritual presence become especially clear. More precisely, the great significance of Christian proclamation and theological teaching, of the indispensable tasks of truth- and justice-seeking communities, in addition to the church's concrete engagement in welfare work, and beyond–all of this becomes clear in the dimension of the prophetic office.

The three dimensions of Christ's spiritual presence are entangled and *perichoretically* bound within one another.[25] I have proposed to speak of the *"threefold Gestalt of the reign of Christ" or the "threefold Gestalt of the reign of God."*[26]

---

[24] Cf. Welker, *God the Revealed*, Part 3.

[25] See Staniloae, *Orthodoxe Dogmatik* II, 90ff; on perichoresis, see Eberhard Jüngel, Art.: Perichorese, *RGG*4, vol. VI, 1109–1111.

[26] Cf. Welker, *God the Revealed, 209-216;* Paul Tillich, *Systematische Theologie*, Vol. III, 25ff, suggested that when describing the processes of life we should replace the commonly used metaphors of "layers" and "levels" with that of "dimensions." Dimensions allow for different weightings while avoiding the need to define set hierarchies.

The resurrected Christ reveals the triune God and thus also himself as the divine Word, as the eternal Logos, but he also reveals the Holy Spirit and the loving Creator and New Creator. In this revelation, he is "not without those who belong to him." In a Christian perspective, "those who belong to him" cannot be reduced simply to the churches. It becomes particularly clear in the prophetic and kingly Gestalten of the reign that this reign of Christ is far broader and far more encompassing than the domain of the churches. The diaconical and prophetic cultural orientations radiate widely into civil societal, academic and legal dimensions of societal life.

It is dangerous to overemphasize any particular one of these spiritual dimensions. Too heavy a stress in theologies or churches on the kingly presence or the corresponding Gestalt of the reign of God might lead to a powerful profile of church service and welfare–but it can also pave the way for the humanistic self-secularization of piety and the churches and a cultural loss of spiritual powers. A strong emphasis on the prophetic dimensions can promote the development of spirited political and shrewd academically analytical forms of theology and piety and civil societal engagements–but it can also lead to moral exhaustion and spiritual burnout. A strong privilege of the priestly spiritual dimension can contribute to the development of powerful liturgical ecclesial profiles–but it can also lead to ecclesiocentric self-isolation and liturgical rigidity and even stale paralysis.

The respect for the three dimensions of spiritual presence and for their perichoretic connection, and the differentiated cultural radiation can help to combat these widespread, skewed overemphases. First, a *theological humanism* is supported in the orientation towards the caring and sustaining and rescuing God whom Christians see revealed in the brotherly lordship and "*kingship of Christ*", starting with the care for the very basic human needs, such as nourishment, healing and fellowship, intensely correlated with the familial and educational systems, with health care and the establishment of basic social routines and human rights.

The second dimension brings the revealing and judging aspects of the presence of the divine, which Christians attribute to the "*prophetic office of Christ*" and which should be correlated with the complex understanding of the dimension of the cross. In this respect, not only the co-suffering and kenotic presence of God, but also the disclosure of the principalities and powers by the cross even in religion, politics, morals and public opinion are crucial. Here the real and symbol-political conflicts, the critique and self-critique of religion, the critique of political and moral and legal developments which are not compatible with the search for justice, mercy and truth, and the love of freedom and peace, become important.

Finally, we have to refer to the sanctifying and ennobling presence of the divine, which, again in a Christian perspective, is correlated with the "*priestly office of Christ*" and with the powers revealed in the resurrection. The witnesses of the resurrection reveal very basic spiritual forms of the constitution of the life of the church, such as the breaking of the bread, the illumination and opening of the Scriptures, the greeting of peace, the sending of the disciples etc.–basic forms which Christians connect with the constitution of the body of Christ and its service in the world.[27]

All three dimensions of the spiritual presence of the divine which Christians see revealed in the life and lordship of Jesus Christ show various interdependences and a multitude of specific radiations into the different spheres of our cultures, our individual and social systems of memories and imaginations. They show different modes of support and of critical challenge of the secular cultural shaping powers which have to be investigated in a realistic comparative discourse with topical foci which promise mutual challenge and illumination among our traditions of faith. What might look like a christocentric triumphalism at a first glance could turn into a helpful offer of a threefold pattern of Living Image and a Spiritual Presence, in which, on the one hand, spiritual, liturgical, educational forms and markers of the identity of a specific faith tradition become cultivated.[28] On the other hand, the spiritual realm develops modes of thought and moral and religious orientation which are to be developed not only within a specific faith community but in a much broader context of societies and cultures and which can also challenge convictions and attitudes of specific faith traditions.

The ethos of the search for justice, compassion and truth is at home in all three faith traditions, represented in this book. It has spread into the moral, legal, political and educational institutions, organisations and civil societal contexts. What Christians identify with the reign of Christ and the Spirit of love and forgiveness will be named differently in other traditions of faith. But we will not only see different names but also different modes of thought and practices in the horizon of similar intentions. This will provide many resources of cultural orientations in the form of discourse, dialogue, fruitful difference and mutual challenge.

---

27 Cf. Michael Welker, *What Happens in Holy Communion?* (Grand Rapids: Eerdmans, 2000).

28 I see Michael Fishbane in a similar way relating "Jewish Theology" and "General Theology": *Sacred Attunement. A Jewish Theology* (Chicago and London: The University of Chicago Press, 2008), parts 2 and 3.

The Forces of Good and Evil in 'Islamic' Comic

Susanne Enderwitz

The most influential search engine, Google, has (or used to have) an informal motto with runs: "Don't be evil". But behind Google are businessmen, not supermen. Therefore, the official corporate self-presentation runs slightly different: "You can make money without doing evil." Moreover, when Google first declared its self-censorship move into China, the motto was somewhat replaced with an "evil scale" balancing sytem, allowing smaller evils for a greater good.[1] This relativist attitude is definitively unacceptable for supermen like the "99" with whom my talk is concerned. For them, even the unconditional observance of the motto "Don't be evil" is much too weak. Rather, they adhere to another motto which transforms moral conduct into overt action and could be rendered as follows: "Be good and fight the evil."

However, when speaking about the "99", we also deal with business. Since the release of the first issue of the "99" in 2006 (**1 issue no. 1**), the comic has proved to be an enormous commercial success, or so it seems. It is impossible to figure out numbers via the Internet, partly due to the distribution policies of the company "Teshkeel" which sells not only paper versions of the "99", but also digital ones that can unrestrictedly be printed out, reproduced and circulated in countless copies. At any rate, "Teshkeel" presents its product as a tremendously negotiable brand, and the echo of the "99" in numerous newspapers, journals and magazines supports this image cultivation. The "99" receive attention from the international media including the "New York Times", "The Wall Street Journal", "Time Magazine" and others, and in 2008 "Forbes Magazine" named the "99" as "one of the top 20 trends sweeping the globe".[2] The world-wide attention was rendered possible by the fact that the original Arabic version was immediately followed by an English version which, from 2007 onward, entered the international markets. In the spring of 2009, a "theme park" was opened in Kuwait, and an animated series is currently produced by Endemol UK. The "99"'s inventor, Naif al-Mutawa, gives lectures and interviews all around the globe, particularly in American universities and television channels.

Naif al-Mutawa (**2 Naif al-Mutawa**) is a thirty-something Kuweiti national, who has an Arab international background. As a child, he used to spend his

---

1 http://en.wikipedia.org/wiki/Don't_be_evil.

2 http://www.forbes.com/2008/01/09/internet-culture-global-forbeslife-global-pop08-cx_ee_0109pop_slide_4.html.

holidays in various American summer camps with children from different national, religious and cultural backgrounds. Also in the US, he studied Psychology, History and English Literature and obtained a PhD in Clinical Psychology, a Masters in Business Administration and a Masters in Organizational Psychology.[3] Afterwards, he worked with traumatized persons, particularly prisoners of war in Kuweit as well as in New York. In 2003, he decided to combine his expertise in psychology with his passion for literature in creating the "99": a brilliant idea, as neither the Islamic world in general nor the Arab world in particular has something comparable to the various superheroes in the Western world. In the editorial to the first special issue from 2006 we read: "The 99 is a business undertaking with social underpinnings. Soon to be available on television, in daily newspapers, on stickers and games, The 99 will become friends to the children and young adults of a quarter of the Earth's families." In pursuing his idea to create a brand for the whole Muslim world, al-Mutawa collected enough money to hire an international crew of specialists who had already taken part in the creation of Hitman, Spider Man, The Incredible Hulk, Star Wars, Batman and the like. Soon, the targeted audience of the "99" became truly international, as it was no longer restricted to the Muslim world, but included all the rest as well. In the concluding "notes" of issue no. 12 from 2008, al-Mutawa writes: "I spent the better part of the last few years telling the world that next Ramadan the world would have new heroes. Now it does."

Although the first heroes to show up in the comic, Nawaf al-Bilali, Dana Ibrahim and Amira Khan, came from an Arab or Muslim background, the protagonists of the comic are as international as their creators and audience. For the future it is planned to have 99 heroes from 99 countries, and this internationality extends to an interculturality or interreligiosity as well. The heroes have seemingly no communication problems, neither concerning their languages nor their customs and beliefs. They share the same problems, such as their relations with parents and siblings, learn the same lessons, such as the advantage of teamwork over isolated action, and display an all-embracing tolerance against each other. Less than 30 issues of the "99" have been published so far and the list of the heroes is not yet complete, but the underlying structure is already discernible: Only a few heroes are Muslims, only a few of the Muslim women wear a veil, only one of the Muslim women wears a Burka (**3 Batina**), and there is no mention of religion in general or Islam in particular, of ritual, prayer, or the like. Neither mosques nor churches, synagogues, temples or shrines are visible in the settings. Neither food- nor clothing prescriptions are observed, as the teenagers switch from one clothing to the other according to their respective role. At home, they wear ordinary sportswear, during a mission, they wear their superman's dress (**4 work clothes**), and when they wish to remain incognito, they wear a mask.[4]

---

3 Naif al-Mutawa, Official Website.

4 The wearing of masks was an experiment which was abandoned after a number of issues.

With the increasing international visibility of the "99", the internationality of its personnel and the internationalization of its protagonists, the "Islamic" character of the whole came under discussion. In a guest article which was put under the title "Why I based superheroes on Islam", al-Mutawa, somehow contradictory to this title, wrote: "Only when Jewish kids think that The 99 are Jewish, and Christian kids think they're Christian, and Muslim kids think they're Muslim, and Hindu kids think they're Hindu... I will consider my vision as having been fully executed."[5] When it comes to the market strategy, al-Mutawa is quite clear and unambiguous: "I think our market will be global, not just Muslim. There is nothing religious about these books. Just as Superman is not only for a Judeo-Christian audience, The 99 is not for only an Islamic one."[6] But his co-author Fabian Nicieza, when speaking about the global market, displays again a certain contradiction between his words and his message as al-Mutawa in the quotation above: "It's really nothing of the sort (of an Islamic comic book). It's a comic book featuring Islamic characters, but from all different parts of the world and all different walks of life, no different than the X-Men from Marvel Comics."[7] What are, then, "Islamic characters... from all different parts of the world"? Muslims from all different parts of the world? Certainly not, as neither the Portugese Catarina Barbarossa nor the American John Wheeler or the Canadian Blair Davis, all of whom are members of the "99", are ever mentioned as converts. There has to be another idea behind the notion of "Islamic characters... from all different parts of the world", a notion which internationalizes Islam on some other than the religious level.

The enigma of the "Islamic characters... from all different parts of the world" becomes clearer, when we return to the initial and still most important audience, the Arab and Muslim youths. For them, and not primarily for the Western or South- and Far Eastern teenagers, the title of the "99" was chosen. In the Quran, the Sunna and in other places, God is described by his most beautiful names (*al-asmā' al-ḥusnā*) to which is added as the highest name (*al-ism al-a'ẓam*) the supreme name of God, Allāh. The *locus classicus* for listing the divine names in the literature of Quranic exegesis is Sura 17/110: "Call upon God, or call upon the merciful; whichsoever you call upon, to him belong the most beautiful names". The names of God are traditionally enumerated as ninety-nine epithets, on which Islamic theology based its systematic expositions about the divine essence and its attributes. **(5 God's names)**

Sura 59/22, for example, includes a cluster of more than a dozen of the divine names (adjectives, word constructs, or otherwise), but in general, the divine names can be found all over the Holy Book. In line with the strictly monotheistic understanding of Allah, God is called "the one" (*al-wāḥid*). At the same time, he

---

5 Naif al-Mutawa, *Animation Xpress The Asia Pacific Edition*, Dec. 4h (2009), www.animationxpress.com/asiapacific//anxapac-kr8if01.htm.

6 Philip Schweier, *Comic Book Bin*, Aug. 14th (2008), www.comicbookbin.com/bubble096.html.

7 Ibid.

is God, the living (*al-ḥayy*), the powerful (*al-jabbār*), the glorious (*al-majīd*), the opener (*al-fattāḥ*), the exalter (*al-rāfi'*), the watchful (*al-raqīb*), the bringer of death (*al-mumīt*) and so forth. Although the exact list was never agreed upon and in fact exceeds the number of 99, over time it became custom to recite 99 names of God in their entirety. Due to popular imagination, the list then served either as a ritual like the Catholic litany of saints or as an enumeration of the attributes that the names suggest. In this last sense of a characteristic or standing out trait of a person, the most beautiful names of God were adopted for the comic strip.[8]

Each of the 99 teenagers, when he or she joins the group of the "99", changes his or her original name for one of the "beautiful names" or attributes of God. According to this, Nawaf al-Bilali becomes Jabbar, the Powerful, in the sense of a muscle-man (**6 Jabbar**), Dana Ibrahim becomes Nura, the Light, with an insight into people's inner selves (**7 Noora**), Blair Davis becomes Raqib, the Watcher, because of his abilities of perception of what is going on around him, John Wheeler becomes Darr, the Afflictor, who is able to create pain in others, and Catarina Barbarossa becomes Mumita, the Destroyer, with her incredible fighting technique (**8 Mumita**). To be sure, al-Mutawa and his team are anxious not to violate Muslim sentiments. The Arabic version of the aliases of each of the 99 is written without the definite article *al-*, because use of this precise form is exclusive to Allah. Thus, the names do not read al-Jabbar, al-Noora or al-Raqib, but just Jabbar, Noora, Raqib. This serves as a reminder to the fact that the "99" are only mortals, and defines them as human role models, with their qualities and weaknesses. al-Mutawa adds: "None of our heroes has more than a single attribute and no power can be personified to the degree that can only be possessed by Allah."[9] Nevertheless, the explanation for the notion of "Islamic characters... from all different parts of the world" lies here: We deal with God's names which are understood to be universal principles of mankind. When they are acted out for a common good, and particularly, when they are combined for a common good, the universal problems of the world can be solved. This is also true for God's "less beautiful" names, according to ordinary thinking, such as his afflicting, destroying, and annihilating abilities. The most important feature of the "99" is the teamwork of usually three or four of the characters in combining their efforts (**9 team**).

The "Islamic" character of the "99" is not restricted to the title-giving "most beautiful names of God", but extends to a counter-narrative of what, in Western thought, is usually interpreted as the Western origins of world culture, enlightenment and modernity. In the special issue no. 1 with the title "Origins", the starting point of the whole story is Baghdad in the year 1258. The background story

---

8 Gerhard Böwering, "God and his Attributes," in: Jane Dammen Mac Auliffe (ed.), *Encyclopaedia of the Qur'an* (Leiden, 2002), vol. II, p. 316; Daniel Gimaret, "Ṣifa," (2. In Theology) in *Encyclopaedia of Islam*. Vol. IX (Leiden, 1997), pp. 551b-552a; Harry A. Wolfson, *The Philosophy of the Kalam* (Cambridge, Mass. / London, 1976), pp. 112-234.

9 The 99, Origins, Editorial. For religious criticism, particularly on the side of Saudi-Arabia which is a highly interesting market for Tashkeel, see Sonja Zekri, *Menassat*, Jan. 7th (2008), www.menassat.com/?q=en/news-articles/2585-muslim-superman.

unfolds like a myth: "They were a great people in a great city that was overrun by a greater greed." The great people are the Arabs, the great city is Baghdad, and the greater greed is represented by the Mongols. We find ourselves in Baghdad **(10 Baghdad)** in the year 1258, shortly before the Mongol invasion, and the story goes on: "The forces of Hulagu Khan surrounded Baghdad. The grandson of the Conqueror, Genghis Khan, prepared to besiege the city of millions, the city of life. He planned not only to conquer the greatest Empire the world had ever known, but to eradicate its hope–its potential–thereby destroying its future... That would require destroying the Empire's true base of power. The Abbasid caliphs had constructed it to turn Baghdad into the focus of education and knowledge in the civilized world..." Then, with a cut, we find ourselves in the Dar al-hikma, the house of wisdom, a huge library which was created by the caliph al-Ma'mun at the height of the Abbasid civilization in the beginning of the ninth century **(11 Dar al-hikma)**. The librarians of the Dar al-hikma have to find a solution as to rescue their enormous treasure from the Mongol destruction, and by certain alchemistic procedures, they create 99 gemstones **(12 librarians)**. After the Mongols have destroyed the Dar al-hikma and have thrown all its books into the Tigris river, the librarians wait outside the city with their gemstones which absorb the dissolved ink from the water and transform the original books into concentrated bundles of light **(13 gemstones).** The librarians carry the gemstones with them on their flight to Granada, where they build a dome with the stones **(14 dome)** which lasts until Isabella and Ferdinand of Spain conquer the city in the final Reconquista of 1492, and any trace of the gems is lost until the beginning of the twenty-first century.

At the end of the Muslim rule in Spain, the forces of evil make their entrance for the first time. Neither Hülägü, the brutal barbarian, nor Isabella and Ferdinand, the martial rulers, are depicted as devilish in nature. Instead, the forces of evil come from amidst the Muslim camp. One of the "guardians", the secret society which looks after the dome with the gemstones, is Rughal.The character's name is based on Abu Rughal, a pre-Islamic figure who is said to have guided the Abessynian troops on their way to Mecca when, near the end of the sixth century, they were determined to conquer the city and destroy the Ka'ba.[10] The pre-Islamic Rughal is a traitor, and so is the Andalusian Rughal. Like Dr. Faustus, a scientiest far ahead of his age, he detects the means by which knowledge can be channeled through light. When the forces of Isabella and Ferdinand approach Granada, he uses a lunar eclipse to direct the light through the gemstones onto himself. The result is a huge explosion in which the dome, the gemstones and Rughal disappear **(15 Rughal)**.

But Rughal is not dead; instead, he undergoes a metamorphosis from Dr. Faustus to Mephisto. His nature is from now on pure (and destructive) energy, and he reappears whenever the world-history enters a new age. In the beginnings of the twenty-first century, he resides in the Corporate Headquarters of the world-span-

---

10 http://gulfnews.com/news/gulf/uae/media/superheroes-created-by-kuwaiti-psychologist-prepare-to-fight-evil-1.518397.

ning company "Mamluk International" in Hong Kong which invests in the sciences, finance, real estate and the media. Why Mamluk International, and why Hong Kong? Because the Mamluks stand for the distance of the ruler to his people, Hong Kong for an unrestricted capitalism and both for an uprootedness and selfishness which is the exact opposite of the *mantra* of the "99": teamwork, sympathy and compassion. It is interesting to study the development of the figure in the hands of its creators. The first sketch of Rughal showed him in the garb of the traditional villain **(16 first sketch)**, whereas the final version of the figure bears the marks of a smart businessman **(17 final version)**.

Rughal is a warrior in the international markets and the *nemesis* of Dr. Ramzi, an intellectual in international peace-making. Dr. Ramzi, an alter ego of Naif al-Mutawa in the first issues of the "99", is the head of "The 99 Steps Foundation" located in Paris. Why Paris? Because the Headquarters of the United Nations Educational, Scientific and Cultural Organization (UNESCO) are located here. Like this organization, and in cooperation with it, the ficitonal "99 Steps Foundation" is an attempt to change the world for the better, to a meaningful, responsible and sustainable use of human and non-human ressources.

Dr. Ramzi has heard from informants in his family as well from other sources that, once upon a time, there were 99 gemstones which contained the world's knowledge from medieval Baghdad. However, they are said to have vanished in a huge explosion which took place in the time of the Reconquista in Spain. Not believing this part of the old story, he sets out to find the stones. His efforts are rewarded when he hears about Nawaf al-Bilali, a Saudi-Arabian who turns out to be a gem-bearer. Other teenagers from different parts of the world follow, all of whom bear a gem which they have been given by someone else, or they have found it by chance or inherited from their parents. This personal gem endows them with a special power, but only after they have proved that they deserve it. Dr. Ramzi tries to gather these teenagers in his headquarters where he changes their names according to the respective power (the 99 names of God) and teaches them how to cope with it. Then, in groups of three or four, they set out to accomplish a mission, usually on behalf of an international organization which was founded for helping the poor, rescuing nature or removing land-mines. In short, they fight against criminal forces in general and Rughal's army in particular.

The "99", also an army of some sort, are not omnipotent. They need to work together and, moreover, they are not free from selfish attitudes, rivalry with their siblings and conflicts with their parents. Many of them have lived through traumatic experiences, for example Dana Ibrahim, later called Noora the Light, who was kidnapped by gangsters and had to free herself from prison, as her father refused to pay the ransom money for her. In the "99 Steps Foundation", the teenagers undergo an education or a training in fields like sports or fitness, social behaviour and moral conduct, before they are sent on one of the missions. Even then, their teamwork is not always perfect, or their strength turns into weakness, when it is not used properly in a given situation. They are not always on good terms with each other, and some of them are less sociable than others, like Nizar Babikr, later called Sami the Listener, who is extremely allergic to all sorts of noise. Last but not least, the "99" do not always come to terms with their threefold identity of being teenagers, supermen and helpers, or, as al-Mutawa puts it, what they can, should and want to do.[11]

"Islam is perfect, people are not." Together with his "99", Naif al-Mutawa takes side with the people against an Islamist understanding of Islam. In his words: "At the age of 32... I would go back to the very sources from which others took violent and hateful messages and offer messages of tolerance and peace in their place. I would give my heroes a Trojan horse in the form of the '99'. Islam was my Helen. I wanted her back."[12]At the same time, the "99" are designed in order to regain for Islam its proper place in world culture: "Islamic culture and Islamic heritage have a lot to be proud og and joyful about. The '99' is about bringing these positive elements into global awareness."[13]

In order to achieve this twofold aim and to show that Islam stands for peace, sympathy and justice, al-Mutawa employs rather unorthodox methods. In using the "most beautiful names of God" for his heroes, he clearly states that man, or rather mankind, is indeed created in the image of God, which is a more biblical than Quranic idea. Even more conspicuous is his use of the principle of love. Among the "99", Hope Mendoza, later called Widad the Loving because of her ability to turn bad intentions into good ones, plays a crucial role. al-Mutawa remarks: "The story of Widad parallels... the story of the conceptions of Islam outside the Islamic world. The core of Islam is the core of any religion or way of life. There are basic human values that are shared across the board... The '99''s ultimate fight is against existing misconceptions of Islam, both inside and outside the Islamic world."[14]

In introducing Widad, al-Mutawa the psychologist adapts the instrument of "paradoxical intervention" for his purpose. Paradoxical intervention is a method in psychotherapy which is counterintuitive and runs against the expectations of the client. One of God's most beautiful names is, indeed, al-Wadūd which stems from the same linguistic root as Widad. In Su. 11/90 and 85/14, God is characterized as "loving" in connection with being "merciful" (*raḥīm*) and "forgiving" (ġafūr). But in the classical Islamic–as opposed to the Christian–tradition, this "loving" aspect of God was certainly never one of his most prominent features, although it played a considerable role in the Sufi tradition.[15]

Love, the core of a humanist thinking which is grounded in medieval Baghdad, counteracts not only militant Islamism, but also its dualistic worldview. The antagonism of the forces of good and evil, or rather of Dr. Ramzi and Rughal, never becomes absolute. Both of them, even the 500-year-old Rughal, remain human and don't turn into abstract principles. Dr. Ramzi sometimes shows an impatience which endangers himself and his disciples, and Rughal seems to envy Dr. Ramzi

---

11 Issue no. 7, Naif's Notes.

12 Issue no. 20, Naif's Notes.

13 Issue no. 12, Naif's Notes.

14 Issue no. 9, Naif's Notes.

15 Cf. Annemarie Schimmel, *Mystische Dimensionen des Islam* (München, 1995), p. 252.

for his social embeddedness. Also, his powerful weapon, a reconstruction of his former Andalusian essence, ultimately turns against him and sides with the good forces.

Al-Mutawa does not propagate the classical Islamic universalism which envisaged a pacified world under the umbrella of Islam. Rather, when defining his heroes as an "amalgam of East-meets-West, an appropriate compromise given the foundation of Islam and the geography of the Middle East", he seems to be interested more in an enhancement of the role of the Arabs and Muslims than of Islam. In fact, the "99" transform the Islamic universalism into a transcultural system of values in whose midst Arabs and Muslims are going to act as an important integrative force. The reference of this transculturality is the international community of states in the form of the United Nations, its various sub-divisions and parallel institutions. When the heroes set out in order to fulfill one of their missions, it is usually on behalf of a project of the UN Food, Environment or Development Programs. It is not without reason that some critics have called the "99" a "United Nations Christmas party". This is, of course, an ironic notion, but there is some truth in it. Like Christmas, which has been adopted and adapted in many non-Christian nations all over the world, the "99" are designed to represent a world-wide ethical code which runs along the lines of the UN-Charter. In order to achieve this aim, they have recently joined their forces with the superheroes of the American "Justice League" **(19 Justice League)**.

Re-Thinking Jewish/Christian Divergence on the "Image of the Divine"

The Problem of Intra-Divine Complexity and the Origins of the Doctrine of the Trinity

Sarah Coakley

1. Introduction

The purpose of this chapter is to suggest the possibility of a new systematic model for thinking about the relations of Judaism and Christianity in connection with the Christian doctrine of the Trinity. As will become clear, this will also, and by implication, involve a certain re-thinking of Jewish/Christian relations *vis-à-vis* the more obviously problematic matter of Christology; but it will be a deliberate strategy on my part not to start here with the overt 'skandalon' for Jews of the fully divine status claimed for Jesus by Christians. The chapter has two parts. In the first–systematic–section, I briefly review some recent, and highly sophisticated, attempts at *rapprochement* between Christians and Jews on the matter of the Trinity, and conclude that the relative neglect of the doctrine of the Spirit (the 'third') in these contexts has led to an implicit retraction of the problems straight back to the christological base. The attempt by some 'post-liberal' systematicians to replace classic Christian supersessionism with talk of 'relations' in God (rather than speculative trinitarian ontology), and by narrative 'naming' of God (rather than the Christian metaphysics of *hypostasis*), still ducks the overarching question of why there should, in the first place, be three in God rather than two. Similarly, recent textual discussions of the Jewish background to the Trinity focus on various *mediator* figures in Jewish thought of the period contemporary to Jesus (especially on Torah, or *sophia*, or the Logos in Philo) and compare those with the still-subordinated divine Logos in second century Christian writers such as Justin Martyr. So once again, the emphasis is implicitly on relational twoness in God, rather than threeness. But if the Christian Trinity effectively turns out to be a binity after all, or a *residual* threeness with no very clear or distinct role given for the Spirit in contradistinction from the Son, then the central christological *skandalon* ultimately remains unmetabolized. The only possibility of alleviating it becomes either via some embarrassed liberal 'guilt' maneouvre to try and moderate the supersessionism implied altogether, or by the already-mentioned 'post-liberal' avoidance of divine metaphysics through the collapsing of *hypostatic* distinctiveness into a narrative unfolding of the implications of the divine 'name'. Neither of these alternatives seems ultimately compelling, philosophically or theologically.

In the second part of this chapter I therefore suggest an alternative approach, based on a crucial but neglected strand of Paul's thinking on prayer and divine action in Romans 8. 14-30, which might be dubbed 'proto-trinitarian' in implication. I then prospectively compare this strand in Paul's theology with certain suggestive lines of thinking about prayer, worship and representative office in biblical, Qumran and early rabbinic sources. The hypothesis that emerges, first, is that these two lines of tradition on prayer share a common, and deep, Jewish root: this is not in itself of course intrinsically surprising. The more subtle and contentious proposal is that Paul's 'proto-trinitarianism', founded in prayer, *is as profoundly Jewish as it is Christian.* To see this, however, requires a certain re-thinking of the origins and history of the doctrine of the Trinity. Rather than starting with the presumption that the Christian church first mused on the problem of Jesus's divine status and only thereafter turned to the problem of the Spirit (which is of course how matters appear according to the chronology of the Christian councils), we find in Romans 8 evidence for a different logic, founded from the start in the practices of prayer. This logic places the *Spirit* to the fore at the outset and perceives there to be a primary, and we might say 'reflexive' or 'dialectical', relation between the 'Father' and Spirit in their transforming and incorporative access to the creation which Jesus now infuses. On this vision, a *reflexive movement of divinity into a space of ecstatic human worship* keeps open a future for the elect in which Messianic 'Sonship' remains unfulfilled and uncompleted until the whole creation is included. It is not a coincidence, I shall urge (although this is rarely noted), that this set of reflections towards the end of Romans chapter 8 immediately precedes Paul's excursus on Jewish/Christian relations in Romans 9-11, and this contiguity may be significant for the topic in hand.

Finally, I shall attempt a slightly more extensive exploration of those select strands in Old Testament, Qumran, and rabbinic thought which seem to exhibit the same pattern of 'reflexive' threeness: God (1), his incorporative, 'reflexive' (or 'dialectical') presence in the world [in the form of 'glory', Spirit, or *Shekinah*] (2), and *participatory* human response to this dialectical presence in the form of prophetic prayer or Messianic election (3). In other words, something approaching the prayer-based logic of Pauline 'proto-trinitarianism' preceded it in the Jewish tradition and continued to be witnessed to sporadically thereafter. I shall close by conceding that this proposed ecumenical mode of approach to the 'Trinity' cannot, as such, soften the obvious supersessionism of classic high Christian christological claims by the time of Nicaea and the later Chalcedon; and nor can it mask, correlatively, the idolatrous offense to Jews of any claim that the human elected one *is divine* (as opposed to participatorily sharing in divinity in some way). This remaining supersessionist nettle therefore has to be grasped. What it may do, however, is open up the way that those christological claims are made in Christianity into an unfinished, and shared, future–that of the still-expected *totum Christi* that can only be effected through the unchartable power of the Spirit. Judaism and Christianity remain, according to this view, inexorably joined at the hip; the primary divine pressure of transcendent 'reflexive' presence–not here in the form of a merely under-employed 'third'–encloses Jews and Christians together even as it wrenches open a shared and mysterious eschatological future.

2. Systematic background: Recent Christian Attempts to Alleviate 'Supersessionism'

My remarks about a contemporary Christian systematic framing for this discussion of Judaism and the Trinity must necessarily remain here somewhat brief and selective. I shall concentrate on the so-called 'post-liberal' approach to the Trinity (enunciated by both Christian and Jewish scholars) that has emerged in second-generation Barthianism in America, on the one hand; and, on the other, on recent attempts in textual scholarship to re-construe the relations of Judaism and Christianity at the very point of the emergence of consciously trinitarian thinking in the second century.[1]

Let me start by noting, however, that Christian systematicians' attempts to alleviate 'supersessionism' in post-War systematic theology have been marked by a certain ambiguity about what such 'supersessionism' involves. The setting aside (in virtually all post-War Christian systematics) of the view that Christianity *rejects* the so-called 'carnal' covenant with Israel and replaces it with a new, and spiritual, covenant (what we may call 'Supersessionism 1'), does not as such alleviate the remaining problem for Judaism of christological absoluteness ('Supersessionism 2'). Barth is a supreme case in point, as has been well shown in Katherine Sonderegger's careful study of Barth's 'Doctrine of Israel'.[2] Strong strands of classic anti-Judaism ('Supersessionism 1') still lurk particularly in Barth's early work, as Sonderegger shows; but in the *Church Dogmatics* 'Israel' is precisely front and center, although in a paradoxical role: indeed, as Sonderegger puts it, Israel is 'elected–Barth does not pull back–*for rejection*'.[3] Christ becomes the rep-

---

1 In what follows I shall be looking briefly below at the work of the American theologians Robert Jenson, Kendall Soulen and Peter Ochs to illustrate the first trend. For the second trend, the recent contributions in part III of the German *Festschrift* for Jürgen Moltmann, eds. Michael Welker and Miroslav Volf, *Der lebendige Gott als Trinität* (Gütersloh, Gütersloher Verlagshuas, 2006), are especially relevant and worthwhile: Christoph Markschies, 'Jüdische Mittlergestalten und die christliche Trinitätstheologie', 199-214; Christian Link, 'Trinität im israeltheologischen Horizont,' 215-228; and Bertold Klappert, 'Geheiligt werde dein NAME!–Dein Torawille werde getan! Erwägungen zu einer gesamtbiblischen Trinitätslehre in israeltheologischer Perspektive,' 229-253.

2 Katherine Sonderegger, *That Jesus Christ was Born a Jew: Karl Barth's Doctrine of Israel* (Pennsylvania: Pennsylvania State University Press, 1992) carefully traces the varying written and biographical enunciations of Barth on Israel from the time of his *Epistle to the Romans* on. Her overall thesis is that 'Barth's position has demanded a sustained critique of Judaism; and that from his break with Liberalism to his mature period, Barth's anti-Judaism has reflected his unwavering commitment to the doctrine of justification by grace through faith alone' (ibid, 167).

3 Ibid, 173 (my emphasis).

resentative place where Israel's 'disobedience' is both punished and resolved, through cross to resurrection ('Supersessionism 2').

Our systematic interest in this contribution resides in pressing a question here which may not immediately be obvious in its implications: to what extent is the form of Barth's immensely influential version of 'Supersessionism 2' implicitly affected by his notorious lack of a strong *pneumatology*? It is somewhat ironic that Robert Jenson, who makes one of the most important 'post-liberal' attempts to reconstrue the significance of the Trinity for Jewish/Christian relations post-Barth, should at the same time be the person who has most savagely criticized Barth for holding a weak doctrine of the Spirit.[4] I say 'ironic', because I am not sure that he, or others who follow his 'post-liberal' agenda for the Trinity and Judaism, have yet shown how Barth's version of 'Supersessionism 2' can be effectively moderated or transfigured *except* by a stronger and revisionist doctrine of the Spirit.

Let me explain. What the Lutheran Robert Jenson, the Methodist Kendall Soulen, and the pragmatist Jewish theologian Peter Ochs all share, in their laudably eirenic attempts to realign Christian trinitarianism with Jewish monotheism, is a Yale-school Barthianism which represents *philosophical speculation* as the prime enemy for Jewish/Christian relations in classic Christian trinitarianism. Their proposal is to replace 'timeless being' with divine 'relationship', and 'hypostatic personhood' with 'narrative naming'. And so the remaining 'supersessionist' offense will be relieved, or so it is claimed. All take their cue from Barth's early remark, made already in *Church Dogmatics* 1/I, that the trinitarian God of Christianity is 'nothing other than an explanatory confirmation of the *name*, Yahweh/Kyrios'.[5] In Jenson's case, this project takes the form of a radically historicized Godhead, a God whose own trinitarian 'identity' actually unfolds through the narrative histories of the Old and New Testaments, and will be ratified only eschatologically.[6] It is the 'timeless substance' talk of classic Christianity that constitutes the offense of 'supersessionism', on this view, not the Trinity as such.[7]

In Kendall Soulen's work, in some contrast, a more embarrassed remnant of 'liberalism' makes its appearance amidst ploys that in other respect echo Jenson's. Soulen concludes somewhat evasively in his *The God of Israel and Christian Theology* that the 'Lord's history with Israel ... does not prepare for the gospel but surrounds the gospel as its constant horizon',[8] a concession that seemingly acknowledges more than Jenson does the remaining offense of (what I have called)

---

[4] R. W. Jenson, 'You Wonder Where the Spirit Went', *Pro Ecclesia* 2 (1993), 296-304. For a rather more nuanced account of Barth's pneumatology, see Eugene F. Rogers, *After the Spirit: A Constructive Pneumatology from Resources outside the Modern West* (Grand Rapids: Eerdmans, 2005).

[5] Karl Barth, *Church Dogmatic* 1/I, ET 400.

[6] Robert W. Jenson, *Systematic Theology* vol 1: *The Triune God* (New York: OUP, 1997).

[7] See ibid, 90-114.

[8] R. Kendall Soulen, *The God of Israel and Christian Theology* (Minneapolis: Fortress Press, 1996), 176.

'Supersessionism 2'. Yet Soulen finally appears elusive about how that position might align with his claims elsewhere that 'YHWH's eternal life happens as a communion of 'persons' *reliably identified* as Father, Son, and Holy Spirit'.[9] For if there *is* such a communion of equal 'persons', how can 'Supersessionism 2' not remain a problem? Peter Ochs, the most prominent Jewish collaborator in this line of thinking, attempts a clearer answer of his own. He contributes an enthusiastic endorsement of the 'post-liberal' trinitarian project to repel all borders against 'philosophic intrusions': 'the creeds are misinterpreted' altogether, he announces confidently, 'if they are taken to imply supersessionism'.[10] Once we substitute 'a logic of relations' for Greek philosophical speculation, he claims, we can find a way between and beyond the false 'exclusivist' and 'assimilationist' options, and even read Nicaea in a mode friendly to rabbinic Judaism.[11] The trick is to see that both Jews and Christians first need to understand something akin to the full implications of Charles Peirce's theory of 'sign relations':[12] it is modern American pragmatism, then, not classic pagan metaphysics, that should accompany a proper ecumenical understanding of trinitarian 'naming'. With appeal to Peirce's version of 'relational' pragmatism we can re-construe 'God creating us, redeeming us from suffering, and delivering us to community with one another and in the divine life' as a flow of signification shared with equal conviction by both Jews and Christians.[13]

How are we to assess these various creative attempts to moderate the divisive effect for Jewish/Christian relations of the classic Christian doctrine of the Trinity? The main trouble with this 'post-liberal' option, in its various forms—or so I see it—is that its anti-metaphysical rhetoric diverts us from two remaining systematic problems that will not go away completely: one is the problem of how 'Supersessionism 2' (the claimed absolute Messianic status of Jesus) can be magick-ed away at the same time as 'Supersessionism 1', simply by resisting Greek metaphysical 'intrusions'; the other is the evasion of the systematic significance of the status of the 'third' in the Christian trinitarian vision of divine 'relationality'. To be sure, Peter Ochs is the one member of this 'post-liberal' group who attempts to account for the necessity of relational *threeness* by appealing to the notoriously elusive notion of the 'third' in Peirceian 'semeiotics'. But suffice it to say that, even if the full Peirceian vision can be embraced in all its subtlety and richness, it remains unclear to me that Ochs himself provides a convincing *logical* or *textual* argument against twoness being sufficient for the 'relationality' he claims to be

---

9 Idem, 'YHWH the Triune God,' *Modern Theology* 15 (1999), 25-54, at 50 (my emphasis).

10 Peter Ochs, 'Trinity and Judaism,' in eds. Hermann Häring Janet Martin Soskice and Felix Wilfred, *Learning from Other Faiths, Concilium* 2003/4 (London: SCM Press), 51-59, at 54, 55.

11 Ibid, 56.

12 Ibid, 57. Ochs's extended philosophical treatment of Peirce is to be found in his *Peirce, Pragmatism and the Logic of Scripture* (Cambridge: CUP, 1998).

13 Ochs, 'Trinity and Judaism,' 57.

fundamental in God. It is once more as if threeness-in-God is presumed, and then Peirce brought in, *ex post facto*, to explicate it philosophically.[14]

It is interesting, moreover, that this same systematic problem attends some fascinating recent attempts by textual scholars to cast the original separation of 'Judaism' and 'Christianity' in a new light by reference to the early rabbinic attack on the idea of 'two powers in heaven'. Whereas Alan Segal famously read the eruption of this rhetoric as precisely a riposte to the emergence of Christian bintiarianism/trinitarianism,[15] Daniel Boyarin now claims that this approach gets the chronology wrong, and that even in the second century the lines between 'Judaism' and 'Christianity' still remained blurred. Thus the causal impetus worked if anything the other way, according to Boyarin, Judaism 'creating Christianity' and only then the opposite occurring in dialectical return: 'The Rabbis', he writes, 'by defining elements within their own religious heritage as not Jewish, were, in effect, *producing* Christianity, just as Christian heresiologists were, by defining traditional elements of their own tradition as being not Christian, thereby *producing* Judaism'.[16] However we decide on the issue of the chronological separation of conscious 'Jewish' and 'Christian' identities (and this of course remains contentious), my point is that the systematic problem of 'threeness' cannot be settled by the '*two* powers in heaven' controversy. And Boyarin's concentration on Justin Martyr as his prototype of a Christian identity only scarcely emerging as such at this time, is also revealing: for it is precisely Justin's interest in the Logos as a subordinated, mediatorial 'second God', and his notorious neglect of the Spirit, that makes his thinking unable to help us with this question either.[17] Is there, then, anywhere else in earliest (Jewish) Christianity that the problem of threeness finds its solution? I think so, but it is easy to overlook. To provide an answer, we now move to our second section, and back to Paul.

3. Why Three? The Phenomenon of Deep Prayer and Its Implications for Election

At the climax of his long argument about sin, justification, law, and baptism in Romans, chapters 1-8, Paul suddenly introduces one of the most profound discussions of prayer in the Bible, indeed arguably in the whole classic Christian

---

14 Ochs does mention Kabbalist 'accounts of the various identities of God' alongside strands in both Rosenzweig's and Levinas's thought which appear 'triadic' (Ochs, 'Trinity and Judaism', 57); but these examples appear so briefly that it is difficult to adjudicate whether their apparently triadic structure is three-fold.

15 See Alan Segal, *Two Powers in Heaven: Early Rabbinic Reports About Christianity and Gnosticism* (Leiden: E. J. Brill, 1977).

16 Daniel Boyarin, *Border Lines*: *The Partition of Judaeo-Christianity* (Philadelphia: University of Pennsylvania Press. 2004), 130 (my emphasis).

17 See Boyarin, *Boder-Lines*, 128-147. Justin Martyr refers to the Spirit at one point in his *First Apology* (6. 1-2) as subordinate to the angels.

corpus. The point is that prayer, strictly speaking, is not done by us at all; for when pushed to the edge we realize that we are so weak, desperate, or sin-bound that we do not even know how to begin, or what to ask for. The crucial passage, Ro 8. 26-7, is freshly translated by Joseph Fitzmyer thus: 'Similarly, the Spirit too comes to the aid of our weakness, for we do not know for what we should pray. But the Spirit itself intercedes for us with ineffable sighs (*stenagmois alalētois)*. Yet he who searches our hearts knows what the mind of the Spirit is, because it intercedes for God's dedicated people (*huper hagiōn*) in accordance with his will'.[18] This description of prayer as ecstatic–as beyond human words or comprehension–is important for our systematic purposes in this context because, as James Dunn has well put it, 'God is at both ends of the process'.[19] The Spirit, far from being 'third' in this understanding of divine relations, or a mere continuer of, or testifier to, the revelation of Son (as is the model in John's gospel: Jn 15. 26), is the very means of God 'reflexively' talking to God *in and through the pray-er*. Moreover, it is clear from the surrounding context of this chapter's argument (Ro 8. 12-39) that the effect of such reflexivity-in-God is that of binding the elect ever more deeply into the Messianic event, and opening that event to an eschatological future. The Christian pray-er is destined thus to become a true 'adopted' offspring of God, incorporated into the life of redeemed 'Sonship' (vss. 15-17), and incorporated too into the suffering implications of the Messiah for the whole physical creation, as it 'groans' towards its eschatological end (vss. 18-23). The Christ event remains uncompleted until that participation is assured (vss. 28-30). Not for nothing, then, I now suggest again, does this eschatological vision exactly precede Paul's equally eschatological excursus on the ultimate relation of Judaism and Christianity (Ro chs. 9-11): the inexorable and inextricable connectedness of the two traditions, in ecstatic Messianic prayer as well as in final destiny, links these two visionary discussions back-to-back.

It would be deeply misleading, however, to pretend that Paul enunciates in Romans 8 a developed trinitarianism: such a claim would be obviously anachronistic.[20] But it would be fair, I think, to dub this a Spirit-led, incorporative, '*proto*-trinitarianism', in which the Spirit is by no means a redundant 'third', but a name for one pole in that dialectical reflexivity-in-God which precisely enables the ecstatic participation in God of the elect, and their opening up to an unknown and 'ineffable' Messianic future which includes, and indeed re-binds together, both Jewish and Christian traditions. In short, the Spirit is the wedge, the guarantor, of the apophatic openness of the Christ event to a yet-unknown fulfillment.

---

18 J. A. Fitzmyer, S.J., *Romans: A New Translation with Introduction and Commentary* (New York: Doubleday, 1993), 516.

19 James D. G. Dunn, 'Spirit Speech: Reflections on Romans 8: 12-27', in eds. Sven K. Soderlund and N, T. Wright, *Romans and the People of God: Essays in Honor of Gordon D. Fee on the Occasion of His 65th Birthday* (Grand Rapids, MI: Eerdmans, 1999), 89.

20 Elements of christological subordinationism are clearly still present in Paul (e.g., 1 Cor 15. 28), as well as a confusing shift between the roles of 'Spirit' and 'Christ' in the relevant passage, Ro 8. 9-17, indicating a less-than-clear sense of the Spirit's personal identity.

What happened to this way of thinking about the Trinity *within* Christianity is a story that I have told elsewhere,[21] and which, perhaps not surprisingly, was to became entangled with mystical or sectarian traditions pushed largely to the edges of conciliar Christian 'orthodoxy', with its *penchant* for a more linear, even covertly-hierarchical, account of the relations of 'Father', 'Son' and 'Spirit' with the church and the world.[22] But that intra-Christian story is not the narrative we are concerned with here. Rather, in this context we want to press the particular question that I have now opened up about the origins of the doctrine of the Trinity and its Jewish backcloth in relation to the activity of prayer: did this 'proto-trinitarian' vision of prayer in Paul owe anything to his own Pharisaic training? And indeed, are parallel traces of it to be found anywhere either before or after Paul in the Jewish tradition?

4. Are There Intimations of 'Proto-trinitarianism' in Jewish Understandings of Prayer and Election?

This is a complicated question, and any answer to it will necessarily involve some subtlety of exegesis. Many years ago now Christopher Stead wrote a two-part paper entitled 'The Origins of the Doctrine of the Trinity'[23] which has stood the test of time;[24] it provided a remarkably succinct and clear account of the exegetical problems that have to be faced in any attempt to locate emergent Christian trinitarianism in its original religio-philosophical context, whether Jewish or pagan. In regard to the Jewish backcloth Stead's view was that there was 'only one likely candidate' known to him that represented 'an actual Trinitarian pattern' (i.e., a *clear* enunciation of 'threeness' in relation to God). This was 'the image in which

---

[21] Originally in Sarah Coakley, 'Why Three? Some Further Reflections on the Doctrine of the Trinity', in eds. Sarah Coakley and David A. Pailin, *The Making and Remaking of Christian Doctrine: Essays in Honour of Maurice Wiles* (Oxford: OUP, 1993), 29-56; now more fully in eadem, *God, Sexuality and the Self: An Essay 'On the Trinity'* (Cambridge: CUP, 2013), 100-151.

[22] See again Coakley, *God, Sexuality and the Self*, esp. chs. 3, 6 and 7.

[23] Christopher Stead, 'The Origins of the Doctrine of the Trinity', *Theology* 77 (1974), 508-517; 582-588.

[24] Only consider the outpouring of scholarly writing since then on Jewish 'hypostasizations' within the Godhead: especially interesting are Peter Schäfer, *Mirror of His Beauty: Feminine Images of God from the Bible to the Early Kabbalah* (Princeton: Princeton University Press, 2002); Gedaliahu Guy Stroumsa, 'Le Couple de L'Ange et de l'Esprit: Traditions Juives et Chrétiennes', in his *Savoir et Salut* (Paris: Les Éditions du Cerf, 1992), 23-41; and–more controversially, for its theory about the very late separation of Judaism and Christianity–Daniel Boyarin, *Border Lines* (see supra, nn. 16, 17), and ibid, *The Jewish Gospels: The Story of the Jewish Christ* (New York: The New Press, 2012). It should be added that whereas discussions of incarnational/Logos/Sophia/angelic parallels are legion in this scholarly literature, few probe the more complex question of 'threeness' which is our explicit focus here.

the Lord God sits enthroned, attended by two angels, one on the right hand and the other on the left', whether the 'two Seraphaim of Isaiah's vision' or the two Cherubim 'who mount guard over the Ark'.[25] Stead went on to underscore, however, that in the first century CE, in particular, angel-imagery of this sort remained extraordinarily 'fluid', both in the Jewish and New Testament materials. There is, for instance, no consistent lining-up of the two-angel-idea (usually Michael and Gabriel) with other quasi-hypostatized notions of divine 'Logos' or 'Spirit', whether in Philo or other relevant texts such as *The Ascension of Isaiah*; and no 'firm distinction of roles' for Spirit, Logos, or angelic visitants in the New Testament either.[26] In fact, Stead concludes that at least *six* potentially-hypostasized entities present themselves in the relevant Jewish literature of the period, in confusing interaction with one another and sometimes melding with the parallel angelic tradition: 'the list would include', he says, 'the Son of God, the Spirit of God, his Anointed, his Word, his Wisdom and his Law'.[27] It is in the nature of the discourses that contain these ideas, however, that conflations and swappings of role are endemic to the *genre*; and whilst Stead suggests a gradual 'concentration' of the six ideas into two (Messiah/Spirit and Wisdom/Torah), even this set of couplings still does not line up consistently, of course, with what was later to become normative Christian trinitarian reflection.

The image of God enthroned between the seraphim/cherubim, however, undeniably held a fundamental position in second-Temple reflection on temple worship; so the intriguing question that confronts us (and which Stead himself does not consider) is whether this model related in some way–itself perhaps also pliable in expression and thought-forms–to a triadic perception of the very nature of personal prayer or temple-worship: as animated from within by God, and as simultaneously constituting a special form of human election. Two *caveats* must however immediately be sounded, lest an overconfident quest for Christian parallels to Paul's 'proto-trinitarianism' mislead us. First, any notion of ongoing 'reflexivity-of-God' in prayer is unlikely to be identified straightforwardly as *Spirit* in this Jewish context (since, as Peter Schäfer amongst others has shown, 'Spirit' language in the Old Testament and the early rabbis is most commonly associated with being chosen for a *particular* task or office, sometimes short-term[28]). And secondly, the obvious–and unassailable–point of differentiation from the Pauline model in Jewish writings will be a resistance to the idea of an already-inaugurated Messianism, or the notion of a *fully divinized*, as opposed to an elected and participatory, human agent. Nonetheless, given the very 'fluidity' of thinking that Stead

---

25 Stead, 'The Origins', 514, referring to Is 6. 2-3 and Ex 25. 18-20. Stead refers the reader here to Jean Daniélou, *The Theology of Jewish Christianity* (London: Darton, Longman and Todd, 1964),117-40 for relevant exegetical examples.

26 Stead, 'The Origins', 514-5. Note that Romans 8. 26 is briefly mentioned in this regard.

27 Ibid, 515.

28 See Schäfer, *Mirror of His Beauty*, 92-3, on the special gifts of the Holy Spirit for prophetic purposes; and for more detail on this theme: idem, *Die Vorstellung vom Heiligen Geist in der Rabbinischen Literatur* (München: Kösel-Verlag, 1972).

so insistently highlights, there is still room for a quest for suggestive parallels to Paul's teaching on prayer-as-triadic. Thus, in what follows I want to highlight three rather different such cases, and at the same time to draw attention to accompanying material from rabbinic teaching which further instantiates the crucial sustaining notion of prayer as essentially God-given, 'ecstatic' or 'vatic'.[29]

It may indeed be revealing to frame and sharpen this quest for Pauline parallels, albeit from a later perspective, with a famous question about prayer that is recorded in the Babylonian Talmud (B. Berakhot 7a). Since the rabbinic sayings cited in this passage go back at least to the third century CE, and probably earlier, it might be argued that there is encoded here a key rabbinic insight about the very nature of prayer to God. At stake is the (ostensibly odd) question of whether God prays to Himself:

> R. Johanan says in the name of R. Jose: How do we know that the Holy One, blessed be He, says prayers [sc. prays]? Because it says [in Isa 56. 7]: Even them will I bring to My holy mountain and make them joyful in My house of prayer [*beit tefillati*]. It is not said "their prayer" [*tefillatam*], but "My prayer" [*tefillati*]; hence [you learn] that the Holy One, blessed be He, says prayers. What does He pray?—R. Zutra b. Tobi said in the name of Rab: "May it be My will that My mercy [*rachamay*] may suppress My anger [*ka'asi*], and that My mercy may prevail over my [other] attributes [*middotay*], so that I may deal with My children in the attribute of mercy [*middat rachamim*] and, on their behalf, stop short of the limit of strict justice [*shurat had-din*]."

The suggestion of an intra-divine prayer, here so strongly supported, might seem to be a serendipitous exegetical aside occasioned merely by an oddity in the text of Isaiah; but this interpretation should be doubted. Something deeper is at stake. The concern with the balance of 'mercy' and 'justice' in the divine attributes is of course a particular interest of the earlier tannaitic tradition;[30] and it is not hard to see how it might have been grounded in a spiritual sensibility about the very workings of prayer at its deepest: the balance of God's attributes *must* favour mercy if the creation is to be sustained in being, and this it is solely His to dispose. Thus, if prayer in 'my house (or temple)' is to be the sustaining prayer of life, it must by definition be guaranteed in some way as grounded inwardly by a prior divine propulsion ('my prayer'). The same fundamental insight, we might add, is already suggested by a discussion in the Mishnah (M. Berakhot 5.5) about the special 'fluency' of the prayer of the mystic R. Haninah ben Dosa;[31] and a similar issue is taken up in a discussion in the Babylonian Talmud of Ps 51. 15 ('O Lord, open my lips, and my mouth shall declare your praise'), a verse on which the rab-

---

[29] I owe the suggestive term 'vatic' to Michael Fishbane.

[30] On this theme see the now-classic treatment in Ephraim E. Urbach, *The Sages: Their Concepts and Beliefs* (Cambridge, MA: Harvard University Press, 1979), esp. 452-9.

[31] This is especially the case if the textual reading is preferred (*shagrah* rather than *shegurah*) which suggests an ecstatic form of prayer: on this point see Schlomo Naeh (in Hebrew), 'Creates the Fruit of Lips: A Phenomenological Study of Prayer According to Mishnah *Berakhot* 4.3. 5.5', *Tarbiz* 63 (1994), 185-218.

bis also had reason to comment, in connection with the daily recitation of the *Amidah*, and the implied request to God to inspirit the Prayer throughout.[32] Here too, *in nuce*, is the very insight basic to Paul's more floridly pneumatological rendition: human prayer and praise are always already animated by divine propulsion.

5. Three Jewish Loci of 'Triadic' Prayer: God Praying to God in the Elect

It is in this broader context, then, that I draw attention to three other deeply suggestive *loci* in Jewish tradition for comparison with Ro 8. 26-7. They are all somewhat different in context, but a little probing of their background hermeneutics suggests confirmation of the model we seek. Recall again that the pattern we are looking for, in whatever figurative or narrative way it may be expressed, is one of divine *reflexivity* in prayer or worship, and participatory *election* (Messianic or an equivalent) in and through such prayer.

1. *Exodus 32. 7-14 in Rabbinic Interpretation*: The first example is already to be found in Torah, in the book of Exodus; but read backwards through the Talmudic passages I have just quoted, it may perhaps strike us also as a remarkably daring instantiation of the logic sketched by Paul in Romans 8. The context here is the idolatrous disobedience of Israel in the making of the golden calf. Still on the mountain-top, where he has been communing with the Lord and receiving the tablets of stone, Moses as prophetic representative of his people has to confront the divine wrath:

> The Lord said to Moses, 'I have seen this people, how stiff-necked they are. Now let me alone, so that my wrath may burn hot against them and I may consume them; and of you I will make a great nation'. But Moses implored the Lord his God, and said, 'O Lord, why does your wrath burn hot against your people, whom you brought out of the land of Egypt with great power and with a mighty hand? Why should the Egyptians say, "It was with evil intent that he brought them out to kill them in the mountain, and to consume them from the face of the earth"? Turn from your fierce wrath; change your mind and do not bring disaster on your people. Remember Abraham, Isaac, and Israel, your servants, how you swore to them by your own self, saying to them: "I will multiply your descendents like the stars of heaven, and all this land that I have promised I will give to your descendents, and they shall inherit it for ever"'. And the Lord changed his mind about the disaster that he planned to bring on his people.[33]

---

32 See B. Berakhot 4b, citing R. Yohanan: 'At the beginning of the Prayer, one says "O Lord, open my lips ..."'. For a more extended treatment of the proper mental preparation for prayer in the rabbinic tradition, see Elliot R. Wolfson, 'Iconic Visualization and the Imaginal Body of God: The Role of Intention in the Rabbinic Conception of Prayer', *Modern Theology* 12 (1996), 137-62, esp. 139-142.

33 Exodus 32. 9-14.

Now there is, of course, an entirely straightforward and literalistic reading of this passage that takes it simply at face value: Moses confronts an anthropomorphic and angry God, and pleads with Him until he changes His mind. But even by the period of the early rabbis, it seems, that rendition was becoming less acceptable, precisely because of the more complex and emerging reflection on the tight dialectical relationship of God's mercy and His justice: by appeal to such, the suggestion of a vacillating or inconsistent divinity–famously pilloried by anti-Jewish critics of the early CE such as Marcion–could be averted. As a rich and revealing discussion by Yochanan Muffs has demonstrated,[34] a rendition of Exodus 32 arose in which Moses acted precisely as the human conduit at the base of the 'parabola' of this intra-divine negotiation. In the context of a desperate intercessory prayer, Moses, *qua* prophet, here stands in for the reflexive divine voice of God as the one who *pleads* His 'mercy'; he operates precisely at the painful axis of this intra-divine dialectic, and negotiates it perilously as the elected representative of Israel: 'Turn from your fierce wrath; change your mind and do not bring disaster on your people', Moses says (vs. 12)–thereby becoming the personal locus of the deflection of divine wrath into divine mercy. This interpretation, of course, is already one laden with theological meaning: that God's own *consistency* finally resides in the supervenience of His mercy over His judgement. But in this shift Moses plays a crucial, even quasi-'incarnational',[35] role; as Muffs puts it, 'God allows the prophet to represent in his prayer His own attribute of mercy';[36] thus Moses 'stands in the breach' on behalf of his people. Muffs is able to illustrate this hermeneutic move pointedly from a medieval rabbinic midrash, although the ideas may be much older:

> God said to Moses after the incident of the Golden Calf, 'Let me at them, and my anger will rest on them and I will get rid of them'. Is Moses holding back God's hand, so that God must say, 'Let go of me'? What is this like? A king became angry at his son, placed him in a small room, and was about to hit him. At the same time the king cried out from the room for someone to stop him. The prince's teacher was standing outside, and said to himself, 'The king and his son are in the room. Why does the king say "stop me"? It must be that the king wants me to go into the room and effect a reconciliation between him and his son. That's why the king is crying, "Stop me"'. In a similar way, God said to Moses, 'Let Me at them'. Moses said, 'Because God wants me to defend Israel, He says, 'Let Me at them'. And Moses immediately interceded for them.[37]

---

34 Yochanan Muffs, 'Who Will Stand in the Breach? A Study of Prophetic Intercession', in *Love and Joy: Law, Language, and Religion in Ancient Israel* (New York: Jewish Theological Seminary, 1992), 9-48; Gary A. Anderson takes up Muffs's analysis from a Christian perspective in his remarkable essay, 'Moses and Jonah in Gethsemane: Representation and Impassibility in Their Old Testament Inflections', in eds. Beverly Roberts Gaventa and Richard B. Hays, *Seeking the Identity of Jesus: A Pilgrimage* (Grand Rapids, MI: Eerdmans, 2008), 215-31.

35 This is Anderson's further gloss: 'Moses and Jonah', 231.

36 Muffs, 'Who Will Stand in the Breach?', 33.

37 *Exodus Rabbah* 42.9, as cited in Muffs, 'Who Will Stand in the Breach?', 34, and discussed by Anderson, 'Moses and Jonah', 218.

In this example, then, we see the elusive 'triadology' of prayer worked out in a dramatic form as the elected prophet bears and transforms the dialectic of divine action: at the base of the divine 'parabola' he receives and re-instantiates his election on behalf of Israel, to open its future even beyond apostasy and idolatry. It is in and through Moses that that future is even assured, and the shift from divine judgment to divine mercy is effected: 'And the Lord changed his mind about the disaster that he planned to bring on his people' (Exodus 32. 14).

2. *The Song of the Sabbath Sacrifice* (*Qumran*): The second and third instances of a logic equivalent to the Romans 8 analysis of prayer are to be found not in reflections on the transformative role of a prophet, but in the rather different–and perhaps more expected–context of liturgical prayer. The first of these comes from an earlier period: in the admittedly heterodox world of the Qumran community, as evidenced in the Dead Sea Scrolls. Here, in the remarkable *Songs of the Sabbath Sacrifice,*[38] we read of a perception of Sabbath liturgy as participatory and transformative in a sense that, although ostensibly very different from that of the role of Moses in Exodus, is evocative of the same divine dialectical engagement in prayer we have noted, this time applied initially to the priestly ministers. The seventh Sabbath song enjoins on the 'priestly angels' the task of reflexively 'lift[ing] the divine exaltation on high';[39] and these exaltations are even echoed by the 'animate temple' of the community itself ('all the corners of the temple's structure'), perhaps striking a chord of recognition in Christians who are reminded of Paul's insistence that they should think of themselves as 'temples of the Holy Spirit' (1 Cor 3. 16-17). Implicitly, then, a divine reflexivity occurs here within, and participatorily transforms, the whole worshipping community, catching them up into the angelic realm and rendering them temple-like, as 'wise spirits of light', even in their constitution in the desert. Away from Jerusalem itself, and substituting a putatively corrupt earthly temple with a vision of the heavenly temple, the Sabbath community at Qumran becomes the corporate elect shot through with ecstatic divine prayer.

Thus, not only is worship itself here in the *Sabbath Songs* a participation of the *community* in divinity-answering-to-divinity, in the form of quasi-angelic worship; but–as John Collins has hinted in a fine article on this topic[40]–the

---

[38] See Michael Wise, Martin Abegg, Jr., and Edward Cook, *The Dead Sea Scrolls: A New Translation* (San Francisco: Harper, 1996), 365-377.

[39] Ibid, 371: 'Lift His exaltation on high, you godlike among the exalted divine beings– His glorious divinity above all the highest heavens. Surely He [is the utterly divine] over all the exalted princes, King of king[s] over all the eternal councils. By the wise will–through the words of his mouth–shall come into being all [the exalted godlike]; at the utterance of His lips all the eternal spirits shall exist. All the actions of His creatures are by what His wise will allows' ... 'With such songs shall all the [foundations of the hol]y of holies offer praise, and the pillars bearing the most exalted abode, even all the corners of the temple's structure. Hy[mn] the G[od a]wesome in power, [all you] wise [spirits] of light; together laud the utterly brilliant firmament that girds [His] holy temple. [Praise] Him, godli[ke] spirits ...'

[40] John J. Collins, 'Powers in Heaven: God, Gods, and Angels in the Dead Sea Scrolls,' in

Melchizedek Scroll from Qumran may also provide a particular, individualized, instantiation of the same logic. Equivalent to one of the principal angels in this scroll is the mysterious priest/king Melchizedek of Gen 14. 18 and Ps 110. 4, who has the elected status of *elohim*, a god or divine being: it is not clear that he was ever a mortal being according to the interpretation of the *Scroll*. But what he does stand for is an exalted priestly entity transported by his anointing into the closest proximity with God Himself.[41] 'We are reminded', as Collins concludes this article, 'that both Jewish and Christian traditions had common roots in the rich and varied world of Second Temple Judaism'. Thus, although 'For most Jews, the scandal of Christianity was the worship of the man Jesus', ... yet 'Christianity began as a Jewish sect ... and was in some way continuous with its Jewish matrix'.[42] Secondary divine beings, elected manifestations of particular divine incorporation, are in this particular world of Jewish ideas not idolatrous exceptions to the rule, but seemingly almost everyday occurrences. We are clearly here in the realm of hypostatic 'fluidity' presciently spelled out in Stead's earlier investigation of the Jewish roots of the Christian doctrine of the Trinity. If to worship truly is to be raised to angelic status in answering God to God, then the ecstatic union of such priests and worshippers implies some sort of divine participation closely akin to the 'dialectical' model also present in Rom 8.[43]

3. *The Shekinah and the Cherubim in Rabbinic Commentary on the Song of Songs*: Our third and last example of this intra-divine logic of prayer and election returns to Stead's key proposal about an explicit Jewish vision of liturgical 'threeness-in-God' in even more explicit mode. But in the light of the foregoing analysis we may perhaps give it a new and clarifying gloss. We recall that Stead highlighted the importance of the biblical image of the Lord God enthroned, attended by two angels. The systematic question that remained there, however, was whether this visual 'threeness' was somehow arbitrary, rather than intrinsic to some specific divine logic of operation. In the world of rabbinic commentary on the Song of Songs this exegetical question arguably reaches some sort of resolution.[44] What interests me especially here is that, in the comparative Christian

---

eds. John J. Collins and Robert A. Kugler, *Religion in the Dead Sea Scrolls* (Grand Rapids, MI, Eerdmans, 2000), 9-28.

41 William Horbury reminds me that it is here that there is a blending with certain heavenly perceptions of Moses in the Jewish literature of the period, thus making a further link between the different strands of tradition I am tracing here: see e.g., Ecclesiasticus 45.2 (partially preserved Hebrew restored in light of Greek,) God 'honoured him as *elohim*, and made him strong among the high ones (angels)'; or *Assumption of Moses* 11. 17 (*spiritus*).

42 Collins, 'Powers in Heaven,' 28, 9.

43 Philip Alexander also comments illuminatingly on this ecstatic dimension of the Qumranic practice of the *Songs of the Sabbath Sacrifice* in his *The Mystical Texts: Songs of the Sabbath Sacrifice and Related Manuscripts* (London & New York: Companion to the Qumran Scrolls: Library of Second Temple Studies 61, 2006), esp. 116-117.

44 Two texts by Michael Fishbane have especially inspired these reflections: *Biblical Myth and Rabbinic Mythmaking* (Oxford, OUP, 2003), 173-177; and 'Anthological midrash and cultural paideia: The case of *Songs Rabba* 1.2,' in eds. Peter Ochs and Nancy Levene,

context, it is the mystical tradition (represented originally and notably by Origen, in his *Commentary on the Song* and in his text on prayer, *De oratione*) that takes up the implications of Ro 8 most vibrantly, and realizes that prayer at its deepest demands a transformative and incorporative 'trinitarian' logic that the spiritually immature are unlikely to comprehend.[45] Nor is it safe for the immature to *try* and comprehend it, according to Origen, because the erotic metaphors in which such intimacy is necessarily couched could lead to sexual aberration on the part of those who are spiritually immature.[46] Michael Fishbane shows us that, in fascinatingly similar guise–and not coincidentally, since Origen himself was the recipient of such Jewish teaching about the Song[47]–the rabbis will speculate about what we might call a triadic 'divine ontology' above the ark in the Temple, and one with profound 'erotic' overtones of unity and ecstasy.[48] God, according to Rabbi Nathan, is as it were self-contracted as *Shekinah* between the two encircling cherabim (see again Exod 25. 19-20): as Fishbane paraphrases him, "the special nature of the ark was that the *Shekinah* spoke from above it, between the cherubim, and 'there they empower Israel'".[49] The 'dialectical' notion is again in play. Moreover, in a tradition handed down by Rab Qattina, the cherubim are there said to be *erotically* entwined, but only on the presumption and demand that the worshippers at the Temple are themselves suitably prepared by participatory obedience to the Law, and so enabling of this divine erotic fulfillment. In other words, as R. Yohanan may even perhaps have instructed Origen himself, the saying 'Yes' to the Law-in-oneself was not only marked by an incorporative triadic logic, but sealed by a 'kiss ... with the kisses of the mouth' of the Song 1.2 in a way that (one might say) gave back God to God.[50] *Without* suitably obedient preparation in thus

---

Textual Reasonings: Jewish Philosophy and Text Study at the End of the Twentieth Century (Grand Rapids, MI: Eerdmans, 2003), 32-51. Also see the important contextualizing article by Raphael Loewe, 'Apologetic Motifs in the Targum to the Song of Songs,' in ed. Alexander Altmann, *Biblical Motifs: Origins and Transformations* (Cambridge, MA: Harvard UP, 1966), 159-196.

45 I discuss this theme in Origen in some detail in my *God, Sexuality and the Self*, 126-132.

46 See ibid, 129, n. 31, and Origen, *Commentarium in Canticum Canticorum*, Prologue, 2.39-40.

47 On this interaction see the fine article, Reuven Kimelman, 'Rabbi Yochanan and Origen on the Song of Songs: A Third-Century Jewish-Christian Disputation,' Harvard Theological Review 73 (1980), 567-95.

48 See Fishbane, *Biblical Myth*, 174-5.

49 Ibid, 174.

50 See *Song of Songs Rabba* to Song 1.2, II, in eds. Ochs and Levene, *Textual Reasonings*, 45.: 'Another interpretation of the verse, *O let him kiss me with the kisses of the mouth*. Said R. Yohanan, "An angel would carry forth each Word [viz., Commandment of the Ten Commandments] from before the Holy One, blessed be he, and bring it about to every Israelite and say to him, 'Do you accept upon yourself this Word?' ... And the Israelite would say, 'Yes'. ... Immediately, [the angel] would kiss him on his mouth, as it says: *You have been shown, that you might know* (Deut. 4.25)–that is, by means of [an angelic] messenger".'

approaching God, however, the effects on the worshipper could be damaging and dangerous. In short, this rich mythological reflection on the intra-divine complexity of the presence over the ark again had its incorporative logic and flow. To be drawn into this triadic flow was to manifest true, 'erotic' obedience to a complex, erotically-entwined God; to offend against it was to driven out the by angels facing out the other way.[51]

6. Conclusions

What are we to conclude from this brief survey of relevant Jewish texts? The preliminary analysis I have attempted in this text of the possible 'triadic' prayer-based Jewish background to Christian trinitarianism has speculatively covered a considerable amount of territory; but its aim has been to open up a fresh investigation into the indissoluble relatedness of Judaism and Christianity in this fundamental arena of worship, and specifically in connection with those problematic realms of Christian doctrine (Trinity, Christology) which seem most to divide the two traditions. If I am now to attempt a succinct account of the systematic implications of this investigation in closing, I think they must be these:

1. What I earlier called 'Supersessionism 1' (the idea of an actual exclusion of the Jews from the Christian covenant with God) has been, I have noted, largely expunged in the post-Holocaust period from contemporary Christian systematic theology. But this still leaves a remaining problem with the Christian claim for a *divine* Jesus who has purportedly completed all the promises of Israel ('Supersessionism 2').

2. Christian theology cannot effectively deal with the difficulties of this 'Supersessionism 2' by evasive talk of a trinitarian 'relationality' that gives no proper account of the distinctive role of the Spirit, especially in prayer and worship.

3. A prayer-based model of reflexive divinity and incorporative election evidenced in Ro 8 does, however, provide an alternative model of considerable ecumenical potential, one in which the 'Spirit'/third is no ineffectual afterthought, but the very wedge in God that opens up the prayerful elect, both Jewish and Christian, to a shared, but ineffable, future of Messianic hope.

4. This model, in turn, provides a way, as 'Supersessionism 2' does not, of thinking of the Christ event as itself still in the *process* of cosmic completion. The christological offense for Jews of the naming of Jesus as already Messiah still has to be grasped rather than denied, to be sure; but it is pneumatologically inflected in a special way and thus opened up to a shared future which is for now unknown.

5. Perhaps then in closing we may dub this proposed position for Christian theology a new 'Supersessionism 3'. It does involve a remaining and emphatic Messianic claim for Jesus by Christians, yet one which is radically demanding in

---

51 See again Fishbane, *Biblical Myth*, 175, citing *BT Baba Batra* 89a on the difference between the angels on either side of the ark facing inwards or facing outwards (cp. Exod 25. 19-20 and 1 Kings 6. 23-7), as signs of divine pleasure or displeasure, respectively.

its openness to final trinitarian fulfilment, a fulfilment that implies a compelling sharing of Jesus's sufferings on behalf of a struggling cosmos, still opened to the Messianic eschaton (see Ro 8. 15-25; 31-39). This is not, as we have seen, a spiritual option for the faint-hearted in either tradition; for as the rabbinic materials we have just surveyed make clear, the realm of prayerful intimacy-in-God (which tends to lead back to reflection on the *Song of Songs*, one way or another, in both traditions) is a perilous realm, delightful certainly to the initiated, the pure, and the spiritually mature, but dangerous indeed to those not yet prepared to be the fragile, suffering and ecstatic receptors of God's own prayer to God. This is the shared Jewish/Christian inheritance on which we have reflected in this chapter; its ecumenical implications, I plead in closing, are still open to further exploration and fulfilment.[52]

[52] I want to express my thanks to a number of scholars who have greatly helped me in the development of this text, most especially Mark Nussberger (who gave invaluable research assistance to me at Harvard), Gary A. Anderson, Michael Fishbane, William Horbury and Andrew Chester, without whose insights, suggestions and corrections this would have been a very different product. My sincere thanks too to Michael Welker and William Schweiker for the rich Heidelberg symposium from which this discussion arose, and for their considerable patience in allowing me to develop the research further after the event.

Part III

The Divine and the Elevation of Life

‘God as Light’ in the Christian Moral Imagination

William Schweiker

1. Introduction

The purpose of this volume is to explore how images of the divine relate to and/or provide guidance for cultural orientation. The challenges confronting cultural life in our global age are well known: environmental endangerment, grinding and unjust poverty, the disappearance of languages and species, struggles for human rights, genetic manipulation of species, legacies of violence and warfare, and the global spread of disease–just to name a few. More the ever before, life on this planet is vulnerable before the power of supra-human global dynamics and systems. Of course, the account of our situation in terms of those challenges, and others as well, is merely one way to describe the present situation. It is a description of our age from within global dynamics rather than from some supposed “bird’s eye” view. It is thereby contestable from other perspectives. However, for anyone concerned to develop an ethics drawn for the resources of a religious tradition, the root question is this one: how, if at all, can global forces be rendered responsive to norms and values aimed at respecting and enhancing the integrity of human and non-human forms of life? The moral and religious challenge of this age is to live responsibly amid powers which shape the destiny of this world. This is why cultural orientation is needed in theological and ethical reflection.

Thankfully, over the last decades several proposals for developing global ethics have been offered. These proposals usually focus on the “grounds” for global ethics.[1] That is, they seek to clarify common values and principles in order to insure that the norms proposed are not imposed on other peoples by one culture’s or one religion’s outlook. Global ethics aims, in other words, to articulate a framework for cooperation, tolerance, and judgment. It provides what is sometimes called a “thin” or “minimal” ethics of shared norms rather than proposing a “thick” or “robust” vision of human flourishing and excellence.[2] The point of

---

1 On the topic of global ethics, see *For All Life: Toward a Universal Declaration of a Global Ethic*, ed. Leonard Swidler (Ashland, OR: White Cloud Press, 1998), *Prospects for a Common Morality*, edited by Gene H. Outka and John P. Reeder (Princeton, NJ: Princeton University Press, 1992), and *A Global Ethic: The Declaration of the Parliament of the World’s Religions*, edited by Hans Küng and Karl-Josef Kuschel (New York, NY: Continuum, 1994).

2 See Michael Walzer, *Thick and Thin: Moral Argument at Home and Abroad* (Notre Dame, IN: University of Notre Dame Press, 1997) and *Interpretation and Social Criticism*

dispute is whether or not "global ethics" so conceived thereby denies cultural particularities in the search for general, minimal norms of justice.

Granting the importance of those concerns about "global ethics," I want in the following pages to address a matter too often neglected in the discussion. In an age of worldwide dynamics, what is the nature, freedom, and also right formation of moral consciousness and how does this relate to conceptions of the moral space of life? That is, I am interested in the formation and deformation of moral consciousness in and through the images, concepts, and narratives used by people to make sense of their world and the orientation of life in that world.

Human consciousness is always socially and historically located and thus always in relation to some socio-temporal construal of reality. So the question then becomes, how can and ought we to test the specific ideas, particular values, distinctive beliefs, and communal narratives that shape consciousness, provide peoples' picture of the world, and guide how to live?

Moral and political thinkers have long worried about the ways value systems and ideologies define and distort human consciousness. Recall Greek thinkers like Plato and his criticism of the "artists," the Hebrew prophets and their denunciation of social injustice, and also distinctive modern critiques of morality, say in Friedrich Nietzsche or Karl Marx. These modern, Western thinkers, one would include J.S. Mill as well, grasped the ways in which ideological forces can lead to a tyranny of the minority by the majority without recourse to brute power. In other words, thinkers have realized that values, beliefs, narratives and the like must be submitted to criticism if they are to be worthy of guiding human life.

In the global age this problem is writ large. Human consciousness is bombarded by cultural forms through the global media. These images saturate peoples' perceptions of the world and others. Global dynamics are shaping peoples' interior lives with a stream of images, perceptions, and feelings; they increasingly define the moral space of life. One can, thereby, engage these dynamics as the way to examine forces currently shaping human inwardness. The strategy of thought is thereby decidedly hermeneutical in the sense that one interprets social and cultural forms in order to articulate the structure and dynamics of human life and action.[3]

A good deal of contemporary ethics have forsaken attention to the dynamics of moral consciousness and perception in order to focus on rules and principles of just social interaction, or, in a related way, to explore the moral discourse of a community. The turn to action and language in modern thought has virtually eclipsed the focus in ancient ethics on moral consciousness and spiritual practices. This is not the time or place to chart the history of this shift in philosophy and theology. It is enough to note the fact and also to acknowledge that a variety

(Cambridge, MA: Harvard University Press, 1993). Also see Jonathan Sacks, *The Dignity of Difference: How to Avoid the Clash of Civilizations* (New York, NY: Continuum, 2002) and Amartya Sen, *Identity and Violence: The Illusion of Destiny* (New York, NY: Norton, 2006).

3 On this see William Schweiker, *Theological Ethics and Global Dynamics: In the Time of Many Worlds* (Oxford: Blackwell Publishing, 2004).

of thinkers, myself included, grant the importance of the turn to language and action but insist that the question of consciousness remains important.[4] This seems required in the examination of the religions as ways of orienting life. Of course, what we call the "religions" involve many things: myths, ritual patterns, some communal existence, norms and values for conduct. Yet the religions are likewise interested in the tenor and direction of human inner-being even as they conceive of this interiority in ways exceedingly different than modern conceptions of subjectivity.[5] This is the case even with those religions that focus more on the collective than the individual precisely because consciousness must be socialized into or formed by the community. Further, the religions typically explore supra-human forces that impinge on human life, whether in ideas about karma or the spirit world or divine providence. Ideas about how one ought to live are always set within some picture of encompassing reality and its powers.

There is a complex interrelation between the dynamics of consciousness and a construal of reality and supra-human forces. This fact brings me to the specific focus of this essay, namely the image of God as "light."

2. The Ubiquity of Image of Light

Importantly, the image of "light" is widespread in the world's religions. Christians, drawing on the Johannine corpus, speak of God as the "light of the world" and Christ as the "light that enlivens every man." Sometimes, as in I John, this image demarcates the boundaries between the Church and "the world," and thereby limits the scope of care and responsibility to the "brothers and sisters." The image provides Christians with orientation vis-à-vis the wider social world. And yet at other times, Christians have used the image to speak about the human condition as such and the universal intention of moral claims, namely, that every human being created by God and endowed with moral reason, say natural law, is due moral respect and care. This too provides cultural orientation but in a way markedly different than its use in demarcating those in the light (the Church) and those in darkness (the world). Importantly, the image of "light" is also found well-beyond the confines of the Christian tradition. In distinctive ways, Jews and Muslims draw on the image of light, say in claims within Islamic mystical poetry about the "light of Muhammad" or in what Michael Fishbane calls "rabbinical mythmaking."[6] The idea is also key to forms of thought arising out of Platonic philosophy

4 For examples of this kind of work in ethics see *Iris Murdoch and the Search for Human Goodness*, eds. M. Antonaccio and W. Schweiker (Chicago, IL: The University of Chicago Press, 1996).

5 For a discussion see the chapters on "Agents and Moral Formations," "Ideas of Ethical Excellence," "Practices" and "Moral Development" in *The Blackwell Companion to Religious Ethics*, ed. William Schweiker (Oxford, UK: Blackwell Publishing, 2005).

6 See Annemarie Schimmel, *And Muhammad is His Messenger: The Veneration of the Prophet in Islamic Piety* (Chapel Hill, NC: University of North Carolina Press, 1985) and

and also ancient Gnosticism. If one casts a glance even wider, the idea is found in claims about "enlightenment" in Persian, Roman, and Germanic religions. Of course, the sheer presence of an image in history, religion, and culture says nothing about its saliency for current thought, but it is cause for one to wonder.

My wonderment is about the possible meanings of this image in the Christian moral imagination. Part of the puzzle is to sort out the linking of the image of "light" to God and also to the "world," where "world" in Christian thought is an image, a symbolic construct, for the socio-temporal space of human life. The main problem I need to explore is how the image of light provides two different–even opposed–possibilities for Christian relation to adherents of other religious traditions, or no tradition at all. The task for the theologian interested in ethics, accordingly, is to sort out this ambiguity and to help to determine how responsibly to inhabit beliefs and practices. One must assess the images that saturate religious consciousness and orient life in terms of their meaning and validity for actual life. What then is the problem?

As noted above, one interpretation of this image, especially in the Johannine corpus, uses it to distinguish the Church from others, the "world," and, historically speaking, the emergent Christian movement from the "Jews" (*hoi Ioudaioi*) (cf. John 8:13-42).[7] On this reading, the image of "light," and especially Christ as the "light of the world," is used as a social boundary-marker of inclusion and exclusion. That interpretation of "light" provides cultural orientation but in ways that communities are set off from each other, often in relations of antagonism and supersession. So, the "world," that is, all non-Christians, dwell in the dark, the regions of sin, while Christians live in the light. In contrast to this interpretation which at root is soteriological, there is, I argue, another and more distinctly ethical interpretation. This account marks connections between the Christian imaginary and other moral traditions that also use the image of "light." Here the image of "light" is about God as the Good and source of moral insight, and, further, that moral goodness–not restricted of any specific community–is a possibility and demand on every human being. This account of the image of "light" implies, in other words, a way of inhabiting religious sources and practices that shape moral consciousness beyond the pitch of inclusion and exclusion. The question nowadays, I suggest, is which interpretation of this image of God as light can and ought to guide Christian thought and action. And it is the second option that I will attempt to advance throughout these reflections.[8] In order to do so will require

---

Michael Fishbane, *Biblical Myth and Rabbinical Mythmaking* (Oxford: Oxford University Press, 2003).

7 For a recent discussion see Amos Yong, "The Light Shines in the Darkness: Johannine Dualism and the Challenge for Christian Theology of Religions Today," in *The Journal of Religion* 89:1 (2009), 31-56.

8 For this approach see David E. Klemm and William Schweiker, *Religion and the Human Future: An Essay in Theological Humanism* (Oxford: Wiley-Blackwell, 2008). Also see,

later connecting the image of "light" to other images and ideas in the Christian imaginary, specifically world, life, and love.

The remainder of my argument moves in several steps. I turn next to some matters of method in ethics and also the types of images about ethical reflection itself arising in the West. Those matters in hand, I then explore the image of God as light, and, finally, conclude with some thoughts on what moral meaning it might provide today. At that point we will see how this image can structure moral consciousness and provide orientation in life. That being said, I need to start at some distance from the image in order to clarify the shape and purpose of my reflections.

3. Images in Moral Thinking?

There are a number of ways that the theme of this chapter could be approached within ethics. For instance, the question of the relation between God and morality, as it is often put, is longstanding in Western thought. Sometimes, as in the Platonic dialogue the *Euthyphro* or in Immanuel Kant's thought, religion and claims about God are grounded in ethical ones. Other times, one thinks of theologians like Karl Barth, valid moral obligations are defined as the "commands of God." And in still other cases, religious ideas are dismissed as insignificant for morality–maybe even a danger–(e.g., David Hume), or they have a complex relation to different dimensions of moral thinking (say, Thomas Aquinas, the Protestant reformers, or current thinkers like Charles Taylor, Iris Murdoch or Paul Ricœur).

However, the general and foundational question of the relation of God and morality is not a helpful focus for this contribution, and for two reasons. First, the general question is so broad that it disallows economical treatment in a short essay. And as some might say, posing the question of "God" and "morality" presupposes a conceptual framework of the moral imaginary arising within Hellenistic thought that really blocks, rather than illuminates, what one is exploring through the imagery of "light" and cultural orientation. Second, so posed–that is, what is the relation between God and morality?–the question misses a crucial point, namely, that there are different images of the divine and these could, at least in principle, have markedly different relations to moral reflection and the orientation of life. This possibility would confound any attempt to reduce the question to a single answer. For instance, if God is imagined as a judge, then the pertinent intersection with moral thinking is different than (say) the idea of God as one's highest good or God as redeemer or God and the voice of conscience. A certain religious outlook, then, would intersect with what we now call ethical reflection in different ways. And, further, one would want carefully to sort out the difference between an "image" of God and an "idea" of God.

William Schweiker, *Dust That Breathes: Christian Faith and the New Humanisms* (Oxford: Wiley-Blackwell, 2010).

So, my purpose, again, is not the question of God and morality, but, rather, to explore the "image" of light and how it might intersect with reflection on the orientation of human life, and so the purview of ethics. The implication is that the Christian imagination is more complex than usually granted precisely because it draws on and uses a wide and even confusing range of images of God for the sake of orienting life. One task of theological ethics, on this conception, is to bring some coherence to the moral imagination by articulating and clarifying its dynamics for the sake of orienting life. How then to explore "images?" That too has been a debated issue within moral theory.

The question of images in ethics, at least in the legacy of Western thought, arises at three different points of ethical reflection. The first point at which the question of "images" in ethical reflection arises is in terms of the method of moral thinking, that is, how one carries out the task of moral reflection. There are contrasting ways theologians and moral philosophers have treated images. One longstanding tactic is to say that the task of the thinker is to critique and then conceptualize the images and beliefs found in a culture or community in order to grasp their rational content and to assess their validity. When Kant, for instance, in the dialectic of *The Critique of Practical Reason*, argues that "God" is a being with understanding and will and thus a causal agent on moral principles, he has, we can say, sought to purge images of God in order to conceive the rational and moral meaning of the idea of God. Or one could also attempt, as Paul Tillich did, to "correlate" religious symbols (and so images of ultimate concern) with philosophical concepts (as conditions of meaning). For this line of thought, the ambiguity and endless potential for re-interpretation which surrounds cultural forms, and so images and metaphors, threatens the precision and validity of moral reason. One needs to grasp the conceptual import of (say) an image in order to give structure and direction to moral reason. Call this a *method of conceptualization.*

Second, some argue that moral thinking is dependent on the pool of beliefs and values in a community, and so its stock of images, because the moral life is in part a process of socialization. The moral thinker seeks to articulate the social imaginary in ways that can aid living in the present. The idea here, as old as Aristotle, is that human beings need to be educated and formed as virtuous people and this process of formation is complex and life-long. What it will entail is something like learning a natural language. That is, moral formation entails learning the forms of thought and values in a community to the point that one has facility with them in moral reasoning and also enacts them in one's life. For Christians this would require becoming the kind of Church that can live out and re-tell the story of God's action in Christ. Other communities would have a different moral vocabulary and set of beliefs and stories and thereby form persons in different ways. It is quite popular nowadays among neo-Aristotelians, communitarians, and narrative theologians to call this the *socialization method.*

Finally, one can begin with the trove of images (symbols, metaphors, narratives) of some community, in this case the Christian community, and attempt to show how they articulate features of human existence otherwise mute and yet operative in life, often enough in dangerous ways. This would require an account of the non-reducible place of "images" in moral thinking, and so resist the method of conceptualization, and yet also seek to demonstrate the realistic intention of thinking with images in a way quite different than the socialization method. In this essay, I adopt, rather than defend, this *hermeneutical method*.

However the question of the place of "images" in moral thinking is more vexing than questions of method. It also touches, second, on the very conception of ethical thinking itself, whether philosophical or theological. If one holds that ethical reflection is sufficiently defined as the articulation and application of norms for specific human actions, including cooperative action, then the pool of images found in a society or community are morally irrelevant. They might form background outlooks, worldviews, or comprehensive beliefs, as John Rawls called them, but they are not the stuff of rigorous and strict moral reflection and deliberation. Suffice it to say, that such a narrow conception of "ethics" is, in my judgment, hardly sufficient to address the complexity of Christian or any other form of human life. Iris Murdoch was more on the mark when she noted: "Man is a creature who makes pictures of himself and then comes to resemble the picture. This is the process which moral philosophy must attempt to describe and analyze."[9] I would add that any "picture" of the human entails a construal of reality, and, accordingly, ethics, in its broad and proper sense, seeks to articulate and to analyze the structures of live reality in order responsibly to orient human life. "Images" are thus crucial in the conception of ethics since (1) human beings strive, as Murdoch noted, to inhabit cultural conceptions or pictures of existence, and (2) our understanding of the space of human existence exceeds direct, immediate, and total apprehension and so is given imaginative construal. The path to self-knowledge and the orientation of life is always by way of interpretation. What we are seeking to understand in order to orient life responsibly are the morally salient features of lived reality.

Now, if one works with that conception of "ethics" then, third, some interesting things come to the fore. For instance, one could explore the significance in the history of cultures and religions of images that have been crucial for moral thinking: mountains (Sinai; Sermon on the Mount, Nietzsche's Zarathustra), trees (Eden; the Bo Tree in Buddhism), deserts and wastelands, urban versus rural (where the "city" is often pictured as morally dangerous), caves (see Plato's myth), the school, the garden (Epicurus), the moral life as a battle against vice (Erasmus) or the soul as the field of battle, and the like. Similarly, the various forms of moral thinking are keyed to different images: a dialogue (for example) is different than an "Enchiridion," that is, a little-knife to help in the battle of life. Likewise there are a bewildering number of images used to picture the human in Western thought, religious and otherwise: the courtroom of conscience, between beast and angel, made of dust (*humus*; Adam), a sensible machine (Hobbes), the *cogito*–and so a thinking being, etc. The same is true of images of God, my topic here. The point being that the question of the moral imaginary fans out to a vast

---

9 Iris Murdoch, "Metaphysics and Ethics," reprinted in *Iris Murdoch and the Search for Human Goodness*, 252.

array of images that begs for historical and comparative analysis. I obviously cannot undertake that task in this chapter.

Mindful of the method, conception of ethics, and also the limitation on the present reflections each of which turns on the place of "images" in thinking, I want to explore one image of the divine and its place in the Christian moral imagination. Yet it is an image, I note, that allows comparative analysis and, in fact, arises at the intersection of Hebraic and Hellenistic thinking, the precise origin point of Christian reflection itself. It is the image of God as the light of the world.[10] In this essay I will only be able to begin to sort out its moral meaning. Much will remain to wonder about in this image.

4. God as Light in Christian Thought

In this history of Christian theology, God as light of the world has often been associated with metaphysical forms of theology, say, in the Catholic Church, and, whether in Catholic or in purely philosophical forms, in what is known as "natural theology." The image of God as light of the world captures the immediate openness to a universal religious symbol of the divine. In *The Republic*, Plato's Socrates distinguishes between changing, mutable *things* that exist, and the eternal, immutable *forms* of those things. How is it possible for us to know these things *as* the kind of things they are (after all, we can identify this thing as a chair or a dog)? We can do so because the thing appears to us as an instance of its form; the eternal form is the condition of the intelligibility of a thing. The form makes it possible to formulate the judgment, "this is a chair." The form is the light in which the mind's eye conceives what the physical eyes perceive *as* the kind of thing it is. The eternal world of forms inhabits and also grounds the changing world of appearances. Questions of "form" continue through the history of Western thought taking decidedly expressions, especially with the so-called turn to language. The basic claim is that reflection can penetrate and grasp basic forms of thought and/or discourse which are elementary and thus structure and provide some integrity to human thought and action.[11]

However, beyond its use in metaphysical and epistemological considerations, Plato's image has also been of crucial importance in Western ethics, and in two ways. First, since forms imply a standard of goodness as perfect correspondence ("participation" or "imitation") between appearance and reality, the form of the good is the highest form and the ultimate object of knowledge: "the end of all

---

10 I am drawing freely from Klemm and Schweiker, *Religion and the Human Future*, Ch. 3.

11 For this argument in recent practical philosophy see Michael Thompson, *Life and Action: Elementary Structures of Practice and Practical Thought* (Cambridge, MA: Harvard University Press, 2008).

endeavour, the object on which every heart is set."[12] When called on to give an account of the Good, Socrates says, "I'm afraid it's beyond me, and if I try I shall only make a fool of myself and be laughed at."[13] The form of the good, as first principle, cannot be defined, although we use it in making judgments of value and worth. Accordingly, Socrates fashions similes and analogies to show what the Good might be like. He begins with the simile of the sun. Just as the experience of seeing something requires not only eyes endowed with the power to see and something to be seen, but also a "third element," the light of the sun, so the experiences of understanding something requires a mind endowed with intelligence, something to be understood, and a third thing–the form of the Good.[14] Here we have a classical reference point for metaphysical theology and a metaphorical cluster of God as light of the world.

The second way in which the image of "light," and even more the Sun, arising in Plato's thought has helped to shape Western ethics is a specific picture it generates of human life itself. As Murdoch puts it commenting on Plato's theory of art and, specifically, the "myth of the cave" in the *Republic*, "Plato pictures human life as a pilgrimage from appearance to reality... The sun represents the Form of the Good in whose light the truth is seen; it reveals the world, hitherto, invisible, and is also a source of life."[15] The pilgrimage of life is through different types of awareness whereby the higher reality is first grasped in images and shadows on the way to direct, immediate vision. The movement, we can say, is a purgation and an ascent. This image of the moral life as a form of *askesis* and movement to the truth is longstanding in Christian thought. It is seen, for instance, in St. Bonaventure's *Itinerarium Mentis ad Deum–the Minds' Road to God*–and other Christian mystical writings. Thus not only does the image of "light" imply a specific metaphysical picture in the relation and difference of form and matter, but also a diagnosis of the human problem–blindness to the truth through illusion and fantasy–and a picture of the moral life, a pilgrimage to the good as a purgation of the self from illusion and false love.

Consider St. Augustine's *Soliloquies* in which the basic form of thinking is Platonic (or neo-Platonic).[16] Augustine wants to know God and the soul, and reason (*logos*) addresses him as the interface between the two. In knowledge something transcends us, so the goal of knowledge is somehow already present at the start; it needs to be brought into clarity. There is, he admits, no necessity in sensory experience, so he negates it in terms of providing knowledge of how God and the soul necessarily are. Only through intellectual knowledge can one know

---

12 Plato, *The Republic*, trans. with intro. Desmond Lee (New York: Penguin Books, 1987), 238 (502c) and 243 (505e).

13 Plato, *The Republic*, 244 (506d).

14 Plato, *The Republic*, 245-7 (507a-509c).

15 Iris Murdoch, *The Fire and the Sun: Why Plato Banished the Artists* (Oxford: Oxford University Press, 1977), 3-4.

16 *Augustine: Earlier Writings*, J.H.S. Burleigh, ed. (Philadelphia: Westminster Press, 1953), 17-63.

how things necessarily have to be; we know the flux only in light of eternal realities, which are in the mind of God. Human thinking has an intrinsic obligation to the highest standards–truth and goodness–and so the human thinker stands in the presence of God as he or she reflects these standards in thinking and doing. What this means morally, as he argues in *On the Morals of the Catholic Church*, is the need for the proper ordering of loves so that the soul might rest in God as its highest good. More recently, this line of thought is neatly summarized by Servais Pinckaers, O.P, in his *The Sources of Christian Ethics*. "Christian ethics is that branch of theology that studies human acts so as to direct them to the loving vision of God seen as our true, complete happiness and final end." He adds: "This vision is attained by means of grace, the virtues, and the gifts, in the light of revelation and reason."[17]

Rejecting the discourse of virtue and the ascent of the mind or soul to God, the image of God as "light of the world" has been more problematic for Protestant thinkers. Kenneth Kirk, the great Anglican moralist, did argue that the "vision of God" was the core of Christian faith and life. And John Wesley, drawing on patristic thinkers in the East, emphasized a vision of the Christian life as a pilgrimage to perfection in love. Much more typical, on my understanding, is a claim such as Karl Barth's: "No more and no less than God himself is there, in that this Word, i.e., Jesus whose story the Gospel wishes to tell, is there as the light in the darkness which comprehendeth not the light (John 1, 2:4-5)."[18] That is to say, Protestants have been interested in God's actions in Christ–and so Christ as the light of the world–rather than the ascent of the soul to God, an account of the Christian life that seems to smack of "works righteousness." The emphasis is decidedly on the atoning work of God done in Christ. The Christian life is then a response to God's action. This might entail, in some versions, an "overcoming" of the world as the realm of darkness, or, conversely, a picture of how to live in the world but not of the world.

A full treatment of the image of light in the history of Christian thinking would, of course, be pulled into Christological questions and problems about Gnosticism and doceticism, the relation between Johannine material and the rest of the New Testament, and a host of comparative connections to the surrounding Hellenistic and Jewish context. That is obviously not possible here.[19] Yet my admittedly too brief history of the use of the image of "light" and God as "light of the world" is meant to show that this image, like all images, is not self-interpreting. Whether used metaphysically, epistemologically, as a picture of the moral life, with respect to our relation to God or God's action in Christ, the image is set within divergent frameworks which it funds and supports but also which help

---

17 Servais Pinckaers, *The Sources of Christian Ethics*, trans., M. T. Noble (Washington, DC: Catholic University of America Press, 1995), 8.

18 Karl Barth, *Church Dogmatics* I/I, trans. G. T. Thomson (Edinburgh: T&T Clark, 1936), 459.

19 On some of these matters see Robert A. Spivey and D. Moody Smith, *Anatomy of the New Testament* (New York, NY: Macmillan, 1974).

to provide its meanings. The oddity, of course, is that the image can migrate between frameworks and thereby be present in decidedly different visions of how one can and ought to orient life. And this shows us, again, why theologians often adopt the method of conceptualization or socialization, as noted above. That is, one can attempt to clean up the messiness of the image through conceptual labor or show how it is used within the Church's form of life. Adopting those methods thereby relieves the interpreter of the image's messiness, as I am calling it. Yet it is crucial to see that the method of socialization coheres with one possible set of meanings of the image found in the Christian tradition. That is, it coheres with the Johannine dualism of Church overcoming the World where "world" can mean the whole domain of non-Christian existence or specific other religious beliefs and practices. In this respect, the image of "light" pushes back on the method, as it were, and provides determinate orientation for life. Christians ought to separate from the "world," witness to others, and imagine themselves as the people of peace, goodness, and "light."

What, we might ask, of a hermeneutical engagement with this image, especially an engagement mindful of the messiness of its meanings? Might it allow us to access different registers or meanings of this image of light and thereby provide a different cultural orientation? To recall, I argued above that theological ethics must bring some coherence to the moral imagination and clarify its dynamics but with the wider purpose of articulating and analyzing the structures of lived reality for the sake of orienting human life responsibly within that space. What could that mean for making sense of the image of God as light in a way that might escape the oppositional logic of Church vs. the World?

5. Orienting Life

It should be clear at this point that the various "methods" for exploring images within ethics noted above are of a piece with the different meanings of the image of light itself. The principle contrast I have been drawing is with respect to this image as underwriting, on the one hand, a sociological view that puts the Church in high contrast to the "world" as a domain of darkness and sin. On the other hand, there is a strand of interpretation that takes the image as a metaphysical and pedagogical idea and uses it to conceive of the moral life as a movement from appearance to reality under the power of the Good and love. Granting that human beings and even communities dwell within different stages or levels of goodness, this account holds that in principle the pilgrimage of the moral life is open to all. Accordingly, one cannot draw the distinction light/dark sociologically, that is, in terms of religious membership, but, morally, that is, in the actual lives of persons and communities. And, in fact, this account would seem to abort the first more sociological interpretation: growth in love would simply mean growth in the capacity to respect and enhance the life of anyone, whether a co-religionist or not.

To interpret the image of God as "light" in ways that contrast with its specifically sociological reading could follow the method of conceptualization or a hermeneutical approach. Later I will show why I follow a hermeneutical path. At this point it is important to grasp that shifting from a sociological reading of the image of "light" means at least three things. First, it means a decisive shift in how the moral space of existence is perceived, understood, and evaluated. That is to say, the structure of lived reality is not defined in terms of the opposition Church/world where the "world" is the domain of sin and darkness, but, rather, the "world" as symbolic construct for the moral space of life becomes the arena of service with and for others and thus also the domain for the struggle for goodness. Stated christologically, the idea is that Christ came not to condemn but to save the world, and this provides orientation for Christian existence. Rather than allowing the distinction Church/world to interpret the scope of Christian moral concern and the context for valid claims, the image of light can also be used to articulate the structures in which the moral life is to be lived and thus the scope of the responsibility to respect and enhance the integrity of life. In a word, this account provides a different interpretation of morally relevant features of lived reality.

If the first move is to show how the image of "light" can provide a distinctive interpretation of the "world" as the moral space of life, then, second and related, it also signals a specific ethical intentionality. Rather than the intentional object of Christian living being the upbuilding and distinction of the Church from the world, the account here implies a kind of "universalism" wherein the object of moral concern is the integrity of life, human and non-human. In other words, the intentionality of moral goodness is not a particular community but a more comprehensive or cosmopolitan good. This is, admittedly, an intentionality or horizon of moral concern. It is obviously the case that no one person or even one community can in any realistic sense love the whole world or all humanity. What we could call the cosmopolitan conscience is about the intentionality of the moral life, not an actual fact. Careful and discriminating judgments must be made about specific decisions, courses of actions, and policies. That too is part of the work of moral reflection. The point is that for any decision, course of action, or policy to withstand moral assessment, it must have, as its inner-intentionality, reference to a comprehensive concern for the integrity of life. It must be moved and judged by the cosmopolitan conscience. This is warranted, we can say, because of the intimate connection in the Christian moral imaginary between the image of light and that of "life." That is, within the Christian tradition the idea of God as living and the source of created life, redeemed life, and even eternal life can provide the intentional object to the image of "light." One might capture this by saying that God's life is the light of the world, that is, divine life is the source and end of the moral space of existence, the "world," but apprehended as living and not a mere idea or abstract Good which too easily infests Platonized uses of the image of light.

I have been making my case for a specific interpretation of the image of "light" by, first, disconnecting it from the "Church/world" logic and showing its connection to another conception of "world" as a moral space and the moral struggle within the world. Second, I have also made the connection, found in the biblical texts, between "light" and "life" in order to clarify an inclusive ethical intentionality beyond the kind of moral particularism too often lodged in the Johannine outlook. These two hermeneutical moves allow a final and decisive one. Recall that the Johannine logic placed love at the center of a Christian orientation in life. And yet because of its connection to the account of "light" and "world," the source of love is God and the object of love is God and fellow Christians. "The commandment we have from him is this: those who love God must love their brothers and sisters also" (1 John 4:21). Yet when the image of "light" is interpreted in relation to a different account of world and life, then the object of Christian love is extended. The motive and object for orienting life shifts to what will respect and enhance, and so to love, the integrity of all life. Further, that is seen as the way to orient existence in the light of the love of the living God, the source and giver of life.

Clearly, an entire theological ethics would be required to work out carefully and coherently the symbolic re-alignment I am suggesting among the images of light, world, life, and love. My point has been to establish within the Christian imaginary the possibility and resources for doing so. This clarifies the hermeneutical work Christian thinkers must undertake in our age of global cultural forms. Stated differently, there are no doubt times in which a stark distinction between Church and World is needed and then one can draw on resources in scripture and tradition to do so. Yet in our age, I am suggesting, a different hermeneutic is needed and I have tried to show that it is fully present in and warranted by scripture and tradition. That point having been established, one question remains. I will conclude these reflections with it. It turns on the reason why the method of conceptualization is insufficient for theological ethics.

6. Conclusion

A question remains at the end of these reflections in virtue of the possibility of the symbolic re-alignment of the image of "light" and its import for orienting existence in the global age. Why ought Christians to interpret and inhabit their beliefs and practices in the direction I have suggested rather than remain within the binary logic of Church/world and light/darkness? To be sure, in an age of wild global dynamics and expanding planetary consciousness, there are powerful forces at work to move people to seek to preserve social boundary-markers. In this age, would it not be foolish to think otherwise? And if the uniqueness of the Church is eroded, is there anything distinctive about a Christian orientation in life? The temptation is to imagine that a theologian can answer these questions by formulating criteria of validity and showing that religious symbols and images can be conceptualized in order to determine whether or not they meet those criteria. This tactic, if adopted, would allow me to show the greater adequacy of my account of the image of "light" in the Christian imagination than particularist readings now popular among many theologians. In a word, the temptation is to adopt the method of conceptualization, as I called it above.[20]

Refusing to adopt that method, as I have done, means that the only case that can be made for the account provided about the orientation the image of "light" can give to life rests, interestingly, on the insight it affords to understanding the Christian imaginary and our current situation. That is to say, the only way to make the case for the greater cogency and adequacy of one interpretation of the image of light over another one is to show how it can isolate problems in that other interpretation and also provide guidance for life in ways that meet the challenges now faced. And that is what I have attempt to do in these reflections, namely, to show that the image of "light" in the Christian imaginary can provide cultural orientation in our age of global endangerments to life in way that avoid the problems which can and do arise within the binary logic of Church/world. The hope is that in the pilgrimage of the Christian life faithful people come to see in and through the images of their faith the wider horizon of love that is now endangered in our global times.

20 For an example of that method, see Franklin I. Gamwell, *The Divine God: Moral Theory and the Necessity of God* (Dallas, TX: Southern Methodist University Press, 1996).

Paradise as a Qur'anic Discourse

Late Antique Foundations and Early Qur'anic Developments

Angelika Neuwirth

1. Introduction

Eschatology is certainly among the central discourses of the Qur'an. Its prominence is largely due to the challenge encountered by the Qur'anic community that had to outbalance an extremely powerful mundane pagan ideology, predominant in its Arabian milieu: the ideology of *murū'a*, i.e. "virile pride", expressing itself in a hedonist, "*carpe-diem*-life style", embodied by the Bedouin hero, the persona of the ancient Arab poet. This anthropocentric understanding of the world, particularly eloquently voiced in ancient Arabic poetry, is taken up as a primary target of the early Qur'anic message. Excessive worldliness, unlimited confidence in man's abilities in the Qur'an is countered by a new, theocentric, eschatological thinking. Qur'anic eschatology is projected through multiple images that, during the first Meccan period of the Prophet's ministry, crystallize into an elaborate drama[1] often conjured up in the Qur'an. Yet, although the diverse events leading up to the Last Day–such as the cosmic cataclysm, the awakening of the dead and the ensuing punishment of the sinners in Hell–all play an important role in the message of eschatology, these are secondary textual employments when compared with the core piece of Qur'anic eschatology: the image of paradise.

As a prevalent Qur'anic motif, paradise not only exerted a sustainable influence on both the spiritual life and the socio-political *Weltanschauung* of the Prophet's contemporaries and of the later recipients of the Qur'an[2], but it also equally inspired classical Arabic literature and art. Whereas this complex reception history of the Qur'anic paradise has been amply studied, the particular literary shape of the Qur'anic paradise itself has seldom been submitted to investigation. Traditional Islamic scholars as well as Western critics have usually taken the numerous impressive descriptions of paradisiacal scenarios simply for a Qur'anic "peculiarity", an iconic *fait accompli*. They usually do not enquire into these narratives' possible dialectical relation vis-à-vis earlier images of paradise[3], let alone their ideological function within the Qur'anic message. Instead, a teleological approach is pursued: not late antique, but Islamic exegetical texts are consulted –

1 Smith, *Eschatology*, 44-54.

2 Jarrar, *Martyrdom*, 87-108.

3 As an exception, Horovitz, *Das koranische Paradies*, 1-16 deserves to be mentioned.

texts that are built on a much later and very different vision of the world and the Hereafter[4]–to explain the unique features of the Qur'anic paradise.

Though it is true that this kind of anachronistic approach is prevalent in contemporary scholarship, there are remnants of an earlier scholarly tradition still alive. This tradition, which was established in the nineteenth century, succeeded during the short period of one century–between 1833 and 1935–to lay the foundation for a historically conscious model of Qur'anic studies both in terms of methodology and the selection of comparative material. This scholarly tradition, initiated by Abraham Geiger (1833)[5], one of the founders of the movement of the *Wissenschaft des Judentums*[6], focused on late antique intertexts of the Qur'an, primarily the Jewish and Christian traditions, but equally paid attention to the pagan Arabian traditions. It was Josef Horovitz whose path-breaking essay "Das Koranische Paradies" (1923) that was to open scholars' eyes to the multiple literary layers that underlie the Qur'anic imaginations of the eschatological Beyond. Furthermore, it is the merit of the last representative of that tradition, Heinrich Speyer (1931)[7], to have thrown light on the primordial paradise, submitting its narrative references to a source-critical investigation. Some modern contributions on the subject–by Walid Saleh[8], Patricia Crone[9], Gabriel Reynolds[10] and the present writer[11], have proceeded in a similar vein though with very different preconceptions concerning the literary artifact 'Qur'an'. The historical approach based on the search for "intertexts", i.e. late antique traditions echoed in the Qur'an, is pursued systematically in the recently established research project *Corpus Coranicum*[12] which, however, goes an important step further. Beyond the identifying of formal and semantic convergences between pre-Qur'anic and Qur'anic texts, it endeavors to reconstruct the peculiar negotiation processes that appear mirrored in the individual Qur'anic reflections of the earlier, Jewish, Christian and pagan traditions. It thus pays attention to the "Sitz im Leben" of individual reworkings of Biblical and post-Biblical traditions in the Qur'an, i.e. their theological and moreover educational function in the process of the emergence of a Qur'anic community.

The following exploration of the Qur'anic paradise will follow the same approach. The strikingly different features of the Qur'anic imagination of paradise vis-à-vis the Jewish and Christian imaginations have until now not been investigated neither regarding their historical foundations nor their impact on the Qur'anic community. The two vantage points, Jewish/Christian and Qur'anic images of paradise, evince conspicuous divergences: whereas the Jewish and

---

4 Kinberg, *Paradise*, 12-20.

5 Geiger, *Judenthume*.

6 Hartwig et al., *Geschichte*, and Hartwig, *Anfänge*, 234-256, and Hartwig, *Gründerdisziplin*.

7 Speyer, *Erzählungen*, see about Speyer Rosenthal, *History*, 113-116.

8 Saleh, *Etymological Fallacy*, 649-698.

9 Crone, *Quranic Pagans*, 387-399.

10 Reynolds, *Qur'ān and its Biblical Subtext*, cf. the review by Neuwirth.

11 Neuwirth, *Symmetrie*, 445-480, and Neuwirth, *Psalms*, 733-778.

12 Marx, *Ein Koranforschungsprojekt*, 41-54.

Christian traditions–essentially following the narrative of Gen 2–focus on the primordial paradise, it is noteworthy that the Qur'an, first and foremost, presents the Hereafter as a utopian place awaiting the Just in the future, telling us only few details about the lost primordial garden, whose inhabitants, Adam and Eve, become significant only at a later stage of the Qur'anic development[13]. It is the eschatological paradise in the first place that the Qur'an depicts in vivid and sensual detail[14]. It is true that Judaism and Christianity did equally develop images of an eschatological Beyond[15], late antique Jewish apocalyptic literature as well as rabbinic writings know about a transcendent abode awaiting the Just. The eschatological encounter of mankind with the divine has even been prefigured in a number of ascent accounts ascribed to elect individuals who ascended to heaven often to return as witnesses of particular experiences in the heavenly abodes.[16] Yet their testimonies do not always design the image of a garden, and if they do, there are little more than forward projections of the primordial paradise, not claiming iconographical traits of their own. Though certainly a theologically significant phenomenon, the Jewish and Christian eschatological paradise is primarily a place where the Just among men will be assembled to enjoy the radiance of the Divine Presence[17]. In Christian tradition paradise is loaded with a particular theological function: to repair the broken image of Adam's paradise where his primordial transgression had occurred staining mankind with the birthmark of original sin. In contrast, the Qur'anic eschatological paradise, *al-janna*, is an ideal space of bliss in its own right, disconnected from the locus of Adam's transgression. Only in later periods this depiction becomes loosely connected to that mythical scenario.

---

13 Neuwirth, *Qur'an, Crisis and Memory*, 113-152.

14 Saleh, *La Vie future;* Smith and Haddad, *Death and Resurrection*; Afsaruddin, *Garden*, 282-287; al-Azmeh, *Rhetoric*, 215-231.

15 Brock, *St. Ephrem*, 49, refers to the First Book of Henoch (second century) 61,12; it is however hard not to realize that the entire corpus of "apocalypses of ascension" is primarily interested in the heavenly representations of the temple, not in a garden scenery, cf. Schäfer, *Ursprünge*, and Rosenkranz Verhelst, *Himmel und Heiligtum*. Brock further refers to the Jewish Palestinian Targum on Gen 3:24: "He drove out Adam. Now He had caused the Glory of His Shekhina (Divine Presence) to dwell above the Garden of Eden from the very beginning, between the Cherubim... he created the Law and established the Garden of Eden for the righteous, so that they might eat from it and enjoy its fruits, seeing that they had kept the commandments of the Law in this world".–There is more ample evidence of a vivid imagination of the eschatological paradise in Christian tradition as Ephrem and his predecessors attest.

16 For the so-called hakhalot literature see Peter Schaefer, *Ursprünge*.

17 bBer 17a.

2. About the methods and the texts

Only a flashback to the earlier developed images of paradise can help to disclose the intertextuality of the Qur'anic paradise with its diegetic predecessors and/or referents. This is a necessary undertaking. Comparative textual studies on the tropological similarities between the Qur'an and other extant texts at the time of the Qur'an's transmission can help to clarify the peculiar descriptions of paradise within the Qur'an. We have to imagine that the Qur'an–or rather the community of the Prophet–debates and re-adapts earlier pagan and monotheistic images. This is not accomplished by simply copying such images but by negotiating them and moreover occasionally "cleansing" them of their allegorical dimensions. This understanding of the Qur'anic genesis implies a process, not of authorial writing but of intra-communal debate, one that extended from the beginning of the Qur'anic proclamation until the death of the proclaimer. It is therefore necessary to regard not only extra-Qur'anic intertextuality but also intra-Qur'anic intertextuality as well, i.e. the constant revisiting of earlier proclaimed texts that during the proclamation are reviewed under newly discovered theological aspects.

It is noteworthy that this negotiation is carried out without any polemical bias vis-à-vis the earlier traditions; these are not explicitly rejected but rather amalgamated into a new overall imagery. Paradisiacal imagery for the Quranic community acquires surplus momentum, however. First of all, paradise narratives constitute a crucial instrument in promoting the new eschatological theology[18]. But they also possess another even more momentous function, which has until now been ignored in scholarship: paradise imagery serves to counterbalance and ultimately to replace particular powerful pagan perceptions of reality that were predominant in the minds of the contemporaries of the Qur'an. I am referring here to the ancient Arab poet's lament about the contingency of reality and the transitoriness of human achievements in particular. Qur'anic descriptions of paradise, as will be demonstrated, serve to invert the predominant imagery of pagan thought by re-arranging its elements to form the counter-image of everlasting bliss.

The following observations will be limited to early Meccan suras which have been thoroughly studied in the recently published Concise Commentary[19], i.e. Q 78, 88, 83 and 55. Q 55, which presents the climax of Qur'anic descriptions of paradise, will occupy particular attention. Due to our limited space, the two Meccan suras that chronologically succeed Q 55 immediately, Q 56 and Q 52, also discussed in the Concise Commentary, have to remain excluded from our present investigation. Nor will there be reference to the numerous later Meccan paradise-related texts. A summary of the peculiar features of the later paradise

18 Wild, *Virgins of Paradise*, 627-647.

19 Neuwirth, *Der Koran I*. This work attempts to establish a reliable chronological sequence of the early suras.

depictions has been given by Stefan Wild[20], yet their intra-Qur'anic development and their theological status within the later proclamation still await investigation.

3. Qur'anic Developments

From early times onward the Quranic community is concerned with the fate that awaits men after the Last Judgment. Since the earlier–cyclical–perception of time had been replaced by the new view of time as passing in linear motion from creation to the eschatological rendering of account[21], the door was open for an imagination of life in the Beyond. Already in early Meccan suras, the eschatological fate of the condemned, the 'Evildoers', as well as the acquitted, the 'Just', is discussed. Yet, it is not the Just, the God-fearing, *mani ttaqā*, who are placed in the foreground, but rather their negative counterparts, the arrogant, *mani staghnā*, who are blamed for refusing to accept, *kadhdhaba*, the monotheist message and who at the same time are accused of neglecting their social duties, i.e. those contemporaries who still adhere to the anthropocentric worldview of ancient Arabia. They are threatened with punishment in the future, a future that in the earliest texts is still abstract. Even in such suras like Q 102, *al-ḥuḥama*, "The Clatterer", which is completely dedicated to the condemnation of a reprehensible type of contemporary, punishment is not yet located in a determinable space but remains confined to the mythical realm, connected to the image of a gluttonous monster prepared to devour the blameworthy individual.

Only midway through the early Meccan proclamation[22] do we find a stronger focus on the eschatological events in detail. Already some of the first suras, Q 80, 79, 75 and 70, had thrown light on the situation of humankind on the Last Day, focusing in particular on the isolation of man from his clan as the most menacing prospect. Short sections of these suras, Q 80:38-39, 40-42, Q 79:37-39, 40-41 and Q 75:22-23, 24-25, had already presented contrastive verdicts on the fates of the Condemned and the Blessed. These texts did not yet, however, involve iconic depictions. More differentiated diptycha[23] (contrastive images) are found only later, in Q 78:21-26, 31-36 and Q 88:2-7, 8-16. It is Q 78 that is the first Quranic text to depict the situation of the Blessed in terms of a banquet (Q 78:31-36)–an image that will be more fully developed in the slightly later Q 88:8-16. In both cases, the depiction of paradise is preluded by a mirror image depicting the space of the Condemned. Only in Q 78 and Q 88, thus, is the breakthrough achieved: the Qur'anic Beyond has accumulated sufficient imagery to become congenial with earlier imaginations of a transcendent place of bliss, be it the Jewish and Chris-

---

20 Ibid.

21 Tamer, *Zeit und Gott*, see also Neuwirth, *Koran als Text der Spätantike*, 211-214 and 607-612.

22 We are following here the sequence proposed in Neuwirth, *Der Koran I*.

23 For a detailed description of the literary genres and subgenres of the Quran see Neuwirth, *Studien zur Komposition*.

tian place of consummate nature, be it the pagan late antique *locus amoenus*, the "delightful place", although this place in the Qur'an always remains understood as a counter-place to Hell. Paradise and Hell constitute a diptych.

4. The early Meccan paradise descriptions previous to Q 55

The earliest detailed paradise description is found in Q 78:31–36, it is preceded by its negative mirror image, a depiction of hell, Q 78:21–26[24]:

21 *inna jahannama kānat mirṣādā*
22 *lil-ṭāghīna maʾābā*
23 *lābithīna fīhā aḥqābā*
24 *lā yadhūqūna fīhā bardan wa-lā sharābā*
25 *illā hamīman wa-ghassāqā*
26 *jazāʾan wifāqā*

21 Behold, Gehenna has become an ambush,
22 for the insolent a resort,
23 therein to tarry for ages,
24 tasting therein neither coolness nor any drink,
25 save boiling water and pus,
26 for a suitable recompense.

31 *inna lil-muttaqīna mafāzā*
32 *ḥadāʾiqa wa-aʿnābā*
33 *wa-kawāʿiba atrābā*
34 *wa-kaʾsan dihāqā*
35 *lā yasmaʿūna fīhā laghwan wa-lā kidhdhābā*
36 *jazāʾan min rabbika ʿaṭāʾan ḥisābā*

31 Surely, the God-fearing awaits a place of security,
32 gardens and vineyards,
33 and maidens with swelling breasts like of age,
34 and a cup overflowing.

The depiction is limited to only a few features, which together evoke the scenario of a banquet: the inmates of the *mafāz*, the place of bliss, will be accommodated in gardens and vineyards to enjoy wine drinking in the presence of beautiful maidens, being aloof from the idle talk and false accusations put forward by their erstwhile opponents. Though this depiction is constructed as a reverse projection of the image of Hell promised to the evildoers, who are offered nothing to cool the heat they suffer from the blaze surrounding them but only hot and disgusting libation, it should not be understood as a mere inversion of the description of Hell. Whereas the image of Hell seems to follow a novel, Qur'anic design, paradise, in contrast, partakes in the imagery of Biblical heritage: the filled cup, *kaʾs dihāq*,

24 The translation is that of Arberry, *The Koran.*

resounds Ps 23:5 *kosi rewayah,* the vineyard, *aʿnāb,* whose shade is enjoyed by the Just alludes to Micha 4:42. As to the framework of a banquet, there are predecessors in the imagery of the Qumranic community. Their "ritual meal (...) is both a foreshadowing and a quasi-sacramental anticipation of the great eschatological messianic banquet that is often referred to in other religious writings of the period, e.g. the New Testament."[25] As against that, Horovitz[26] has pointed to the closely related depictions of banquets in pagan ancient Arabic poetry equally featuring young and beautiful women. The image of women accompanying or receiving the dead in their *post-mortem* abode is known not only from Iranian tradition[27] but equally from Greco-Roman culture[28]. The image should have been familiar to the listeners of the Qur'an since the maidens seem not in need of introduction, they are only alluded to through the mention of their characteristic attributes. In Q 78, they simply form part of the luxurious equipment of the "Garden", and it is only in the somewhat later text Q 55 that they are assigned to the Blessed as partners, and in Q 52, the last text in the first Meccan period, that they are finally married to them.

The next following detailed depiction of paradise is Q 88:8–16, it is again preceded by a description of Hell, V. 2–7:

1 *hal atāka ḥadīthu l-ghāshiya*
2 *wujūhun yawmaʾidhin khāshiʿa*
3 *ʿāmilatun nāṣiba*
4 *taṣlā nāran ḥāmiya*
5 *tusqā min ʿaynin āniya*
6 *laysa lahum ṭaʿāmun illā min ḍarīʿ*
7 *lā yusminu wa-lā yughnī min jūʿ*

1 Hast thou received the story of the Enveloper?
2 Faces on that day are humbled,
3 labouring, toilworn,
4 roasting at a scorching fire,
5 watered at a boiling fountain,
6 no food for them but cactus thorn,
7 unfattening, unappeasing hunger.

8 *wujūhun yawmaʾidhin nāʿima*
9 *li-saʿyihā rāḍiya*
10 *fī jannatin ʿāliya*
11 *lā tasmaʿu fīhā lāghiya*

---

25 Klausner, *Eschatology*, 623.

26 Horovitz, *Das koranische Paradies*, 1-16.

27 Tisdall, *Original Sources*, 235-238.

28 Jarrar, *Martyrdom*, 87-108, Saleh, *The Woman*, 123-145.–In Jewish tradition–as attested in the late compilation *Yalqut Shimoni*–the presence of sexuality can at least be deduced from the statement that the Blessed will be granted to experience the enjoyments of the three stages of the human life cycle every day, cf. Rosenkranz Verhelst, *Himmel und Heiligtum*, 44.

12 *fīhā ʿaynun jāriya*
13 *fīhā sururun marfūʿa*
14 *wa-akwabun mawḍūʿa*
15 *wa-namāriqu maṣfūfa*
16 *wa-zarābiyyu mabthūtha*

8 Faces on that day jocund
9 with their striving well-pleased
10 in a sublime garden,
11 hearing there no babble;
12 therein a running fountain,
13 therein uplifted coaches
14 and goblets set forth
15 and cushions arayed
16 and carpets outspread.

This paradise description responds to a particularly cynical description of Hell, where the inmates, again, are refused cool drink to ease their suffering from the heat of the blaze that surrounds them. In this text, furthermore, they are fed not with food edible for humans, but with the fodder of animals, bushwood, which is cynically presented as "unfattening, unappeasing". In contrast, the Just are promised entrance to an elevated place (whose particular status, however, remains unspecified). It is—like in Q 78—a place safe from disturbing idle talk. Like in Q 78 it is a garden, which in this text is watered by a fountain. No mention of female companions is made, whose presence may perhaps be assumed as self-understood. Instead the focus is placed on the equipment of the space with urban furniture: there are sofas in the style of antique *klinai*, cushions, *namāriq*[29], carpets, *zarābiyy*[30]—both obviously, as their foreign names suggest, precious Iranian import ware. In Rabbinic descriptions the "righteous (are) sitting at golden tables" (bTaan 25a) or under elaborate canopies (Ruth rabba 3:4) and participating in lavish banquets (BB 75a)[31].—There are also the indispensible vessels of any banquet scenario: cups awaiting the guests. Nature retreats into the background, urban furniture and equipment taking its place. Paradise acquires the character of a courtly banquet.

In contrast to these images, Q 83:22, a text that within the proclamation process immediately follows Q 88, contains only a brief reminiscence of the pomp laid bare in Q 88. The depiction, this time, is not preceded by a reverse image describing Hell:

22 *inna l-abrāra la-fī naʿīm*
23 *ʿalā l-arāʾiki yanẓurūn*
24 *taʿrifu fī wujūhihim naḍrata l-naʿīm*

---

29 For *namāriq* see Jeffery, *Foreign vocabulary*, 181.

30 For *zarābiyy* see Jeffery, *ibid.*, 150.

31 Bamberger, *Paradise*, 628 (there "Ruth rabba 3:4" is erroneously rendered as "Ruth 3.4"), cf. Rosenkranz Verhelst, *Himmel und Heiligtum*, 46.

25 *yusqawna min raḥīqin makhtūm*
26 *khitāmuhu miskun wa-fī dhālika fa-l-yatanāfasi l-mutanāfisūn*
27 *wa-mizājuhu min tasnīm*
28 *ʿaynan yashrabu bihā l-muqarrabūn*

22 Surely, the pious shall be in bliss
23 upon couches gazing:
24 thou knowest in their faces the radiance of bliss
25 as they are given to drink of a wine sealed,
26 whose seal is musk–so after that let the strivers strive –
27 and whose mixture is Tasmim,
28 a fountain of which do drink those brought nigh.

In this case the depiction is tied to the reality of the addressees of the Qur'an who are made observers of the Blessed in paradise: their bliss is recognizable from their faces, as the addressees would immediately discern. Paradisiacal recompense is particularly generous and attractive. This should be an incentive for the Qur'an's audience to emulate the earthly behavior of the Blessed. In this description, no trace of a particularly lush nature, nor any mention of the female companions is found. Instead the entire scene is filled with a description of the urban aspects of the place: the paradisiacal wine, its seal, its water of mixture[32], the luxurious furniture[33]–and the pleasant looks of the inhabitants of paradise.

The desire to recover 'Lost aspects of the world in the Hereafter' is certainly in the focus of the Qur'anic presentations of paradise. Yet there is also the reverse image of the world offering glimpses of paradise. Both these references to Paradise are mirrored in Qur'anic texts which built on individual Psalms.

5. Sura 55–a hermeneutical turning point

Q 55, *Sūrat al-Raḥmān* contains the most elaborate description of paradise in the entire Qur'an. Hence, a brief introduction is necessary. The sura is one of the most poetic texts in the Qur'an and exemplifies a central *theologoumenon*: the symmetry of the divine order of creation, not only on the semantic level, but equally in grammatical and phonetic terms. Symmetry is thus not only pointed out to the listener as part of the content of divine speech, it is equally displayed in terms of structure, a procedure made possible by a unique device offered by Arabic morphology, i.e., the dual form. The excessive use of the dual, by virtue of its prominent position in pre-Islamic poetic compositions, implies an aesthetic claim that is unfamiliar to most Jewish and Christian scriptural texts: a claim to poeticity. The poetic character of the Qur'an has often been dismissed as merely

32 The promise of flavoured wine–deduced from Cant 8.2–is part of a rabbinic (though later compiled) description of Paradise, see Rosenkranz Verhelst, *Himmel und Heiligtum*, 32.

33 For *arāʾik* see Jeffery, *ibid.*, 52.

"ornamental," constituting an obstacle to the reader's immediate grasp of the message. In the case of Q 55, the poetic style is clearly part of the message itself. Symmetry in this text is as much a characteristic of the signified as it is of the sign itself. For the harmoniously balanced order is manifest in binary structures exhibited in the "clear speech" of the Qur'an itself. The prooemium of the sura even gives precedence to the communication of word over creation:

1 *Al-Raḥmān*
2 *ʿallama l-Qurʾān*
3 *khalaqa l-insān*
4 *ʿallamahu l-bayān.*

1 The All-merciful –
2 he taught the Koran,
3 he created man,
4 he taught him clear speech/clear understanding.

In view of the fact that the divine Word, qurʾān, and by extension the recitation of the Qur'an itself, is considered as the most sublime speech act, *bayān* can be understood as an evocation of Qur'anic language. At the same time it may denote the human capacity of clear speech based on clear understanding. Thus, two phenomena that are inherent in the world since the act of creation itself–namely, the harmonious order of beings, and the distinctness and clarity of speech as a medium of communication–thematically permeate the entire sura.

The text thus can be read as an exposition of the interaction of the primordial ensemble evoked in the beginning–*khalq,* creation, and qurʾān, divine instruction–which, according to the Qur'anic paradigm, in a linear motion leads up to the dissolution of both elements at the end of time. The duality thus constitutes an intrinsic part of the Qur'an's natural theology: that God has created the world as a manifestation of his presence, as a "text" no less than his verbal manifestation in revelation, and that he has created man in order that he may understand both his verbal and his "creational" self-expression. Both readings gain their urgency from their eschatological objective. Q 55, with its insistence on symmetry and dualistic structures, is the poetic orchestration of a theological claim. On the basis of these observations, the sophisticated linguistic shape of the text proves highly significant, and indeed functional, something that the sura has been continuously denied in Western scholarship that has consistently found fault with the dual forms dismissing them as merely resulting from rhyme constrains.

6. The paradise sections of Q 55

46 *wa-li-man khāfa maqāma rabbihi jannatān*
47 *fa-bi-ayyi ālā'i rabbikumā tukadhdhibān*
48 *dhawātā afnān*
49 *fa-bi-ayyi ālā'i rabbikumā tukadhdhibān*
50 *fīhimā 'aynāni tajriyān*
51 *fa-bi-ayyi ālā'i rabbikumā tukadhdhibān*
52 *fīhimā min kulli fākihatin zawjān*
53 *fa-bi-ayyi ālā'i rabbikumā tukadhdhibān*
54 *muttaki'īna 'alā furushin baṭā'inhua min istabraqin*
wa-janā l-jannatayni dān
55 *fa-bi-ayyi ālā'i rabbikumā tukadhdhibān*
56 *fīhinna qāṣiratu l-ṭarfi*
lam yaṭmithhunna insun qablahum wa-lā jānn
57 *fa-bi-ayyi ālā'i rabbikumā tukadhdhibān*
58 *ka-annahunna l-yāqūtu wa-l-marjān*
59 *fa-bi-ayyi ālā'i rabbikumā tukadhdhibān*
60 *hal jazā'u l-iḥsāni illā l-iḥsān*
61 *fa-bi-ayyi ālā'i rabbikumā tukadhdhibān*

62 *wa-min dūnihimā jannatān*
63 *fa-bi-ayyi ālā'i rabbikumā tukadhdhibān*
64 *mudhāmmatān*
65 *fa-bi-ayyi ālā'i rabbikumā tukadhdhibān*
66 *fīhima 'aynāni naḍḍākhatān*
67 *fa-bi-ayyi ālā'i rabbikumā tukadhdhibān*
68 *fīhimā fākihatun wa-nakhlun wa-rummān*
69 *fa-bi-ayyi ālā'i rabbikumā tukadhdhibān*
70 *fīhinna khayrātun ḥisān*
71 *fa-bi-ayyi ālā'i rabbikumā tukadhdhibān*
72 *ḥūrun maqṣūrātun fī l-khiyām*
73 *fa-bi-ayyi ālā'i rabbikumā tukadhdhibān*
74 *lam yaṭmithhunna insun qablahum wa-lā jānn*
75 *fa-bi-ayyi ālā'i rabbikumā tukadhdhibān*
76 *muttaki'īna 'alā rafrafin khuḍrin wa-'abqarīyin ḥisān*
77 *fa-bi-ayyi ālā'i rabbikumā tukadhdhibān*
78 *tabāraka smu rabbika dhī l-jalāli wa-l-ikrām*

46 But such as fears the Station of his Lord, for them shall be two gardens --
47 O which of your Lord's bounties will you and you deny?
48 abounding in branches–
49 O which of your Lord's bounties will you and you deny?
50 therein two fountains of running water -
51 O which of your Lord's bounties will you and you deny?
52 therein of every fruit two kinds -
53 O which of your Lord's bounties will you and you deny?
54 reclining upon couches lined with brocade, the fruits of the gardens
nigh to gather --
55 O which of your Lord's bounties will you and you deny?

56 therein maidens restraining their glances, untouched before them by any man or jinn
57 O which of your Lord's bounties will you and you deny?
58 lovely as rubies, beautiful as coral –
59 O which of your Lord's bounties will you and you deny?
60 Shall the recompense of goodness be other than goodness?
61 O which of your Lord's bounties will you and you deny?
62 And besides these shall be two gardens –
63 O which of your Lord's bounties will you and you deny?
64 green, green pastures --
65 O which of your Lord's bounties will you and you deny?
66 therein two fountains of gushing water –
67 O which of your Lord's bounties will you and you deny?
68 therein fruits, and palm-trees, and pomegranates –
69 O which of your Lord's bounties will you and you deny?
70 therein maidens good and comely –
71 O which of your Lord's bounties will you and you deny?
72 houris, cloistered in cool pavilions –
73 O which of your Lord's bounties will you and you deny?
74 untouched before them by any man or jinn --
75 O which of your Lord's bounties will you and you deny?
76 reclining upon green cushions and lovely druggets –
77 O which of your Lord's bounties will you and you deny?
78 Blessed be the Name of thy Lord, majestic, splendid

After an elaborate portrayal of creation (v. 1–36) and judgment (37–45) with their *binary* juxtapositions, there is the promise (v. 46) *li-man khāfa maqāma rabbihi jannatān* ("but for such who fears the Station of his Lord, for them shall be two gardens"). This is the only verse where the dual form cannot be explained in terms of any of the paired phenomena mentioned earlier in the text. This exception calls for an explanation. A parallel case appears in the second description of paradise, where again *two* gardens are mentioned (v. 62), *wa-min dūnihimā jannatān* ("and besides these shall be two gardens"). *Jannatān* (literally,"two gardens") is best interpreted with reference to the conventions of ancient Arabic poetry, which often uses dual forms in topographic contexts to denote only one extended place, or–even more probably–with reference to the understanding of some classical Arabic philologists as an expression of infiniteness: "garden after garden, infinite gardens."[34] The text depicts (twice: vs. 46–61; 62–77) the image

[34] The understanding of the dual form *jannatān* (Q 55:46–76) proposed in Western scholarship as due to constraints of rhyme is found already with al-Farrā', *Ma'ānī al-qur'ān*, 118 and al-Suyūṭī, *Itqān*, vol.3, 299; the latter instance is quoted by Wansbrough, *Quranic Studies*, 25. Wansbrough, however, fails to mention that the use of dual forms for a singular *metri causa* is a most frequent phenomenon in ancient Arabic poetry, where even fixed conventions emerged like the poet's stereotypical address of two friends in the *nasīb* (see e.g. Nöldeke, *Delectus*, 8.5, 12.14 etc.) or the phenomenon of two slanderers (ibid., 8.8); see the additional examples collected by Gandz, *Mu'allaqa*, and Goldziher, *'Ijādat al-mariḍ*, 185–200. Dual forms without numerical value are particularly frequent in toponyms; once

of the Blessed residing in a garden with lush nature; v. 48: "abounding in branches", and plenty of fruit; v. 52: "therein of every fruit two kinds". In the first garden scenario (vv. 46-60), one might understand v.50 *ʿaynāni tajriyān* ("two fountains of running water") as a mechanistic concession to congruence with *jannatān*; however, this is clearly impossible in the case of the phrase *min kulli fākihatin zawjān* ("therein is a pair of every fruit") that immediately follows v.52, since in this case a basic Quranic perception is evoked that is expressed in various texts, cf. Q 51:49: *min kulli shayʾin khalaqnā zawjayni, laʿallakum tadhakkarūn* ("and of everything we have created a pair, that perchance you might remember"). The blessings of lush vegetation and plenty of water are complemented by the presence of beautiful maidens.

In accordance with the sura's characteristic construction of the created world from *paired* elements these maidens are compared to *two* complementary objects, in the one case presenting a variation of an observation expressed in the hymnal part, v. 58: *ka-annahunna l-yāqūtu wa-l-marjān,* "lovely as rubies, beautiful as coral" (cf. v.22: *yakhruju minhumā l-luʾluʾu wa-l-marjān*), in the other case being described by *two* qualifications (v. 72). In spite of the prominence of the maidens' virginity (vv. 56.74), no erotic dynamics is perceivable between them and the blessed, who remain as motionless as the maidens themselves, fixed to their luxurious seats. The last verse of the second description focusing the furniture and textile equipment of the space again introduces a *binary* juxtaposition: v. 76, *muttakiʾīna ʿalā rafrafin khuḍrin wa-ʿabqarīyin ḥisān* ("reclining upon green cushions and superb rugs"). The final proclamation introduces a last contrasting *pair*: the antithetical manifestations *jalāl* ("majesty," comparable to the rabbinic *middat had-dīn,* the power of exerting judgment and thus punishment) and *ikrām* ("generosity," comparable to the rabbinic *middat ha-raḥamīm,* the power that manifests itself in the generous forgiveness). The text closes with a doxology.

The description in Q 55:46-78—uniquely in the Quran—according to its literal sense thus presents a "double paradise image": Not only are there "two gardens" instead of one, but the duplicated garden is also presented twice, figuring in two subsequent, slightly divergent descriptions (vs. 46-61; 62-78). Expectedly, these duplicated paradises are replete with paired topics—a phenomenon that has long puzzled scholars. As said before, the frequent dual forms should not be taken in their literal, numerical sense, but as figures in a highly poetical and playful demonstration of linguistic virtuosity. One has to remember that Q 55 pursues a particular hermeneutical trajectory: to demonstrate the harmonious and balanced structure of creation. It follows that any proper description of the symmetry of creation demands an equally sophisticated, "dual-loaded" language to match its

these dual forms are transferred into extra-poetical contexts, they continue to convey their poeticity. This fact has been noted by a number of Arab classical philologists, see Neuwirth, *Symmetrie,* 447-480. The apparent doubling of the gardens is less extraordinary than it may look. The play with the possibilities of Arabic morphology, familiar from poetry, should have caused far less problems to contemporary listeners than to the later readers, who were pre-disposed and limited by the positivist approaches of Islamic exegesis.

ontological harmony. The thesis that language is on par with creation is a major topic of the sura and has been discussed in detail elsewhere[35].

Furthermore some semantic peculiarities that seem to have exerted considerable influence on the later readers' perception of the Qur'anic paradise should be noted. What was already looming in the earlier paradise descriptions becomes evident in the elaborate portrayal of Q 55: the Quranic paradisiacal abode presents itself surprisingly distinct from both the Jewish and Christian eschatological paradise[36]. Though it is meant as a reward granted to the Virtuous in general, the space is obviously a gendered space. Those invited to enter the garden are male persons, who are honored according to the *decorum* of contemporary courtly hospitality. Part of their reward is the enjoyment of the erotic company of beautiful maidens, whom they find present at the site; vs. 56, 58: "therein maidens restraining their glances// lovely like rubies, beautiful like corals", vs. 71, 73: "therein maidens good and comely// houris cloistered in pavilions"[37]. They are–indirectly–assigned to be their sexual partners, this thought seems to underlie the assertion that they are "untouched before them by any man or jinn", vs. 56, 74. No surprise that this gendered social image of paradise later called for an adjustment: later suras and even secondary additions to early suras (Q 52:21) contain promises securing the participation of the families (Q 13:23; 36:56: wives) of the inhabitants of paradise, as well, in the eschatological Bliss. Yet, the image of the eschatological paradise first arises in the shape described above: as a space promising courtly enjoyments to privileged male elect.–Another peculiarity unknown from the Jewish and Christian imagination of paradise is the fact that the Blessed are surrounded by luxurious furniture and precious textiles; vs. 75: "green cushions and lovely druggets", as well as furniture of courtly luxury; v. 84: "couches lined with brocade". These observations raise the question: How can the presence of the corporally erotic, on the one hand, and the traces of material civilization, even luxury, on the other hand, be explained? More precisely: What is their function?

---

35 Neuwirth, *Koran als Text der Spätantike*, 433-448.

36 Within Judaism, eschatological perceptions of paradise had been developed in particular in apocalyptic works such as the first book on Enoch (second century BC), and the targums (Aramaic translations) at Genesis. In Christianity, the Genesis story in the Pshitta (Syriac Bible) itself reflects an understanding of paradise as both primordial and eschatological.

37 The designation "Houri" used by Arberry is derived from the plural form "ḥūr" of the Arabic adjective *aḥwar, ḥawrāʾ*, meaning "having eyes in which the contrast between black and white is particularly intense". In Q 55:73 the word *ḥūr* is not yet the designation of "virgins of paradise" but rather a qualification of the "maidens good and comely" mentioned in Q 55:71. The word which had not been known as a technical term before its introduction through the Qur'an has been questioned as to its traditionally accepted meaning designating women, see for the controversy raised by the hypothesis of Luxenberg who claimed a completely different meaning ("grapes"), Wild, *Virgins of Paradise*, and Saleh, *The etymological fallacy*.

7. Paradisiacal Imaginations in Late Antiquity

It is sometimes forgotten that the Quran is neither directly derived from the Bible nor necessarily from Biblical tradition exclusively. This is particularly evident in the case of its depiction of paradise. Here, other textual precursors need to be taken into account. The presence of the erotic in the hereafter–looked upon from a broader perspective–is not as extraordinary as it may appear on first sight. Once we leave the Biblical model of the afterlife aside, there is ample evidence for the presence of women who accompany men *post mortem*. For example, in the Hellenistic pagan context, the ancient goddess of victory, Nike, carries off the dead worrior to his *post-mortem* abode[38]. Iranian lore knows of female figures taking care of the male dead as well[39]. And even within Biblical tradition, Church fathers such as Irenaeus (third century CE) discussed the question if corporeal sexual relations should be imagined as continuing in paradise[40]. Proto-monastic ideals would, however, eventually win the day. Later authorities, such as the Syrian theologian Ephrem of Nisibis (303-373) in his "Hymns on Paradise", rigorously spiritualized sexuality; yet Ephrem's poetry at the same time leaves no doubt that he too imagined paradise not free from erotic terms. He states in his second "Hymn on Paradise":

Ṭūbaw l-man da-hwā rgīgā l-pardaysā
d-rā'eg w-bāla' leh b-tar'eh l-šappīrā
b-'ūbeh mḥabbeb leh b-karseh mnaṣṣar leh
ṣārē w-sā'em leh b-gaw mā'aw
w-en dēn g'aṣ men (')nāš pāleṭ w-šādē leh
d-tar'eh hū d-buḥrānā d-rāḥem bnay (')nāšā

"Blessed be he for whom Paradise yearns.
Yes, Paradise yearns for the man whose
goodness makes him beautiful,
it engulfs him at its gateway,
it embraces him in its bosom, it caresses him in its very womb;
for it splits open and receives him into its inmost parts.
But if there is someone it abhors,
It removes him and casts him out;
This is the gate of testing
That belongs to Him who loves mankind"[41].

In the seventh Hymn eroticism becomes even more explicit:

Aynā d-men ḥamrā ṣām hwā b-puršānā
leh ṣāwḥān yattīr gupnaw d-pardaysā
wa-ḥdā ḥdā sgūlāh mawšṭā tettel leh

---

38 Adolf Lumpe, Hans Bietenhard, *Himmel*,173-212.

39 Tisdall, *Original Sources*, 235-238.

40 Jarrar, *Martyrdom*, 87-108.

41 Brock, *St. Ephrem*, 84.

w-en dēn bṭūlā hwā tūb a ʿlīh
l-gaw ʿūbhen dakyā d-meṭṭūl īḥīdāyā
lā npal b-guw ʿūbā w-ʿarsa d-zuwwāgā.

"The man who abstained, with understanding, from wine,
will the vines of paradise rush out to meet, all the more joyfully,
as each one stretches out and proffers him its clusters;
or if any has lived a life of virginity, him too they welcome into their bosom,
for the solitary such as he has never lain in any bosom nor upon any marriage bed"[42].

Of the two imaginations of paradise, the Qur'an's, however, is distinctly diverse. In comparison with Ephrem's allegorically tuned poetry, the imagination of the female eroticism in the Qur'an appears rather realistic and hence more in line with its pagan predecessors. This anti-allegorical trend fits with a common characteristic of the Qur'an, one that may be described as a textually critically program of analysis intending to de-allegorize Christian readings of Biblical narratives[43]. So Ephrem's poetry, though probably not unfamiliar to the Qur'anic community as other parallel evidence would suggest, and bears little resemblance in its treatment of paradise to the Qur'anic scenario of an assembly of privileged men and beautiful women in a luxurious ambience. Thus it is not Ephrem's hymns that can explain or solve the quandary regarding both the physical presence of women as well as the traces of material goods and worldly culture in the Qur'anic paradise. Both of these latter traits are difficult to reconcile with the vision of a purely spiritual abode.

Nor is an explanation available through a reference to the Rabbinic imagination of the heavenly abode, "Gan Eden", where "the Righteous are sitting at golden tables or under elaborate canopies", since here the two elements of lush nature and the erotic companions are missing—according to bBer 17a there will be no sensual enjoyment in Gan Eden[44].

8. The Pagan Subtext

It is helpful to remember, that the Qur'an is last but not least the heir to the most sophisticated pagan Arabic poetry. As early as 1923[45], Josef Horovitz assumed that Qur'anic paradisiacal scenarios reflect banquet scenes from ancient Arabic poetry. Looking closely at the Qur'anic descriptions we do not, however, find a banquet in the vein described by the ancient poets, but rather a static tableau portraying groups of men and women in a place of lush nature that bears at the same time courtly traits, being furnished with aesthetically refined artifacts. Although

---

42 Brock, *St. Ephrem, 125* (I owe the transcription of the Syriac original to the kind support of my cooperators Yousef Kouriyhe and David Kiltz, *Corpus-Coranicum*).

43 Neuwirth, *Koran als Teyt der Spätantike*, 590-595.

44 Bamberger, *Paradise*, 628.

45 Horovitz, *Paradies*, 1-16.

this is not a reference to any particular episode of ancient poetry, it is a poetical reference and quite a universal one at that. Descriptions of paradise–this is the thesis raised in our contribution[46]–are a response to the more general outlook expressed in the ancient Arabic *qaṣīda*. They constitute an nothing less than an inversion of the image presented in its initial part, the elegiac and nostalgic *nasīb*, which depicts the previously inhabited encampments revisited by the poet as a wasteland, a landscape of ruins, stripped of its civilization, relinquished by its inhabitants and inaccessible to communication. One of the most famous ancient Arabic *qaṣidas*, by the poet Labid, sets out with the words: "Effaced (literally: extinguished) are the abodes", *ʿafati l–diyāru*. These words, or similar uses of the same cultural metaphor[47], formulate and evoke in the audience's mind the stereotypical beginning of a large number of poems, all of which conjure up the emptiness of space and a loss of communication. Frequently these descriptions of deserted campsites are metaphorized as inscriptions on the body: The traces of the deserted campsites are reminiscent of the faint lines engraved on a wrist, or–which is even more revealing–they develop into the evocative trope of rock graffiti or inscriptions, *waḥy*. There is, then, a meaningful message immanent in the writing and in the deserted space, which is hidden from the beholder. To the poet-hero, both the extinguished campsite and the lost beloved, who is the second main topic of the *nasīb*, are negations: allegories of irreversible time, irretrievable meaning, and unrecoverable emotional fulfillment. The place is perceived as desolate since the luxuriously furnished caravans have taken the women, and with them the poet's beloved, away to be swallowed by a mirage[48]. The *nasīb* thus serves to express an *aporia*.

Nature defies the poet, not responding to his ever repeated question of "*ubi sunt qui ante nos in mundo fuere,*[49]" about the whereabouts of the formerly pulsating social life, the reliable social structures, the aesthetic equipment of the living space with its promise of erotic pleasure. All culture and human achievement falls prey to time or are obscured by nature. In the end, the familiar topos of popular Hellenistic philosophy reminds the listener that nature alone is capable of cyclically renewing itself; man is destined to perish and decompose. For the ancient Arabic poets, it is nature's eternity that underscores the transitoriness of man and his achievements. The poet Labīd, an older contemporary of the Prophet, says:

Balīnā wa-lā tablā l-nujūmu l-ṭawāliʿu, wa-tabqā l-jibālu baʿdanā wa-l-maṣāniʿu.

"We vanish but the rising stars do not, mountains remain when we are gone and fortresses". Time does not affect nature, which is eternal, *khālid*, allowing repeat-

46 It has been put forward earlier in Neuwirth, *Psalms*, 711-717.

47 See an inventory in Montgomery, *The deserted encampments*.

48 See Stetkevych's interpretation of Labid's poem, in her *The Mute Immortals Speak*.

49 The sustained presence of the late antique topos has been aptly demonstrated by Becker, 'Ubi sunt'.

ed recurrences ad infinitum. In contrast, man is caught and "consumed" by time, the concept itself popularly associated with *dahr*, fate.

It is this perception of nature as overwhelming man and his culture that the Qur'an has come to refute: God himself commands fate and re-shapes the time of man, which now ranges from the primordial creation of the world and the coincidental creation of the logos–i.e., divine instruction and man's innate faculty of understanding, *bayān*–to the end of the world on Judgment Day, when man will redeem the pledge of divine instruction; it even extends into the Hereafter, which the Qur'an diegetically transforms into the spatial image of paradise. The Qur'anic description of paradise not only reverses the erstwhile bleak and threatening conception of nature into something ever-green and fruit-bearing, but it also preserves civilization: precious cushions and carpets, cups filled with wine that had been sealed with musk, and moreover the presence of beautiful young women, known from the *nasīb* as icons of a meaningful and enjoyable life. Paradise is a space where man is reinvested with his cultural paraphernalia.

9. The plural functions of the Qur'anic paradise

This hypothesis which tries to offer an explanation as to why the Qur'an introduces such a courtly image of paradise would remain mere guesswork were it not for the second connection between the *nasīb* of the *qaṣīda* and the Qur'anic paradise, which we already alluded to: the Qur'anic re-interpretation of *waḥy*[50]. What has seldom been recognized in scholarship is the fact that the *qaṣīda* both laments the transitoriness of human achievements *and* complains of the "non-readabilty" of reality, which is regarded as a situation of collective loss. The poet who has halted to trace the deserted campsite of his former sojourn with his beloved is confronted not only with his loss, but with a hermeneutical *aporia* as well: Where have those people gone who used to furnish the place with social life and its pleasures, why has the erstwhile populated place fallen into ruin? The poet turns to the traces of the campsite in order to "ask them", to search for the meaning of his present apprehension of reality. The ruins he addresses, however, remain mute, thus reminding him of an unreadable inscription, a *waḥy*, which bears a message linguistically incomprehensible to him. *Waḥy* is an important term in ancient Arabic poetry, denoting any non-verbal "sign language". Yet this term bears a pronouncedly negative connotation due to its prominent employment in the poet's lament about the contingency of worldly reality. In its Qur'anic re-employment, *wahy* receives a new inverted meaning: it comes to denote the most important medium of communication to be imagined: communication with the divine articulated in the Qur'anic message. One might have expected the introduction of a term to denote God's communication to his elect as something familiar or shared with other monotheist cultures, such as an Arabic rendering of the Greek *apokalypsis*, or the Syriac *galyutha*. The Qur'an however refers to the core

50 Neuwirth, *Koran als Text der Spätantike*, 711-716.

corpus of Arabic literary articulations by ingeniously using the local poetic term *waḥy* and inverting its meaning. *Waḥy* thus has come to denote the exact opposite meaning of unintelligible sign language. The poet's bleak psychological state and his inability to comprehend reality are obsolete discursive fields. The new Qur'anic definition of *waḥy* has henceforth rendered the term a positive force, one that clarifies existential and material ambiguity through the divine and definitive knowledge and inspiration of God.

Q 55 has been demonstrated to be a re-working of a Biblical psalm, Ps 136[51]. The psalm text like the sura in its introductory section records the events of primordial creation; it shifts however, in its core section, to a completely different topic, i.e. God's interventions in the history of his elect people. It is at this point that the sura diverges from the psalm; in the Qur'anic perspective God's presence is less manifest regarding his care for his people in situations of political crisis in history than in the universal act of creation with its eschatological fulfillment in paradise on the one hand and the communication of his word on the other. Yet the Qur'an does engage in a discourse of history as well: Qur'anic descriptions of paradise provoke reflections on history and historical consciousness by rewriting ancient Arabic poetry. The refrain of Psalm 136 "God's grace lasts forever", echoed in the refrain of Q 55 "O which of your lord's bounties will you and you deny?"—connects with an inversion of the ancient Arabic conception of all-overpowering time, claiming that "God disempowers devastating time".

This shift in interest from history to eschatology is accompanied by a particular and well-defined meta-discourse: the hermeneutical accessibility of the cosmos, God's presence in language. The Qur'an attempts nothing less than to render the undecipherable understood, to decode the message of enigmatic writing, *waḥy*, that so haunted the ancient poet. *Waḥy* re-appears in the Qur'an in a rigorously inverted meaning, it is used to introduce revelation, the hermeneutical field of communication par excellence. With this paradigmatic turn, the Qur'an offers its listeners a new promise: divine faithfulness is not derived from the biblical narrative of salvation, where God intervenes in human history, but rather from God's liberation of man from the aporetic crisis that is so expressively pronounced in ancient Arabic poetry. Subsequently, in this new conceptualization of paradise, an equally new plenitude of meaning is staged: The old pagan poetic tropes of loss, the campsites lying in ruins, the beloved having departed, are inverted and reinterpreted to provide a comprehensive and socio-historical relevant narrative. Thus the hermeneutical inaccessibility of reality's "sign language", as propounded poetically in pre-Islamic Arabic poetry, is discursively reversed. The Qur'anic manifestation of paradise, though amalgamating different well established traditions, thus introduces a substantially novel dimension into the eschatological thought of its time. It thus clearly betrays its late antique pluricultural milieu of genesis, but it equally proves essentially new and challenging.

---

51 Neuwirth, *Psalms*, 733-778.

"So that he could not bear the sweetness"

Imagining the Unimaginable in Medieval Ashkenaz

Johannes Heil

Jewish cultures in the past were extremely dynamic. Due to the interplay of internal and environmental factors they underwent repeated transformations, accompanied by changing formative centers and manners of cultural expression. Yet, whether moving between the poles of Jerusalem and Alexandria in the classical period, between Sepharad, Italiy and Ashkenaz in the Middle Ages, or between Hassidism and the Haskalah in modern times, these distinct cultures all share some basic characteristics. Aside from the central meaning of the Torah as the binding and constitutive factor in Judaism and Jewish cultures,[1] one further basic characteristic is the resolution to keep the prohibition against images as given in the Ten Commandments (Exod. 20, Deut. 5). The book of Exodus even goes so far as to remember the veneration of the Golden Calf (Exod. 32) as another original sin and preserves this moment in history as an enduring admonition to keep the commandments. As a consequence, rabbinical literature (especially in the tractate *Avoda zara* of the Mishnah and the Talmud[2]) formulated far-reaching restrictions against images, not to mention any form of veneration of images.[3] Whereas Christian theologians when speaking about "images of the Divine" may actually be speaking about drawings, pictures or sculptures as epistemic or educational tools or even as effigies and representations of the Divine, with regard to Jewish traditions and cultures the topic "images of the Divine" simply does not make sense, at least at a first glance.

Thus, this contribution is about the second glance. To be sure, this more far-reaching view will not change what is obvious at the first glance. We can discuss Jewish approaches to "images of the Divine" only by introducing a wider concept of what "image" means, moving from material images (הנומת-לכו לספ =

1 See for example David Biale (ed.), *Cultures of the Jews. A New History* (New York, 2002); see also Ross Brann and Adam Sutcliffe (eds.), *Renewing the past, reconfiguring Jewish culture: from al-Andalus to the Haskalah* (Philadelphia, 2004); Gad Freudenthal, *Science in Medieval Jewish Cultures* (Cambridge, UK, 2011); Alan T. Levenson (ed.), *The Wiley-Blackwell History of Jews and Judaism* (Chichester etc., 2012).

2 Easy access to the English translation is available at https://www.jewishvirtuallibrary.org/jsource/Talmud/avodahzara_toc.html.

3 See Kalman P. Bland, *The Artless Jew. Medieval and Modern Affirmations and Denials of the Visual* (Princeton, NJ, 2000).

sculpture or any image, Exod.20,2) to the imagination and insight, or as Max Weber put it: aniconism contributes to rationalization of religious thinking.[4] Weber's observation about the paradoxical relationship between the prohibition against images and a more analytical understanding of the Divine points in the right direction, yet it ignores that aniconism may not only lead to rationalization but also to an intensified imaginative understanding, even to the extent that we consider both as being deeply interrelated. This can be illustrated by many examples from Jewish history. One starting point would be the almost complete restriction against the access to the interior of the temple, with only the High Priest allowed to enter this space, but the encouragement of all the other believers to seek a deeper understanding of the Divine, or to use the appropriate term: the *Shekhina* (הָנִיכְש).

I will focus here on examples from the formative period of Ashkenaz, the Jewish culture of Latin Europe, and present some considerations with examples from roughly 950-1300 CE. I will also emphasize that even though the general prohibition against images and iconographic expressions was eventually broken in late classical and medieval times by displaying images of human beings (to mention a few, the wall paintings of Dura-Europos[5] and the many examples of figurative illustrations of medieval Jewish manuscripts such as the Mahzors of Worms and Amsterdam and the Darmstadt Haggadah[6]), not a single attempt to create a figura-

---

4 Max Weber, *Wirtschaft und Gesellschaft* (1922), in *Max Weber Studienausgabe* I.22, Tübingen 2005, p. 140f.: "Die ursprünglich magisch bedingt gewesene jüdische Scheu vor dem 'Bildnis und Gleichnis' deutet die Prophetie spiritualistisch aus ihrem absolut überweltlichen Gottesbegriff heraus um. Und irgendwann zeigt sich dann die Spannung der zentral ethisch religiösen Orientierung der prophetischen Religion gegen das 'Menschenwerk', die aus dessen, vom Propheten aus gesehen, Scheinerlösungsleistung folgt. Die Spannung ist um so unversöhnlicher, je überweltlicher und gleichzeitig je heiliger der prophetisch verkündete Gott vorgestellt wird [...] Für uns ist nur wichtig die Bedeutung der Ablehnung aller eigentlich künstlerischen Mittel durch bestimmte, in diesem Sinn spezifisch rationale Religionen, in starkem Maße im Synagogengottesdienst und dem alten Christentum, dann wieder im asketischen Protestantismus. Sie ist, je nachdem, Symptom oder Mittel der Steigerung des rationalisierenden Einflusses einer Religiosität auf die Lebensführung. Daß das zweite Gebot geradezu die entscheidende Ursache des jüdischen Rationalismus sei, wie manche Vertreter einflußreicher jüdischer Reformbewegungen annehmen, geht wohl zu weit. Daß aber die systematische Verdammung aller unbefangenen Hingabe an die eigentlichen Formungswerte der Kunst, deren Wirksamkeit ja durch Maß und Art der Kunstproduktivität der frommen jüdischen und puritanischen Kreise genügend belegt ist, in der Richtung intellektualistischer und rationaler Lebensmethodik wirken muß, ist andererseits nicht im mindesten zu bezweifeln."

5 On the Synagogue of Dura-Europos, see Steven Fine, "Jewish Identity at the Cusp of Empires," in idem, *Art, History, and the Historiography of Judaism in Roman Antiquity* (Leiden, 2014), pp. 101-22; see also Joseph Gutmann (ed.), *The Dura-Europos Synagogue. A re-evaluation (1932–1992)* (Atlanta, 1992). Mediev Manuscripts.

6 See *Die Darmstädter Pessach-Haggadah*, 2 vols. (Berlin, 1971); *The Worms Maḥzor* (London, 1985); Gabrielle Sed-Rajna, "The decoration of the Amsterdam Mahzor," in Albert

tive image of the Divine or Divine appearances such as the *Shekhinah* throughout the classical, medieval and early modern periods is known. This applies even to the depiction of a *sol invictus* in the mosaic floor of the ancient synagogue at Hammath Tiberias and other late Roman synagogues in the area around the Sea of Galilee, which appears to be more of an ironic symbol than a simple hidden message for "highly acculturated circles" (Levine) or even an image of the Divine in a very real sense.[7]

Basically, the question about images of the Divine with regard to Judaism addresses the textual rather than the iconographic level. The textual level, then, offered and offers possibilities for a broad variety of imaginations of the Divine.

These possibilities even included negative approaches–an attitude that will be illustrated with an example taken from the *Siwuv* (Round Trip), the "Travels of Rabbi Petachiah." This early thirtheenth-century text is an account of the journey of the Ashkenazic scholar Petachiah, who traveled from his native Ratisbon or Prague to the east. Contrary to his Sephardic contemporary, Benjamin of Tudela, whose travel account described various and rather practical issues, including providing geographical information for travelling merchants[8], Petachiah clearly wrote and reported as a pilgrim who had visited the holy places–mostly the shrines of venerated sages and biblical heroes (or meaningful events). His account as delivered in later manuscripts starts immediately, without any further preface, with a geographic description:

> These are the travels undertaken by Rabbi Petachiah, who travelled through all the countries. He set out from Prague, which is in Bohemia going to Poland, from Poland to Kieff in Russia, and from Russia he went in six days to the river Dniepr ...

---

van der Heide et al. (eds.), *The Amsterdam Mahzor. History, Liturgy, Illumination* (Leiden, 1989), pp. 56-70.

7 See Lee I. Levine, "Contextualizing Jewish Art. The Synagogues at Hammat Tiberias and at Sepphoris," in R. Kalmin et al. (eds.), *Jewish Culture and Society under the Christian Roman Empire* (Louvain, 2003), pp. 91-131, 100, 115; Günter Stemberger, *Juden und Christen im spätantiken Palästina* (Berlin, 2007), p. 30f.; Emmanuel Friedheim, "Sol Invictus in the Severus Synagogue at Hammath Tiberias, the Rabbis, and Jewish Society: A Different Approach," in *Review of Rabbinic Judaism* 12 (2009), pp. 89-128; Rachel Hachlili, A*ncient Synagogues, Archaeology and Art. New Discoveries and Current Research* (Handbook of Oriental Studies–Handbuch der Orientalistik; Sect.1, vol 105; Leiden), pp. 358-82.

8 *The Itinerary of Benjamin of Tudela: Travels in the Middle Ages*, transl. Marcus Nathan Adler, with Introductions by Michael A. Signer et al. (Malibu, CA, 1993); see Joseph Shatzmiller, "Jews, Pilgrimage, and the Christian Cult of Saints: Benjamin of Tudela and His Contemporaries," in Walter A. Goffart et al. (eds.), *After Rome's Fall: Narrators and Sources of Early Medieval History* (Toronto, 1998), pp. 337–347; David Jacoby, "Benjamin of Tudela and his 'Book of Travels'," in Klaus Herbers et al. (eds.), *Venezia incrocio di culture; percezioni di viaggiatori europei e non europei a confronto* (Rome, 2008), pp. 135-64; François-Xavier Fauvelle-Aymar, "Desperately seeking the Jewish Kingdom of Ethiopia. Benjamin of Tudela and the Horn of Africa (twelfth century)," in *Speculum* 88 (2013), pp. 383-404.

It also concludes unspectacularly:

> In the village of Usa is buried Honah, son of Amittai, [and] in Bosra, of Babylon, Ezra, the scribe. Rabbi Chana, the Bagdadian, who wrote in the Talmud, was of Bagdad, the great city as mentioned before. At Babylon there are no stones, but everything is of brick.–End of the words of Rabbi Petachiah, brother of Rabbi Yizchak, the White, author of the Tosaphot, and of Rabbi Nachman, of Ratisbon.

In between, the pious traveler had described many places and names, mostly of Jews he had met on his journey, and he reported about curiosities and his personal observations. But he mentioned God rarely at best. However, in what and how he reported about details and events, God was continuously present. Worshipping God by avoiding his name was a widespread pattern in the earlier, norm-oriented period of Ashkenazic culture. Rabbi Petachiah's hesitation to directly address the Divine is therefore not unique but characteristic according to what we find in the writings of many of his contemporaries. And we can better understand this when considering the conditions of Jewish life in the formative period of Ashkenaz on the banks of the Rhine River or elsewhere in the north.[9] The first generations of sages (the *rishonim*) were primarily occupied with adjusting the written and the oral Torah to the new conditions in the far north and to the requirements of daily life in an environment that was extremely different from that in the Mediterranean world, from where most of the immigrants who arrived from the tenth century and onwards had come. A good example is the Kalonymos (*Shemtov*) family who probably came from the Byzantine south of Italy.[10]

Normative discussions of how to deal with an environment that was sometimes hostile, and at best not aware of the importance of keeping the Torah and the meaning of following the food purity requirements in daily life, are among the oldest witnesses to Jewish life in Northern Europe from roughly 950 onwards.[11] Having only these sources, one could gain the impression that medieval Jewish scholars were primarily occupied with manifold questions related to food, especially to wine, its production and transport.

This was already true for the responses of the first great Ashkenazi scholar, R. Gershom ben Jehudah me'or ha gola ("the illuminator of the Diaspora", who died in 1028) and the *taqqanot* ("community rules") ascribed to him by later generations. The same applies for the great scholar Rashi of Troyes (R. Shlomo ben Yitzhak, ca. 1040-1105) whose responses to the questions submitted to him

---

9 Michael Toch, "The formation of a diaspora. The settlement of Jews in the medieval German 'Reich'," in *Aschkenas* 7 (1997), pp. 55-78; Ivan Marcus, "A Jewish-Christian Symbiosis. The Culture of Early Ashkenaz," in David Biale et al. (ed.), *Cultures of the Jews. A New History* (New York, 2003), pp. 449-516; Jonathan Elukin, *Living Together, Living Apart. Rethinking Jewish-Christian Relations in the Middle Ages* (Princeton, 2007).

10 Avraham Grossman, *The Early Sages of Ashkenaz: Their Lives, Leadership and Works* (Jerusalem, 1981), pp. 27 ff. [Hebrew].

11 Assumptions in favor of continuous Jewish life in northern Europe from the Roman and medieval periods remain without foundation.

repeatedly dealt with the production, transport and preservation of kosher wine. Still in the thirteenth century, in the works of another great Ashkenazi scholar, Meir of Rothenburg (who died in 1297), civil matters such as marriage, divorce, inheritance, business rules and so on were clearly dominant; further discussions dealt with food and other matters of daily life, almost all of this with no explicit reference to the sphere of the sacred.[12]

To be sure, the early sages of Ashkenaz were by no means halakhic bureaucrats ignorant of God. They were and had to be masters of the Halakhah, dedicated to the normative interpretation of the sacred law. Interestingly, Rashi started his career in the centers of learning along the Rhine River and became an outstanding halakhist and commentator on the Talmud, whose decisions and opinions became part of the core content of the Ashkenazic intellectual tradition. However, his biblical commentaries were probably even more important; Rashi wrote only after he had left Worms in about 1075 and returned to his native town of Troyes in Champagne, where he established his own school.[13]

However, it seems that Rashi was less interested in another area of textual productivity of the early Ashkenaz sages, liturgical poetry. This field is also full of textual images of the Divine. Rashi made use of liturgical poems for his commentaries (mostly with reference to older texts from the corpus of the pre-medieval classical piyyutim from Palestine), and some piyyutim have been ascribed to him by later medieval traditions (probably in order to legitimize more recent compositions and their use in the service by attributing them to the venerated sage from Troyes).[14]

In view of the precarious state of the emerging Jewish culture of Ashkenaz during the High Middle Ages, it is astonishing to find poetry as one of the oldest monuments of this culture. We may ask why did a generation of immigrants—mostly from southern Italy but also from the former Roman areas in southern Gaul via the Île de France and the former Frankish capital Metz—sit down and

---

[12] See Ephraim Kanarfogel, "Preservation, creativity, and courage. The life and works of R. Meir of Rothenburg," in *Jewish Book Annual* 50 (1992) 249-259; see also Elisheva Baumgarten, *Mothers and Children: Jewish Family Life in Medieval Europe. Jews, Christians, and Muslims from the Ancient to the Modern World* (Princeton, 2004).

[13] See Michael A. Signer, "God's love for Israel: apologetic and hermeneutical strategies in twelfth-century biblical exegesis," in Idem et al. (eds.), *Jews and Christians in Twelfth-Century Europe* (Notre Dame, IN, 2001), pp. 123-49; Ivan G Marcus, "Rashi's choice: the Humash commentary as rewritten Midrash," in David Engel et al. (eds.), *Studies in Medieval Jewish Intellectual and Social History; Festschrift in Honor of Robert Chazan* (Leiden, 2012), pp. 29-45.

[14] See Albert Van der Heide, "Rashi and early Ashkenazi piyyut," in *Zutot* 1 (2001), pp. 77-83; Elisabeth Hollender, *Piyyut Commentary in Medieval Ashkenaz* (Studia Judaica 42) (Berlin, 2008), pp. 119f.; Idem, "A Commentary on a Lost Piyyut. Some Thoughts on Transmission and Fixing of Texts in Rashi's Bet Midrash," in Hanna Liss et al. (eds.), *Raschi und sein Erbe* (Heidelberg, 2007), pp. 47-63.

compose poems when arriving at the banks of the Rhine River?[15] Probably the main factor inspiring this astonishing poetic activity was that, arriving in the lands north of the Alps, the Jews found their own textual heritage alienated and exploited. For example, for the monks of St. Albans, Mainz, Lorsch and other places (following the Carolingian reform with its impact on the development of monastic life), chanting the psalms with their Christological interpretations had become a major element in structuring and nourishing the daily life cycles of the monasteries.[16] Under such conditions "Sing unto [the Lord] a *new* song; play skillfully" (Ps. 33.3) could be understood in a far stricter sense by the Jewish community: that the biblical traditions needed to be re-actualized by the addition of new compositions, thus attaining a renewed, undivided ownership of the text. The texts of these compositions have few images of the Divine in a stricter sense (the rock, the shield, the king, the guide and teacher, the delight), but are rich in meaningful expressions, leaving much room for the individual imagination. One of their major characteristics is the directness of the speaker. Many texts operate in the singular form, sometimes changing to the plural and including the community for which the individual is speaking. The speaker addresses God in a personal, direct manner. Speaking to his invisible counterpart and correspondent, he uses changing motifs and images, whereas the addressee remains silent. The words of the speaker therefore become increasingly demanding, urging and even imperative (*timloch*, "Thou shall rule"): as the addressee never answers back or opposes the claim, the words are implicitly verified.

Let us have a look at Meshullam ben Kalonymos' composition, *Moré ha-taïm* (Guide of the Errant), which today is recited during the morning service of *Yom Kippur*.[17] It is a fine example of what we may call the 'progressive Renaissance' of Psalmodic text writing. Here Meshullam wrote a kind of versed super-commentary for the verses of Psalm 145 which are quoted in parts at the end of each stanza. The composition consists of a verse-by-verse commentary on the psalm verses. Thereby, the reader (prayer) is prepared for reading the verse.

---

[15] Jefim Schirmann, "The Beginning of Hebrew Poetry in Italy and Northern Europe. Italy," in Cecil Roth (ed.), *The World History of the Jewish People. The Dark Ages: Jews in Christian Europe 711-1096* (Tel Aviv, 1966), pp. 249-66; Abraham M. Habermann, "The Beginning of Hebrew Poetry in Italy and Northern Europe: Northern Europe and France," in ibid., pp. 267-73; Leon J. Weinberger, *Jewish Hymnography. A literary history* (London etc., 1998), pp. 138ff.; Johannes Heil, "Prayer, Memory, and Identity. On Jewish Liturgical Poetry from Ashqenas 10th to 12th Century," in Roy Hammerling (ed.), *Medieval Prayers. The First to the Fifteenth Century* (Leiden, 2008), pp. 337-65.

[16] See James W.McKinnon, "Book of Psalms, Monasticism, and the Western Liturgy," in *The Place of the Psalms in the Intellectual Culture of the Middle Ages*, ed. Nancy van Deusen (Albany, N.Y., 1999), pp. 43-58; Joseph Dyer, "Psalms in Monastic Prayer," in *ibid.*, pp. 59-89; Idem, "Monastic Psalmody in the Middle Ages," in *Revue Bénédictine* 99 (1989), pp. 41-74; Idem, "The Singing of Psalms in Early Medieval Office," in *Speculum* 64 (1989), pp. 535-78.

[17] Hebrew text Daniel Goldschmidt, *Mahzor le-yamim ha-noraim* [Prayer Book for Rosh ha-Shanah and Yom Kippur], pp. 122-24.

> *Thou showest sinners the path in which they walk; teach me the way to tread.* (Verse 145.1) *I will extol Thee, my God, O King.*

Following the super-commentary, the verses of the psalm became conditioned: readers could understand why they are encouraged to extol the Lord. The following stanzas together with further verses of the psalm work the same way:

> *Fulfill the desire of them who hope for Thy mercy, that Thy faithful servants may rejoice.* (145.4) *One generation shall laud Thy works to another.*
> *With supplication and fasting they draw near to Thee; they were fashioned for Thine honor, to serve Thee.* (145.5) *The glorious splendor of Thy majesty, they shall proclaim.* [...] *God is our rock, yea, our delight. He will subdue our perversity that all may proclaim* (145.9) *The Lord is good to all.*

It seems that with these commentaries, the poet intended to directly address the precarious state of his community and to guard against confusion and despair. Filling the gap between the imperfect present, which at times was a vale of tears, and the metaphysical confidence as expressed in the psalm, the commentary prepared and strengthened the reader for a pure expression of praise.

The next example is more explicit in its relatedness to the present. It deals with the loss of the temple, assuring that current spiritual offerings have the same value as those from past days in the temple:

> *May be their confession as ancient offerings before Thee, and the utterance of Thy witnesses be like sacrifices on Thine altar.* (145.16) *Thou openest Thy hand [and satisfiest the desire of every living thing.]*

Indeed, the meaning of the temple was much discussed in these days (not only during the nineteenth century reform debates). At about the same time, the foundation inscription for the first synagogue in Worms ("the house for His name... little sanctuary, *miqdash me'ad;*" dating to 1034) explicitly stated that God prefers prayers rising from the house of prayer rather than the smoke rising from offerings in the temple.[18]

Things became considerably more multifaceted with the emergence of a broader mystical movement in Ashkenaz in the twelfth century, a movement that arose in the aftermath of the experience of persecutions during the crusades of 1096 and 1146/7. In its formative period, Ashkenaz had always been in contact not only with the centers of rabbinical learning in Babylonia, but also with Eretz Israel. From there, the Jews of Italy and later in the north inherited not only the *piyyut*, but also access to mystical traditions. Based on motifs from the chariot visions in Ezekiel 1 and the temple vision in Isaiah 6, they originated in the (partly anti-rabbinical and priestly) *Merkavah* ("chariot") and *Hechalot* ("palaces")

---

[18] Ernst Róth (ed.), *Festschrift zur Wiedereinweihung der Alten Synagoge zu Worms* (Frankfurt am Main, 1961), p. 97f.

meditations about a mystical ascent into heaven, divine visions, the place of angels and deeper insight into the Torah from the late classical period.[19]

In this context, the work of the mystic Eleazar ben Yehudah of Worms in the twelfth century attempts to determine even the *middot* ("mesures") of the creator, although with the result of inconceivable dimensions. As Hanna Liss shows in her study on Eleazar's *Hilkhot ha-Kawod,* this text provides changing ideas about the Divine for which the traditional Talmudic explanations were found to be insufficient. It addressed the ambivalence between the absolute infinity of the Divine and the visionary revelation of the god-king to the prophets (Is. 6.1: "I saw the Lord seated on a throne" / בשי ינדא־תא הארא). How, Eleazar asked, can the Lord, of infinite dimensions, be seated on a throne, which so obviously is a limited thing? Coming to the conclusion that the prophetic vision was something different from the very being of God, but nevertheless a part of God's unity (*ichud,* like the unity of the various presentations of God visible in various ways to the prophets), Eleazar widened the imaginative horizon and introduced telling images related to the Divine.[20]

Coming closer to the end of my monograph, I would like to return once more to Rabbi Petachiah, the medieval traveler between the poles of what was then the known world. When the wise man from Regensburg, on his way to the tomb of the prophet Ezekiel and to Jerusalem, arrived at Ararat, he reported:

> Rabbi Petachiah said that the mountains of Ararat are five days' journey form Babylon. The mountains of Ararat are high. There is one high mountain, above which there are four others, of which two are opposite two. The ark of Noah was carried between these mountains and could not be removed. However, the ark is not there, for it has decayed. The mountains are full of thorns and other herbs; when the dew falls upon them, manna falls upon them, but when the sun shines warm it melts. Whatever portion of it is gathered in the night, if it be kept, likewise melts. They therefore carry off the manna together with the thorns and herbs, which they are obliged to cut off, since they are very hard. It is like white snow. The herbs and nettles are very bitter. However, when boiled together with the manna they become sweeter than honey and every other sweet stuff. Were it boiled without the nettles the limbs of the partaker thereof would become disjointed for excessive sweetness. They look like small grains.

---

19 See Gershom Scholem, Major Trends in Jewish Mysticism, first pub.1941, ed. Joseph Dan et al. , Tübingen 1993; Peter Schäfer, The *Hidden and Manifest God.* Some Major Themes in Early Jewish Mysticism, Albany 1992; Eliot R. Wolfson, Through a Speculum That Shines: Vision and Imagination in Medieval Jewish Mysticism, Princeton 1994; Vita D. Arbel, *Beholders of Divine Secrets. Mysticism and Myth in Hekhalot and Merkavah Literature* (Albany, 2003); Rachel Elior, *The Three Temples: On the Emergence of Jewish Mysticism* (2005); Moshe Idel, "From Italy to Ashkenaz and Back. On the Circulation of Jewish Mystical Traditions," in: *Kabbalah* 14 (2006), pp. 47-94; Ra'anan Boustan, Martha Himmelfarb, Peter Schäfer (eds.), *Hekhalot Literature in Context. Between Byzantium and Babylonia* (Tübingen, 2013).

20 Hanna Liss, *El'azar ben Yehuda von Worms: Hilkhot ha-Kavod. Die Lehrsätze von der Herrlichkeit Gottes* (Tübingen, 1997), pp. 105ff., 200ff.

> They gave him a few to taste. They melted in his mouth, and they were sweet, penetrating into all his limbs, so that he could not bear the sweetness.[21]

Rabbi Petachiah was a skillful narrator. His account is full of irony in the sense of modern literary theories. Otherwise what would be the point of saying that, although made according to God's instructions, Noah's ark was no longer there, because being manmade it went the way of all human beings and things: it turned to dust. However, Petachiah ignored the obvious and the temporal distance, and he reported about the flood as an event that could have happened only recently. The description that follows is presented in the same way: Petachiah – not caring about the raised eyebrows of his readers then and now – lets us know that the manna was still there: he earnestly claims to have found the heavenly bread far from the places where the Bible tells us this miracle happened in the dim and distant past. To Petachiah it is clear: The manna was still there! With the straightforward description of the manna falling from heaven in its original form (not in its transubstantiated form, as the Lateran council would describe it),[22] he emphasized the continuous presence and powerful acting of the Divine. He thus opened a broad space for the reader's personal imagination, even today.

To me this is one of the most fascinating medieval confrontations with the Divine. We shall not concern ourselves with the question of which manna-like drugs the pious man had consumed to experience shaking body parts. Much more fascinating is the spiritual rationalization he attributed to this unpleasant experience–even as a visionary experience caused by a medieval scholar's drug abuse: That the manna was still there, but "that he could not bear the sweetness"–meaning that the presence of God was attainable through piety and insight, but the time for its fulfillment had not yet arrived.

Therefore, in Petachiah's text "images of the Divine"–or what can better be described as an imaginative textual representation of the Divine open to individual embodiment–existed only on a distant level: on the historic and future levels. In the present, however, "he could not bear" it. Nevertheless, it is foreseeable in the present. Most telling is another episode that Petachiah reports from his visit to Jerusalem:

> At Jerusalem there is a gate; its name is the Gate of Mercy. The gate is full of stone and lime. No Jew and still less a Gentile is permitted to go there. One day the Gentiles wished to remove the rubbish and open the gate, but the whole land of Israel shook, and there was a tumult in the city until they left off. There is a tradition among the Jews that the divine glory (*shekhinah*) appeared through this gate and that through it it would return. It is exactly opposite Mount Olivet. Mount Olivet is lower than it.

---

21 Abraham Benisch (ed.), *Travels of Petachiah of Ratisbon* (with English translation) (London, 1856), pp. 48ff.

22 There is no clear hint whether Petachiah's account on the manna directly opposed the Christian Eucharistic teaching, but since a travel narrative did not require a side trip to the question of the true heavenly food, this episode can be read as a silent dispute with the teachings of the church.

> Nevertheless, whoever stands on that mountain may see it. His feet will stand that day on Mount Olivet. They shall see distinctly when [the Eternal] will return to Zion through that gate. Prayers are offered up there. The Tower of David still exists.[23]

This episode once more connects the witnesses and the reports from the past and the promises for the future with Petachiah and his contemporaries in between.

To summarize, the biblical ban against images did not prevent images of the Divine on a textual level. Therefore, it did not prevent spaces of collective and individual imagination. As we learned from Petachiah's journey, a gifted author could operate perfectly within the given space and its limits. Both the space and limits permitted the introduction of new models of thinking and therefore made innovations and change possible. In the end, the poets and Petachiah's *Siwuv* prove the assumption that the strict ban against material images even expanded the space for imagination and contributed to the emergence of virtual images.

23 Petachiah, pp. 64ff.

Islam as a Cultural Orientation for Modern Judaism[1]

Susannah Heschel

What greater theological intimacy can be imagined to exist between two religions than to have the founder of one be a pious member of the other? Yet Jesus served less often as a bridge than as a contested figure–was he a Jew or a Christian? Or did he transform himself from a Jew to a Christian–even to an Aryan, as Ernst Renan claimed?[2]

The cultural landscape in which modern Judaism developed was primarily Christian (Protestant) Germany. Indeed, the initial steps taken in the development of a new, acculturated Jewish religious worship involved Christianization: the use of an organ, a sermon as the central focus of the service, the music of Protestant hymns used for Jewish texts, and the rabbi clad in long black robes with a white collar, just like a Protestant pastor. Yet beneath that Christianization lay a rebellious ideology. Abraham Geiger, one of the prime architects of liberal Judaism in nineteenth-century Germany, supported changes in the religious practice of Judaism and convened several synods of like-minded rabbis to discuss, determine, and implement those changes. Yet Geiger also developed a wide-ranging, highly-influential theory of Christianity's derivation from Judaism, so that changes in Jewish religious practice were not a Christianization of Judaism but a reclamation of the original, liberal, Pharisaic Judaism of antiquity that had been lost over the generations. Christian persecution of Jews had resulted in a Talmudic legalism, Geiger argued, that suppressed the liberal, progressive spirit of the Pharisees, themselves the originators of the Talmudic tradition. And while Geiger identified Jesus as a Pharisee who preached liberal, Pharisaic teachings, he argued that Jesus's own message was lost to Christianity once Paul mixed that message with pagan ideas, so that Christianity was a religion about Jesus, not the faith of Jesus.

---

1 I would like to express my deep gratitude to the Wissenschaftskolleg zu Berlin for the year-long fellowship I received during 2011-2012, during which I pursued research partially reflected this article. I would like to dedicate this article to the extraordinary staff of the library, and to the directors: Luca Giuliani, Reinhart Meyer-Kalkus, and Joachim Nettelbeck, with gratitude for the warm and intellectually stimulating atmosphere they have created at the Wissenschaftskolleg.

2 On Ernest Renan and the Aryan Jesus, see Susannah Heschel, *The Aryan Jesus: Christian Theologians and the Bible in Nazi Germany* (Princeton: Princeton University Press, 2008), chapter one; Halvor Moxnes, "The Construction of Galilee as a Place for the Historical Jesus," *Biblical Theology Bulletin* 31:1 and 2 (2001), 26-37; 64-77.

That faith, liberal Pharisaism, was what Geiger wanted reconstituted in Reform Judaism.

The arguments Geiger developed were presented in both scholarly and popular formats, and were well-known to contemporary Christian theologians, who reviewed and discussed his work (usually negatively) in the major theological journals and monograph publications of the second half of the nineteenth century. His claims regarding Jesus as an unoriginal Jewish preacher and Paul as the real founder of a Christianity that deviated from Jesus's own faith became widespread and highly popular among Jews ever since, in the United States as well as in Europe. While conservative Jews sometimes accused liberalizers of imitating Christianity in their synagogue services, reformers virtually never made those claims about the changes they advocated. Certainly, the teachings of liberal Judaism often sounded nearly identical to those of liberal Protestants, blurring the boundaries between the two religions so that, at times, tensions were created, as the historian Uriel Tal has pointed out.[3]

Yet if modern Judaism did not identify itself with Christianity, nor claim for itself a Christianizing mantle, how did it position itself within the Christian cultural landscape? The real intimacy, from the modern Jewish point of view, was between Judaism and Islam. The synagogue service, with its organ and hymns, may have bestowed a Christian aurality, but the visual was reserved for the Muslim: European, British, and American synagogues were built, starting in the 1830s, in Moorish architecture. European-trained graduates of rabbinical schools mastered Hebrew, but to a remarkable extent also mastered Arabic and immersed themselves in the field of Oriental Studies. Much of that study was motivated by an interest in the history of Jewish culture and philosophy as it developed in Islamicate lands in the Middle Ages; after all, much medieval Jewish philosophy was written in Arabic, and the nineteenth century also saw the development of the myth of the "Golden Age" of Jewish life in Muslim Spain. However, the interest in Arabic extended further and stands in contrast to Jewish writings on Christianity. Parallels between rabbinic literature and the Gospels were pointed out by rabbis and Jewish historians with the purpose, implicit or explicit, of undermining the originality of Jesus, but studies of the parallels between rabbinic literature and the Qur'an and tafsir were undertaken to demonstrate the influence of Judaism on Islam. Christianity, in nineteenth-century German-Jewish eyes, was a fallen religion, originating with the Jew Jesus, but subsequently dominated by non-Jewish doctrines such as incarnation, trinity, and virgin birth, whereas Islam, in Jewish eyes, had preserved the strict monotheism of Judaism and a commitment to a religious legal system that was derived from or at least bore significant parallels with Jewish law.

One of the greatest of the German-Jewish philosophers, Hermann Cohen, for example, viewed Islam much more favorably than Christianity not only because it cultivated religious tolerance, but because its beliefs were, in his view, philo-

---

3 Uriel Tal, *Christians and Jews in Germany*, trans. Noah Jacobs (Ithaca: Cornell University Press, 1974).

sophically pure, whereas Christian beliefs in trinitarianism, incarnation, and virgin birth were metaphysically erroneous and led inevitably to a society rooted in domination and injustice. Cohen thought of Christianity as a religion of myth and therefore philosophically erroneous and incapable of morality, yet wrote about Islam, "The Jewish philosophy of the Middle Ages does not grow so much out of Islam as out of the original monotheism. The more intimate relationship between Judaism and Islam–more intimate than with other monotheistic religions–can be explained by the kinship that exists between the mother and daughter religion."[4] His voice is echoed by the contemporary historian Bernard Lewis, who writes, "Judaism and Islam are sister religions, with many important resemblances between them. A Jew, particularly a learned Jew, had a head start over his Christian colleagues in the study of Islam, and an immediacy of understanding which they could not easily attain."[5]

Commenting on the study of religion, the nineteenth-century German philologist Friedrich Max Mueller famously stated, "He who knows one, knows none." The study of religion requires comparison, and as Jewish scholars flocked to the study of Islam during the remarkable century from the 1830s to the 1930s, they were examining the meaning of Judaism even as they explored aspects of Islam. Not only was their knowledge of Hebrew helpful in mastering Arabic, their understanding of classical Jewish exegetical modes–such as Midrashic commentaries on Scripture and debates over proper interpretation and enactment of Halakha–were crucial for their sympathetic understanding of tafsir and fiqh, Islamic exegesis and jurisprudence. Indeed, in some ways Islam served as a template for wrestling with questions central to Judaism as well, such as the significance of their monotheism and the historical development of religious law.

The starting point was determining just what constitutes "Islam" as well as "Judaism". In a private letter to his friend, the German scholar Martin Hartmann, written in 1906, Ignaz Goldziher, the Hungarian Jew who is recognized as the greatest scholar of Islam of the past two hundred years, wrote, "Aber machen Sie doch unseren Islam nicht gar zu schlecht; er ist das, wozu ihn die Bekenner machen. Nach dem Buchstaben seiner Litteratur allein wird er nicht gerecht beurtheilt. Fuer jedes barbarische Hadith kann ein humanes angefuehrt werden."[6]

Islam should be defined according to the beliefs and interpretations of its adherents, and not simply through a study of its texts, Goldziher urged. Goldziher made similar claims about Judaism, insisting that its commentaries and inter-

---

4 Hermann Cohen, *Religion of Reason out of the Sources of Judaism, trans. Simon Kaplan* (New York: F. Ungar, 1972), 92; "Die jüdische Philosophie des Mittelalters erwächst nicht sowohl aus dem Monotheismus des Islam, als vielmehr aus dem ursprünglichen Monotheismus, und höchstens kann die Verwandtschaft, die zwischen dieser Tochterreligion und der der Mutter besteht, die innige Beziehung verständlich machen, welche intimer als sonstwo zwischen Judentum und Islam sich anbahnt." *Religion der Vernunft*, 107-08.

5 Bernard Lewis, *op. cit.*, 12.

6 Ludmila Hanisch, *"Machen Sie doch unseren Islam nicht gar zu schlecht": Der Briefwechsel der Islamwissenschaftler Ignaz Goldziher und Martin Hartmann, 1894-1914* (Wiesbaden: Harrassowitz, 2000), 267.

pretive writings be plumbed for the religious life of their authors, and not simply treated as disembodied texts. Here he was participating in the *Wissenschaft des Judentums*, the scholarly study of Judaism that emerged in the early nineteenth century, which was concerned not only with collecting Jewish texts, but also with writing a historical narrative of Jewish political and religious experience.

As the field of Islamic Studies arose and gained enormous momentum in Western and Central Europe during the long nineteenth century, Jewish scholars flocked to the study of the Qur'an and early Islam. Abraham Geiger launched the field with a comparative study of the Qur'an and the Mishnah and Midrash, published in 1833. Other Jewish scholars, such as Geiger's contemporary and fellow student at the University of Bonn in the 1830s, Salomon Munk, turned to the study of medieval Islamic philosophy and its context for medieval Jewish philosophy. Gustav Weil published the first book attempting to demonstrate the chronological sequence of the Suras of the Qur'an, a project subsequently pursued and expanded by Theodor Noeldeke. Goldziher himself pioneered the study of the Hadith, as well as numerous other aspects of Islamic religious texts in work that remains important to this day. By the 1920s, Jewish scholars, as the historian Ludmila Hanisch has demonstrated, had come to dominate the university professorships in Germany, so that the field of Islamic Studies was decimated when National Socialist Germany fired all civil servants, including professors, who were not considered "Aryan".

Goldziher's extensive and fascinating correspondence with Hartmann, recently published by Hanisch, interweaves scholarly concern with classical Islamic texts with contemporary interests, such as the veiling of Muslim women. What stands out in the correspondence is Goldziher's insistence on the positive appreciation of Islam, which is typical for most Jewish scholars in the field, and also his insistence on integrating Islamic exegetical commentaries (tafsir) into the scholarly interpretation of Islamic texts, also common in nearly all Jewish scholarship on Islam. Both are unusual markers of Jewish research: Muhammad and the Qur'an appear in a very positive light, particularly in contrast to the Jewish scholarship of the same period on Christianity and the figure of Jesus, and the attentiveness to Islamic self-understanding that Goldziher urges stands in contrast to Jewish scholarship on Christianity and Christian scholarship on Judaism, neither of which paid particular attention to the indigenous commentaries of the religions they were studying.

The fascination of Jews with Islam during the long nineteenth century has multiple implications: Jews in Europe shaped the modern scholarly methods and topics of research on Islam, concentrating on analyses of the Qur'an and early Islam. Some Jews wrote popular books describing their travels in Islamicate regions, such as Iran, the Ottoman Empire, and Central Asia, and a few converted to Islam. A few Jewish scholars developed significant relationships with Muslim students, colleagues, and political leaders. Scholars of Jewish history emphasized the positive experience of Jews in what they called the "Golden Age" of Muslim Spain, in contrast to persecutions in Christian Europe, and some Jewish theologians spoke of the intimacy between Judaism and Islam. Through their publications and lectures, Jewish writers often used Islam as a template to present aspects of Judaism to a European readership, and they also became mediators of Islam to Christian Europe.

Even as Jews were assimilating into Christian Europe, Islam functioned as their pivot of cultural orientation. They admired in Islam precisely those aspects of Judaism they wished to stress: strict monotheism, rejection of anthropomorphism, and the ethical basis of religious law. If, as the historian Suzanne Akbari has argued, medieval Christians disparaged Islam as a revival of the Judaism they despised for its legalism and its rejection of Jesus as messiah, Jews were now reclaiming that identification between Judaism and Islam in a positive, affirming fashion.[7]

The Jewish affirmation of Islam suggests an additional dimension to the modernization experience of Jews. For a long time, historians of modern Jewry described a process of assimilation into European culture and concomitant decline in Jewish religious observance.[8] Still other historians have celebrated the entrance of Jews into European educational, professional, and cultural opportunities, while Zionists, such as Gershom Scholem, criticized German Jews for abandoning a distinctive Jewish national identity.[9] Already the nineteenth-century Jewish historian Heinrich Graetz had complained that liberal Jews were Christianizing Judaism, writing "Wie es sich christelt, judelt es sich" In more recent years, the historian David Sorkin has described German Jews departing from a traditional, autonomous Jewish community and creating a Jewish "subculture" within Germany, with separate institutions, such as Jewish hospitals and schools, yet based on traditional German values such as *Bildung* (education, culture).[10]

However, modern Jewish thought might also be understood as a variegated process of introjection of, and polemics against, European Christianity. The process of political emancipation from the numerous laws restricting their participation in education, professions, acquisition of property, residency rights, and much more, was a process of liberation for Jews that now allowed them to gradually emerge from a status that might be described as an internal colonization within Germany. Political emancipation did not come unchallenged, of course; outbreaks of physical violence against Jews accompanied the freedoms granted, and full

---

7 Suzanne Conklin Akbari, *Idols in the East: European Representations of Islam and the Orient*, 1100-1450 (Ithaca: Cornell University Press, 2009).

8 See, for instance, Jacob Katz, *Tradition and Crisis: Jewish Society at the End of the Middle Ages* (New York: Schocken Books, 1971); Azriel Shochat, *Im Hilufei ha-Tekufot* (Jerusalem: Mosad Bialik, 1960).

9 Gershom Scholem, "Reflections on Modern Jewish Studies" (Hebrew), *Luah Ha-Aretz* (1944), 94-112; trans. Jonathan Chipman in: *On the Possibility of Jewish Mysticism in Our Time and Other Essays*, ed. Avraham Shapira (Philadelphia: Jewish Publication Society, 1997), 51-71; idem., "The Science of Judaism–Then and Now," (German) *Bulletin, Leo Baeck Institute* III (Tel Aviv, 1960), 10-20; trans. Michael A. Meyer in: *The Messianic Idea in Judaism and Other Essays on Jewish Spirituality* (New York: Schocken Books, 1971), 304-13.

10 David J. Sorkin, *The Transformation of German Jewry, 1780-1840* (Detroit: Wayne States University Press, 1999).

social acceptance by Christians was not experienced by Jews, neither in villages nor cities, not even among the fully assimilated living in cities such as Berlin, as Gershom Scholem describes in his memoir, *From Berlin to Jerusalem*.[11]

Given that background, the Jewish affirmation of Islam offers nuances in understanding modern Jewish experience. If the modern era is an example of assimilation or Christianization, it seems odd to find Jewish identifications with Islam, particularly when expressed not only in learned treatises but in public, physical displays, such as the construction of synagogues in Moorish architecture. The oddness of the Jewish identification with Islam is striking not only because it contradicts the standard assumption that German Jews were committed to full assimilation into Christian society, but also for its contradiction of the common views of Islam held by Christian scholars. Whereas Muhammad was conventionally viewed as suffering from epilepsy, whose seizures he supposedly mistook for an experience of divine revelation, the Jewish scholar of Islam Gustav Weil, who had spent several years in Islamicate countries during the 1830s, insisted in an 1842 article that the question for scholars of religion was not judging Muhammad's medical condition, but studying how Muhammad himself understood his own experience: uncertain if his experience represented divine prophecy, he attributed it at first to a medical condition.[12] Weil further joined his claims to those of the Hadith, the body of Islamic traditions regarding the prophet Muhammad, even as his biography of the prophet was based on Islamic sira (biographical traditions).[13] Another example is the response of the distinguished German scholar of Islam, Martin Hartmann, to Goldziher's plea for a sympathetic understanding of Islam.[14] Hartmann's response to Goldziher's letter came six months later with an insistence on Islam's inferiority to both Christianity and Judaism:

> Im Grunde ist ja diese islamische pretaille nicht schlimmer als die christliche des Mittelalters und als die juedische Pilpel-fexe, aber wir haben den altbabylonischen Priester-Schwindel (denn er steht hinter Judentum, Christiantum und Islam) innerlich ueberwunden, die muslimische Welt ist von ihm toedlich vergiftet und ich sehe keine Moeglichkeit einer Rettung.[15]

1. The First Generation: Geiger's Study of the Qur'an

Jewish scholarship on Islam began with Abraham Geiger (1810-1874), who became one of the most original and sophisticated theologians of his era, as well as a leader of what became known as Reform Judaism. Born in Frankfurt am Main to

---

11 Gershom Scholem, *From Berlin to Jerusalem*, trans. Harry Zohn (New York: Schocken Books, 1980).

12 Gustav Weil, "Sur un fait relatif a Mahomet," Journal Asiatique 14 (July 1842), 108-12.

13 Gustav Weil, *Mohammed, der Prophet* (Stuttgart 1843).

14 On Hartmann's career, see Martin Kramer, "Arabistik and Arabism: The Passions of Martin Hartmann," *Middle Eastern Studies* 25:3 (July 1989), 283-30.

15 Ludmila Hanisch, op. cit., 278.

an Orthodox family that gave him a traditional Jewish education in rabbinic texts, he first became a student at the University of Heidelberg in 1829 for one semester, and then moved to the University of Bonn from 1830-33. There he joined a small group of male Jewish students newly welcome to study at German universities (Jewish women had to wait until women were admitted to German universities toward the end of the century).[16] Several of Geiger's fellow students at Bonn thought of becoming rabbis; in those days, Bonn "seemed to be truly a Hochschule for Jewish theologians."[17] Lacking a rabbinical seminary to attend, they formulated their own course of studies, and gathered regularly to practice delivering sermons to one another. Their studies emphasized Oriental languages and Geiger enrolled in Arabic classes with the philologist Georg Freytag, a student of Antoine de Sacy, who had held the professorship in Arabic Studies at Bonn since 1819.[18]

This was a remarkable group of students at Bonn who subsequently became distinguished scholars: Salomon Munk became the leading scholar of the nineteenth century of medieval Arabic Jewish philosophy; Josef Derenbourg became a historian of Second Temple Judaism and later, with his son, Hartwig Derenbourg, a distinguished Islamicist, wrote on the medieval Arabic texts of Saadia and Averroes; Salomon Frensdorff subsequently published important scholarship on the Masoretic text of the Hebrew Bible; Samson Raphael Hirsch, who remained only one year in Bonn, soon became the leading rabbi of German Orthodoxy; and Ludwig Ullmann translated the Qur'an into German, published in 1840, and widely used during the course of the nineteenth century; the translation saw its ninth printing in 1897.[19] Ullmann's translation of the Qur'an into German was followed by a Hebrew version, translated by Salomon Reckendorf and published in 1857.

Munk is best remembered for having determined, by comparing Latin and Hebrew translations, that the author of the Fons Vitae was the Jewish philosopher Solomon ibn Gabirol (Avicebron), not a Christian, and that the original had been written in Arabic. He also published a critical edition of the original Arabic version of Maimonides' *Guide of the Perplexed*, with a translation from Arabic into

---

16 Monika Richarz, "Juden, Wissenschaft und Universitäten. Zur Sozialgeschichte der jüdischen Intelligenz und der akademischen Judenfeindschaft, 1780-1848," *Jahrbuch des Instituts für deutsche Geschichte*, Beiheft 4 (Tel Aviv, 1982), 55-72.

17 Ludwig Geiger, "Introduction," *Abraham Geigers Briefe an J. Derenbourg, Allgemeine Zeitung des Judentums* (1896), 52. For a discussion of the relationship between the two men, see Michael Graetz, "The History of an Estrangement between Two Jewish Communities: Germany and France during the 19th Century," in *Toward Modernity: The European Jewish Model*, ed. Jacob Katz (New Brunswick and Oxford: Transaction Books, 1987), 159-169.

18 On Freytag's career at the University of Bonn, see Christian Renger, *Die Gründung und Einrichtung der Universität Bonn und die Berufungspolitik des Kultusministers Altenstein* (Bonn: Ludwig Röhrscheid Verlag, 1982), 237-9. Due to loss of university records, it is no longer possible to determine in which seminars and lectures Geiger enrolled.

19 University of Bonn archives, Matriculation Records: Album Academiae Borussicae Rhenanae, D. XVIII Octob. 1829 Album der Universtiät Bonn 1827-1829,1 IMB 1827/2.1839. Consulted March 1993.

French. Munk had traveled to Damascus in 1840, as part of a commission investigating a ritual murder accusation against Jews there, and collected manuscripts for Paris, including Karaite texts, many of which were inspired by Muslim theological traditions. Munk's studies of medieval Islamic and Jewish philosophical traditions bore parallels: he limited his presentation of Islam to Sunni traditions, omitting Shiism and mysticism, and while he mentioned Kabbalah in his survey of Jewish philosophy, he disparaged it as a deviation from Mosaic monotheism and leads to pantheism.[20] In 1865, when he was already 60 years old and blind, Munk was appointed to the professorial chair previously held by Ernest Renan, the Semitic philologist who lost the position after publishing the *Vie de Jesus* in 1863, a work deemed unacceptable by the Roman Catholic church.

Yet another Jewish scholar of the same generation was Gustav Weil, born in 1808 in Sulzburg, Baden, who, like Geiger, was given a strong education in rabbinic texts, and even spent some time studying at the rabbinical college of Metz, France. Weil entered the University of Heidelberg in 1828 and studied Arabic with the Old Testament scholar Carl Umbreit, who was also one of Geiger's teachers. Weil then moved to Paris and continued his studies under Antoine de Sacy, the leading Arabic philologist of his day. During the 1830s, Weil traveled with French expeditionary troops through North Africa and spent four years in Cairo, where he studied Arabic and taught European languages. The years of his stay in Paris and in Cairo overlapped with those of the distinguished Egyptian philologist Rifa'a al-Tahtawi, though it remains uncertain if they met in either city. Weil returned to Heidelberg to complete his Habilitation, hoping to receive a professorship, but was confined to a position as assistant librarian at the university. Only in 1861, at the age of 58 and after numerous important scholarly publications and recurring requests for a professorship, was his professorship at Heidelberg bestowed. The delay was caused by Weil's refusal to be baptized and the university faculty's refusal to appoint a member of the "Israelite" faith.[21]

Weil's scholarship on Islam was prolific. He published a book on Arabic poetry (1837), a German translation of the *1001 Nights* (1838-41); a biography of Muhammad (1843); and a historical-critical analysis of the Qur'an, in which he attempted to place the suras in chronological order (1844); a five-volume history of the caliphates (1846-51); and a *History of the Islamic Peoples* (1866). Weil worked primarily with Arabic manuscripts that had been gathered for the Ducal library in Gotha by an adventurer, Ulrich Jasper Seetzen (1767-1811); a catalogue of the library's collection of Arab manuscripts was published in 1826 by Johann Moeller.

---

20 Alfred Ivry, "Salomon Munk and the *Melange de philosophie juive et arabe*," *Jewish Studies Quarterly* 7 (2000), 124.

21 See the documentation at the University of Heidelberg archives; e.g., UAH PA 2423: Letter from Weil to the Ministry of the Interior, dated Febrary 23, 1843. See also Sabine Mangold, *Eine "weltbürgerliche Wissenschaft": Die deutsche Orientalistik im 19. Jahrhundert* (Stuttgart: F. Steiner, 2004), 156-8.

Both Geiger and Gustav Weil brought historicist sensibilities to their philological work. In contrast to other Arabists of their day, including de Sacy, Freytag, and Fleischer, they were less interested in linguistic analysis of Arabic and instead read texts for evidence of historical data. Weil, for example, concentrated on the sira traditions, that is, biographies of the prophet Muhammed, to reconstruct the history of the early Islamic movement. Geiger examined the Qur'an for historical evidence of religious and political conflicts, but for him the Qur'an was a single unit, whereas Weil sought to establish a chronological sequence in the suras in order to establish even more precise developments that the text reflects. The affinities between Judaism and Islam were stressed by both Weil and Geiger, though Weil went a step further, presenting Islam as superior to both Judaism and Christianity. For Geiger, Islam was a branch of Judaism, and Muhammad was a genuine religious enthusiast who was honestly convinced of his religious message. In Weil's account, Islam was a purified version of both Judaism and Christianity: "A Judaism without the many ritual and ceremonial laws, which, according to Mohamed's declaration, even Christ had been called to abolish, or a Christianity without the Trinity, crucifixion and salvation connected therewith"–that is, Weil constructed Islam after the image of religion of his day: Judaism without law, Christianity without dogma; Islam was the Enlightenment religion.[22] By contrast, the multi-volume *Life of Mohammad* by the Austrian scholar Alois Sprenger, originally published in 1861 and recently reprinted, presents Muhammad as an epileptic suffering from hallucinations and hysterical frenzy.

Yet these superb scholars worked outside the rubrics of the German university. Ullmann, born in 1804, served as a rabbi in Krefeld, but died at a young age, in 1843; Frensdorff was a teacher in Hanover, and Geiger became a rabbi in Breslau, Frankfurt, and Berlin, while Munk, Derenbourg, and Weil moved to France and developed academic careers there. Islamic Studies in Germany began during the 1830s with a brain drain; it ended in the 1930s with a more catastrophic expulsion. By 1933, the fields of Islamic Studies and Arabic Studies in Germany were filled with Jewish scholars and were considered the finest in the world. Some of those Jewish scholars were able to emigrate to Palestine, Britain, or the United States, while others lost their lives. The field of Islamic Studies in Germany was decimated and required decades after the war to reconstitute itself.

Geiger's book, *Was hat Muhammad aus dem Judenthume aufgenommen?*, originally written in Latin and published in German in 1833, began with the encouragement of his teacher, Georg Freytag, who formulated the topic of a prize essay on the Jewish sources of the Qur'an out of deference to him. It was only in the spring of 1831 that Geiger, together with two of his classmates, began studying the Qur'an. He noted in his diary, in an entry dated April 29, 1831: "In der That habe ich zu dieser Arbeit grosse Neigung und darf für diesen Zweck eine ziemlich reiche Ausbeute erwarten, da sich überall Anklänge an das Judenthum und zwar an das durch die Rabbinen und die märchenhafte Grillenfängerei morgenländi-

22 Gustav Weil, *The Bible, the Koran and the Talmud* (London: Longman, Brown, Green, and Longmans, 1846), ix.

scher Juden gestaltete finden."[23] He wrote the essay during the first four months of 1832, won the prize, and was awarded a doctorate by the University of Marburg for it in 1834.

The publication of Geiger's book was hailed all over Europe as inaugurating a new way of understanding the origins of Islam within Judaism.[24] Antoine De Sacy, Heinrich Ewald, Reinhard Dozy, Theodor Noeldeke, Heinrich Fleischer, Ignaz Goldziher, were among the many scholars who praised it as "epoch-making."[25] Indeed, Geiger's work set a pattern that was followed by numerous other Jewish scholars, such as Gustav Weil, Hartwig Hirschfeld, Isaac Gastfreund, Josef Horovitz, Victor Aptowitzer, Israel Schapiro, David Sidersky, Abraham Katsch, who sought to demonstrate rabbinic parallels with early Islamic texts and Judaism's influence in shaping Islamic belief, ritual practice, and law.

Geiger's construction of Islamic origins is simultaneously a study of Judaism. Islam, he argues, was assembled from the building blocks of Jewish ideas and religious practices. By contrast, he argues, Jews possess a "religious genius" and Judaism is a powerful, original religious impulse able to generate offshoots appropriate to primitive cultural settings without losing its essential characteristics and the purity of its teachings. Both Islam and Christianity began as efforts to bring Jewish monotheism to the pagan world, though Islam managed to preserve a strict monotheism whereas Christianity corrupted its theology with pagan ideas, as Geiger later argued in a series of studies of early Christianity, which he published between 1857 and 1874.

The central issue at stake for Geiger, however, was demonstrating that rabbinic literature serves as a scholarly linchpin in understanding Western religions. One of the most despised works of Western civilization, rabbinic literature was suddenly revealed by Geiger to provide the key to understanding Islam, just as he later demonstrated that rabbinic literature was key to understanding both the figure of Jesus and the teachings of the gospel authors. One example is the Qur'anic and midrashic recountings of the tower of Babel (Genesis 9:8-9). In both cases, the biblical punishment of dispersion and confusion of tongues is intensified to a curse according to which those who built the tower will be absolutely annihilated by a poisonous wind or will have no place in the next world (Sura 11:63 and Mishnah Sanhedrin 10:3). Geiger insisted that the Qur'an was not the product of Christian heretics teaching Muhammad falsehoods about biblical narratives, as most Christians through the centuries had claimed (with the exception of Peter the Venerable, who blamed Judaism for producing Islam), but rather that Islam arose as a vehicle for bringing Jewish monotheism to the pagan Arabs. Islam was born of Judaism, and Muhammad, whom Geiger describes in very positive terms,

---

23 Ibid., 39.

24 Abraham Geiger, *Was hat Mohammed aus dem Judenthume aufgenommen? Eine von der Königl. Preussischen Rheinuniversität gekrönte Preisschrift* (Bonn, 1833; reprinted Leipzig: M. W. Kaufmann, 1902; Osnabruck: Biblio Verlag, 1971).

25 See my discussion of the reception of Geiger's book: Susannah Heschel, *Abraham Geiger and the Jewish Jesus* (Chicago: University of Chicago Press, 1998), chapter one.

while convinced of his divine mission, did not want to found a new religion, but to align his teachings with those of the biblical prophets.

Geiger's evaluation of Muhammad's borrowings from Jewish sources is inflected by his assumption that early Judaism was strictly monotheistic. For example, he rejects a Jewish origin for an incident mentioned in the Qur'an, Sura 38:73-77, in which the angels fall down in honor of Adam.[26] The incident cannot reflect Jewish tradition, Geiger argues, because worship of any other being than God would have seemed to any Jewish interpreter inconceivable. Instead, he writes:

> The legend bears unmistakable marks of Christian development, in that Adam is represented in the beginning as the God-man, worthy of adoration, which the Jews are far from asserting. It is true that in Jewish writings great honor is spoken of as shown by the angels to Adam, but this never went so far as adoration; indeed when this was once about to take place in error, God frustrated the action.[27]

The passage is one of the few in which Islamic understandings of God are discussed in this body of scholarship. For the most part, arguments regarding Judaism's influence on Islam focused on matters of law, ritual, or ethical principles. Geiger's discussion is additionally striking as an example of the Jewish insistence that influence was unidirectional: Judaism influenced Islam, Islam was never recognized as influencing Judaism–at least not until the 1912 studies of Shiism by Israel Friedlander, a student of Theodor Noeldeke.[28] Until Friedlaender, Jewish scholars shaped the Islam they studied after the model of their understanding of Judaism. That is, just as mysticism and apocalypticism were considered foreign to Judaism–"Schmarotzengewächs," in Heinrich Graetz's term–so, too, were Sufism and Shiism topics that were generally ignored by Jewish scholars, at least until the work of Friedlander, who argued that false messianic movements in Shiite Islam influenced the rise of false messianic movements in Judaism. For most Jewish scholars, however, both Islam and Judaism were rational religions. Indeed, it was the mystical and apocalyptic traditions within Hellenism that weakened Judaism and ultimately crippled Christianity's ability to retain a pure Jewish monotheism, according to Graetz, Geiger, and most subsequent Jewish historians. Their studies of Judaism and Islam were strictly theological, bound by doctrine and rooted in a positivist, philological approach to texts that left little room for the phenomenological approaches to religion that were beginning to take shape by mid-century. Moreover, a more complex understanding of "influence" in the realm of religious ideas and practices did not emerge until the twentieth century,

---

[26] This account also appears in less complete form in six other passages. Geiger, *Judaism and Islam*, 75-77.

[27] Geiger, *Judaism and Islam*, 77; see T. B. Sanhedrin 29a-b; Midrash Rabbah on Genesis, paragraph 8; Leopold Zunz, *Die gottesdienstlichen Vorträge der Juden*, 291, footnote.

[28] Israel Friedlaender, "Shiitic Elements in Jewish Sectarianism," *Jewish Quarterly Review*, new series 2:4 (April 1912), 481-516.

suggesting that proximity between Judaism and Islam does not necessarily encourage borrowing but, on the contrary, lines of demarcation.

2. The Next Generation

The study of Islam was in its infancy in the 1830s in Germany; the basic scholarly tools had not yet been developed: dictionaries, critical editions of texts, and methods for analyzing them. As Geiger wrote, his analysis of the Qur'an was based simply on the "naked Arabic text." Heinrich Lebrecht Fleischer, who became professor of Oriental languages at the University of Leipzig in 1835, had, like Freytag, trained under de Sacy in France, where scholars were busy analyzing the treasure trove of documents that Napoleon's scholars had brought back from Middle East expeditions.[29] Bonn remained a smaller center than Leipzig for studying Islam; in Leipzig, Fleischer had over three hundred students, Jews and Christians, and of the 131 dissertations he directed prior to his death in 1886, fifty-one were written by Jews, including Daniel Chwolsohn, Morris Jastrow, Immanuel Loew, Wilhelm Bacher, Eduard Baneth, and Goldziher, whom Fleischer considered his greatest student.[30] Fleischer was also the founding editor of the *Zeitschrift der deutschen morgenländischen Gesellschaft* and welcomed contributions by Jews, making his journal one of the only prestigious German academic journals studying religion in which Jews were permitted to publish their scholarship, and creating Islamic Studies as a particularly welcoming field for Jewish scholars.

By the second half of the nineteenth century, some Jewish scholars were also inaugurating contacts with the Muslim world. For example, Weil travelled with French expeditionary forces through North Africa and spent four years in Cairo, studying Arabic and Turkic dialects; Josef Horovitz became professor of Arabic for seven years at the Aligargh Muslim University from 1907 to 1914; Max Herz became a consultant for architectural restoration of mosques and preservation of Islamic antiquities in Cairo at the turn of the century;[31] Gottlieb Leitner helped create the University of the Punjab; and Goldziher established personal relation-

[29] On Fleischer, see Sabine Mangold, *Eine 'weltbürgerliche Wissenschaft': Die deutsche Orientalistik im 19. Jahrhundert* (Stuttgart, 2004); Johann J. Fueck, *Die arabischen Studien in Europa bis in den Anfang des 20. Jahrhunderts* (Leipzig, 1955); Martin Kramer (ed.), *The Jewish Discovery of Islam* (Tel Aviv, 1999); Holger Preissler, "Heinrich Lebrecht Fleischer: Ein Orientalist, seine jüdischen Studenten, Promovenden und Kollegen," *Leipziger Beiträge zur Jüdischen Geschichte und Kultur*, ed. Dan Diner IV (2006), 245-68; on Jena, Stefan Heidemann, "Zwischen Theologie und Philologie: Paradigmenwechsel in der Jenaer Orientalistik, 1770 bis 1850," *Der Islam* 84 (2007), 140-84.

[30] Universitätsarchiv Leipzig, Philosophische Fakultät, Promotionen. Consulted July 2009.

[31] Istvan Ormos, "Preservation and Restoration: The Methods of Max Herz Pasha, Chief Architect of the Comite de Conservation des Monuments de l'Art Arabe, 1890-1914," in *Historians in Cairo: Essays in Honor of George Scanlon*, ed. Jill Edwards (Cairo: American University of Cairo Press, 2002), 123f.

ships with scholars, religious reformers, and political leaders during his trips to Cairo and Damascus, and several of his studies of hadith and Qur'an exegesis were later translated into Arabic and published in Egypt in the mid-twentieth century.[32] Those translations, according to Josef van Ess, came primarily at the direction of Ali Hasan Abdalqadir, who taught at al-Azhar University during the 1930s and 40s.[33] Controversies broke out in Egypt in the 1940s over the use of Goldziher's historicist approach, primarily in conjunction with the rise of the Muslim Brotherhood; Mustafa al-Sibai, founder of the Muslim Brotherhood in Syria, came to al-Azhar to study under Abdalqadir in 1939 and objected to the latter's citations of Goldziher in his lectures on Islamic law. The controversies over historicist approaches to Islamic texts limited the impact of Goldziher's work in Egypt, as of other European historians.[34]

The Jewish scholars and theologians who admired Islam stood in sharp contrast with some of the major Christian scholars of Islam in Germany of the same era. Julius Wellhausen, for example, transferred traditional Christian theological denigrations of Judaism to their evaluations of Islam. C.H. Becker transferred the origins of Islam to Hellenism, not Judaism.[35] Wellhausen, in switching his scholarship from the Old Testament to Islam, intended, he wrote, "to learn about the wild stock upon which the shoot of Yahwe's Tora was grafted by the priests and the prophets."[36] What he hoped to find, Josef van Ess explains, "was religiosity without priests and prophets, that is, without the Law and without institutions."[37] Wellhausen was looking for liberal Protestantism, purged of Judaism. For Wellhausen, the era of classical prophecy was the high point of ancient Israel; the priesthood and religious law were viewed by him as later developments marking a degeneration of biblical Israel's religiosity into Judaism. Similarly, Becker assumed a dichotomy between subjective religiosity and institutionalized religion–an implied dichotomy between Protestantism and Judaism. Van Ess writes, "In his [Wellhausen's] view, the shari'a fosters conservatism and makes progress impossible; its idealistic character makes those who are subject to it despair of adequate accomplishment and thus favors their indolence."[38]

---

32 Josef van Ess, "Goldziher as a Contemporary of Islamic Reform," in *Goldziher Memorial Conference*, ed. Eva Apor and Istvan Ormos (Budapest: Hungarian Academy of Sciences, 2005), 37-50.

33 Ibid., 38.

34 See G.H.A. Juynboll, *The Authenticity of the Tradition Literature: Discussions in Modern Egypt* (Leiden, 1969).

35 C. H. Becker, "Der Islam als Problem," *Der Islam* 1 (1910), 1-21.

36 Julius Wellhausen, *Muhammed in Medina* (Berlin, 1882), 5. See Peter Machinist, "The Road Not Taken: Wellhausen and Assyriology," in *Homeland and Exile: Studies in Honor of Bustenay Oded*, ed. Gershon Galil, Mark Geller, and Alan Millard (Leiden, Boston: Brill, 2009).

37 Josef van Ess, "From Wellhausen to Becker: The Emergence of Kulturgeschichte in Islamic Studies," in Malcolm H. Kerr, ed., *Islamic Studies: A Tradition and Its Problems* (Undena Publications, 1980), 27-51; p. 42.

38 Ibid., 43.

In the entire corpus of scholarship on Islam, Goldziher stands as a singular figure. His work is so wide-ranging, profound, and influential that I can only mention very briefly in this context a few points regarding his significance.

In his scholarship, Goldziher was not simply a philologist but also a proto-phenomenologist of religion, asking how Muhammad experienced being a prophet. On the question of Jewish influence in shaping Islam, Goldziher echoed Jewish denials of Islamic originality: Islam contains "practically nothing original"; "Muhammad's teaching was not the original creation of his genius... but all his doctrines are taken from Judaism and Christianity"; Islam "was the most important manifestation of the Semitic genius ever made." At the same time, Goldziher frequently ignored or denied the possibility of Jewish influence on aspects of Islamic law even when that influence was obvious. Patricia Crone has pointed out that Goldziher "could have made an effortless case for the theory that Jewish law contributed heavily to the Shari'a; yet time and again he opted for the view that it was 'a bygone stage of Roman legal history' which made the contribution."[39]

At the same time, Goldziher's methods show clear signs of Jewish influence. In the redaction criticism he brought to the early textual sources of Islam (and Judaism) he applied the historicist methods of the Tübingen school of New Testament scholarship that he had learned from Geiger's monumental study of Second Temple Judaism, *Urschrift und Übersetzungen der Bibel*, published in 1857. These methods were first applied by Goldziher to his studies of Hebrew myths and later to his lectures on Jewish history, in which he emphasized the progressive development of Judaism–lectures that so outraged his reactionary Hungarian Jewish audience that they canceled his sixth and final talk.[40] Geiger's methods, mediated by the Tübingen School's F.C. Baur and D.F. Strauss, are reflected in Goldziher's distinction between Meccan and Medinan parts of the Qur'an–Meccan being Jewish–and his argument that Hanafite and Malikite schools of legal interpretation reflect a range of social and political layers.[41] As Geiger had done with rabbinic texts, Goldziher demonstrated the conflicting schools that created the Hadith and then attributed their views to Muhammad.

As Geiger had done in the 1860s, Goldziher confronted the work of Ernest Renan and the racial theory that was emerging in some areas of Oriental studies. Renan, who saw Islam, like Judaism, as fixed and incapable of development, shifted from a hereditary to a linguistic definition of the "Semitic" in his writings.[42] Renan's study of Semitic languages, published in 1853 to great acclaim–he was

---

39 Patricia Crone, Roman, *Provincial, and Islamic Law: The Origins of the Islamic Patronate* (Cambridge, New York: Cambridge University Press, 1987), appendix two.

40 Ignac Goldziher, *Mythology among the Hebrews and Its Historical Development*, trans. Russell Martineau (London: Longmans, Green, 1877).

41 Goldziher wrote in an 1868 entry in his diary, "I began to understand Geiger's message after I got acquainted with Strauss and Baur," that is, the radically historicist methods of the Tübingen School. Robert Simon, *Ignac Goldziher: His Life and Scholarship as Reflected in His Works and Correspondence* (Leiden: E.J. Brill, 1986), 134.

42 Ernest Renan, "Nouvelles Considérations sur le caractère général des peoples sémitiques," *Journal Asiatique*, série 5, 13 (1859): 214-282, 417-450.

awarded the Volney Prize by the French Academy–argued that Semites lack mythology because they are instinctually monotheistic. The study set a new agenda for the next decades, sparking a broader European discussion of the value of monotheism and encouraging a redirection of Christianity. Lacking mythology was not viewed as a triumph over paganism, but as a deficit of religion, reflecting the Semites' intolerant and exclusivist nature, standing in utter opposition to Aryans in religion, language, and ways of thinking. Compared to the Aryans, the Semites lacked scientific and artistic originality, had created no national epic or mythology, showed no ability to think abstractly, and could not organize large governments or military campaigns. Judaism was unable to progress and developed a rigid legalism; the mantle of the classical prophets had passed to Jesus, who was transformed, according to Renan, from Jew to Aryan during the course of his life. His claim was passionately refuted by Geiger, who wrote that Renan's negative view of Judaism was not theological but racial in origin: it "is not the opinion of the Christian concerning Jews and Judaism, it is the jealousy of the races of the Aryan ... and the Semite."[43]

Critics of Renan abounded; Max Mueller, in his *Semitic Monotheism*, published in 1859, pointed out that if monotheism was a characteristic trait of Jews, why had ancient Hebrews relapsed into polytheism so often? Similarly, Goldziher asked, much later, if Arabs had first been polytheists, and then monotheists, how can religion be the product of racial instinct? However, defenses of Christianity against Renan, such as Mueller's, ultimately disengaged it from Judaism in order to affirm the uniqueness of Christian monotheism.[44] Those embracing Renan now began to see the move to polytheism as a source of progress, rather than a relapse into evil, so that christology and other Christian dogma were hailed as the transformation of monotheism via polytheism, leaving behind the backward monotheism of the Jews. The Jewish turn to Islam came, in part, to rehabilitate Judaism through a link with Islamic monotheism. Goldziher's response was to uncover mythology within Islam, insist on the purity of its monotheism linked to its ethics and religious law, and demonstrate its progressive development, just as he had earlier argued about Judaism in his study of its mythologies, originally published in 1876.[45]

Renan's arguments against Islam continued. In 1883 Renan gave a lecture at the Sorbonne, *L'Islamisme et la science*, in which he argued that neither the Arabs nor Islam, to say nothing of Jews and Judaism, are scientific and capable of philosophical thinking. He spoke of "the terrible simplicity of the Semitic spirit, closing the human brain to every subtle idea, to every fine

[43] Abraham Geiger, *Judaism and Its History*, trans. Maurice Mayer (New York: M. Thalmessinger, 1865), 338.

[44] George Williamson, *Longing for Myth: Religion and Aesthetic Culture from Romanticism to Nietzsche* (Chicago: University of Chicago Press, 2004), 225.

[45] Ignaz Goldziher, *Der Mythos bei den Hebräern und seine geschichtliche Entwickelung. Untersuchungen zur Mythologie und Religionswissenschaft* (Leipzig: F. A. Brockhaus, 1876).

sentiment, to all rational research, in order to confront it with an eternal tautology: God is God."[46]

The emergence of racial theory within the field of oriental studies in the second half of the nineteenth century, directed against both Islam and Judaism, led Goldziher to emphasize historical change within Islam. For Goldziher, the inability to prove an early dating for the Hadith, for example, was a sign of Islam's progressive development beyond the Meccan and Medinan periods. A cautious historian, Goldziher recognized that isnads, chains of transmission, cannot be relied upon to authenticate historical data: "Minute study soon reveals the presence of the tendencies and aspirations of a later day, the working of a spirit which wrests the record in favour of one or the other of the opposing theses in certain disputed questions."[47] In other words, isnads were used to legitimate later teachings by projecting them into the past. Goldziher's Muslims were like the rabbis of the Talmud, who attributed their teachings to noted rabbis of earlier eras and who modified their rulings in accordance with the political, social and economic environment of the Jews: Goldziher emphasized that even Muhammad had to adapt his teachings to the circumstances of the Arabs to whom he was preaching. Religious practice was malleable, and interpretations of the Qur'an were bound to vary in different eras, a sign of the religion's vitality–the same argument Goldziher made with regard to Judaism.

Goldziher's emphasis on Muhammad's lack of originality should also be seen in the context of refuting the static, racially-based arguments of Renan: "From the point of view of cultural history it is of little account that Muhammed's teaching was not the original creation of his genius which made him the prophet of his people, but that all his doctrines are taken from Judaism and Christianity. Their originality lies in the fact that these teachings were for the first time placed in contrast to the Arabic ways of life by Muhammed's persistent energy."[48] A year after Renan's death in 1893, Goldziher was invited by the Hungarian Academy of Sciences to deliver a memorial lecture, later published as *Renan as Orientalist*, a devastating critique. Goldziher delineated the prejudice that governed Renan's approach, his insistence that creative movements of Arabic learning in the past and political efforts in the present stemmed either from rebels against Islam or from Iranians–namely, Aryans.[49]

---

[46] Ernest Renan, *L'Islamisme et la science* (Paris: Calmann Levi, 1883). See Albert Hourani, *Islam in European Thought* (Cambridge, New York: Cambridge University Press, 1991), 29.

[47] Ignaz Goldziher, "The Principles of Law in Islam," *Muslim Studies* (New Brunswick, N.J.: Aldine Transaction) vol. 2, 302. Note that D.S. Margoliouth, a contemporary of Goldziher's, took the argument even further, as did Henri Lammens and Joseph Schacht.

[48] Ignaz Goldziher, "Islamic Theology," in: *Muslim Studies*, op. cit., 21.

[49] Robert Simon, *Ignác Goldziher: His Life and Scholarship as Reflected in His Works and Correspondence* (Budapest: Library of the Hungarian Academy of Sciences; Leiden : E.J. Brill, 1986), 390-2.

3. Conclusion

The Jewish affirmation of Islam, and assertion of influences of Judaism on early Islam, and of parallels between the two religions, stands in marked contrast to Christian evaluations of Islam of the same era, and also marks an important, neglected aspect of modern Jewish self-understanding. For many of Germany's leading Christian scholars, Islam was another unfortunate example of Judaism—a religion of law and cultic ritual—as reflected, for example, in Wellhausen's work. Since Christianity does not bear a component of Islam within it—in contrast to the Jewish ideas, texts, and persons that stand within the heart of Christianity—polemics against Islam could proceed without impinging on Christian theology. In addition, the philological methods that dominated Christian scholarship were designed to examine the text as the creation of scribes, so that the Qur'an could be studied in isolation from the social and religious setting in which Islam emerged. For Jewish scholars, beginning with Geiger, Islam was not only an object of admiration; it was a template for presenting Judaism to the European world. Through their admiration for Islamic monotheism and its rejection of anthropomorphism, their explanations for the rise of Islam and the emergence of the Qur'an within the milieu of rabbinic Judaism, and their studies of the rationality of Islamic law and ethics, Jews were defending the rational and ethical basis of Judaism's legal system and the importance of its commitment to monotheism and religious law. By arguing for the overwhelming influence of rabbinic Judaism on Islam's ideas and religious practices, Geiger, Weil, Goldziher, and others were also using historical method to provide a theological substitute for traditional belief in divine revelation: perhaps God had not revealed the text of the Jewish Scriptures and rabbinic commentaries, but those Scriptures and commentaries were powerful enough to have created the three monotheistic religions of the West.

Ultimately, Jews saw in Islam that which was important to them within Judaism, an ethical monotheism, and just as they created a *Kulturjudaismus*, they did likewise for Islam. Their scholarship created a *Kulturislamismus*, describing Islam as a rational, philosophical, law-adhering, family-centered, highly moral religion with particularly strict sexual mores and its women firmly under male control. Yet could we not also imagine the reverse: Judaism reconceived by Jewish thinkers after the image of Sunni Islam: a religion without mysticism, apocalypticism, or anthropomorphisms, and rooted in rational philosophy, monotheism, sexual restraint, patriarchal family, ritual law, and stringent morality. German-Jewish thinkers created an alliance between Judaism and their idealized image of Islam to bolster their definition of Judaism as a religion of ethical monotheism. And always, Jews insisted that Islam, like Christianity, was born of Judaism, even as their modern Judaism was born, as we can recognize today, out of their image of Islam.

Christology

The Images of the Divine in USA and South African Black Theology

Dwight Hopkins

One of the 1960s developments in American and South African societies was the rise of black consciousness–an ideological renaissance of identity and new recognition of the self. Though manifest in disparate areas (such as, the economy, social relations, and political engagements), the black consciousness awakening was, primarily, a reorientation of dislocated subject populations self-critically interrogating the question–who are we? Such a new discourse or practical orientation spanned material culture and language. For instance, new clothing, hair styles, reconstructed histories, African kinships, naming processes, music, slogans, and languages were brought into play. Moreover, culture, as lived out in this epoch denoted a broader understanding, one underscoring how left out populations bring to bear their own experiences of history, tradition, language, and identity into the larger discursive narrative of the collective memories and contemporary practices of a nation. Such a definition of culture allows for political revelations of fluid existence. Yet it incorporates comprehensive realities within an integrated web of a total way of life, which is, precisely, the expansive definition of culture.[1]

During the 1960s vibrant and creative cultures, Christianity and theology were also impacted. Specifically, a few African American and black South African academics and pastors attempted to discern what was the relationship between the Christian gospel and the new self-identity process. In a word, what was the image of Christ in this new cultural orientation of black consciousness?

This chapter examines three of the USA and three of the South African founders of black theology who offered responses to these queries. Albert Cleage, James H. Cone, and J. Deotis Roberts offered distinct answers to the Christological and cultural relationships in the United States. Similarly, Manas Buthelezi, Allan Boesak, and Simon Maimela engaged such assertions from the South African contextual perspectives. For our larger purpose, we want to discern the image of the divine inter-continentally and inter-contextually.

---

1 See Randwedzi Nengwekhulu, "The Dialectical Relationship Between Culture and Religion In The Struggle For Resistance And Liberation," in *Culture, Religion, and Liberation*, ed. Simon S. Maimela (Pretoria, South Africa: Penrose Book Printers, 1994), p. 19. Also see Raymond Williams, *The Long Revolution* (Harmondsworth: Penguin, 1965), p. 63.

1. The Image of the Divine in the USA

Albert Cleage was a local pastor of a United Church of Christ church in Detroit Michigan during the 1960s and 1970s. In fact, the cultural movement of inner city Detroit directly defined his understanding of what he called and what he named his local church, the Black Messiah.

For Cleage, the historical Jesus was a black revolutionary Zealot, leading the fight against a "white Rome" in order to realize a revolution for the black nation of Israel. When Cleage writes "black Jesus" he does not mean ontologically, symbolically, or psycho-culturally. Christologically, he means a Jesus with a *literal* African or a black phenotype.

> When I say that Jesus was black, that Jesus was the black Messiah... I'm not saying, "Wouldn't it be nice if Jesus was black?" or "Let's pretend that Jesus was black" or "It's necessary psychologically for us to believe that Jesus was black." I'm saying that Jesus WAS black. There never was a white Jesus.[2]

With the death of John the Baptist, in Cleage's opinion, Jesus assumed the political leadership of the revolutionary Zealots. This black movement waged war against the white oppressor, Rome, in order to reconstitute the black nation. The black scribes and Pharisees collaborated with "white" Rome to preserve their privileges. Consequently, Jesus came as a revolutionary and an organizer of the black revolution. He had to be crucified for political reasons because "this is the kind of life that Jesus lived." He died due to his sole purpose–making black revolution to reconstitute the black nation.[3]

It is something of a misnomer to classify Cleage's interpretation of Jesus as Christology in the classical conception of the doctrine of Christ. Cleage hardly displays any interest in the resurrected Christ. For him the messiahship belongs to Jesus not because of Good Friday and Easter, but strictly as a result of Jesus' life and earthly activity in attempting to reconstitute the black nation. Thus Cleage apparently avoids a dichotomy between the Jesus of history and the Christ of faith. With Cleage's black Messiah, the Jesus of history is an identical twin with the Jesus of faith.[4]

---

[2] Quoted in Alex Poinsett, "The Quest for a Black Christ," *Ebony Magazine* (March 1969), p. 174.

[3] Albert Cleage, *The Black Messiah* (New York: Sheed and Ward, 1968), pp. 62, 72, 85, 91, 124.

[4] For Cleage's doctrine of Jesus, see his *Black Christian Nationalism* (New York: William Morrow & Co., 1972), p. 42; also see his statement: "Not in his death, but in his life and in his willingness to die for the Black Nation. To say that God was in Jesus reconciling the world unto Himself at a particular moment on Calvary when Jesus died upon the cross is not the same as saying that God reconciled men unto Himself in the life and teachings of Jesus, which gave men a new conception of human dignity and inspired them to fight to be men instead of slaves" (ibid., p. 188).

What was the material cultural orientation that allowed Cleage to pastor a local church with such a Christological image of the divine? It was the culture determining the theology. For instance, during Cleage's time various elements in the black cultural renaissance were attempting to build a black nation. (In hindsight, this was obviously a quixotic fantasy.) Some were organizing a nation that would go back to Africa. Others were planning to establish a nation in several of the states in the southern USA. And still others, like Cleage, were calling for a black nation constituted by urban areas dominated by a majority of African Americans. In this sense, the "nation" would not have contiguous borders. Conferences were held on "nation time" or "nation building time". A flag was adopted; a national anthem was voted on, "national" colors were recognized, and various political parties argued over which one represented the emerging nation. Caucuses were established in major professional organizations. And, whether or not it was empty rhetoric or fact, some even called for the nation to have its own army.

In other words, a Christological image arose out of a specific materiality of a people in crisis and creativity. This image of the divine was local, history-bound, and specific. The cultural orientation gave rise to the perspective of the divine.

If Cleage's Christology describes a literal black-skinned Jesus, James H. Cone's image of the divine portrays a completely different cultural orientation. God's liberation of black people through Christ's cross and resurrection marks the centrality of Cone's Christology. For Cone, the Christian Scriptures or New Testament witness reveals Jesus' person as the Oppressed One. Because black people experienced extreme afflictions, the locus of Jesus' work is a black Christ identified with liberation from black suffering. The Bible tells the story of Jesus' oppression; the contemporary story tells of black people's oppression. In a word, the Oppressed One in black suffering expresses divine being and divine activity. Christ is black because of how Christ was revealed and because of where Christ seeks to be. Having intersected the liberation of the oppressed with the person and work of Christ and having situated that liberation in the African American community, Cone boldly asserted in his first published book, "Christianity is not alien to Black Power, it is Black Power."[5]

Cone cites a distinction between the literal and symbolic nature of Christological blackness. In explicating the contrast, Cone offers a proviso for the possible interim nature of a black Christology. "I realize," he confesses, "that 'blackness' as a Christological title may not be appropriate in the distant future or even in every human context in our present." But today (1969) the literalness of Christ's blackness arises from Christ literally entering and converging with black oppression and black struggle. Furthermore, Cone continues, Christ's symbolic status of blackness resides in Christ's "transcendent affirmation" that God has never left the universal oppressed alone.[6]

---

5 James H. Cone, *Black Theology and Black Power* (New York: Seabury Press, 1969), pp. 35, 38, and 120; also see Cone, *A Black Theology of Liberation*, 2nd edition (Maryknoll, N.Y.: Orbis Books), pp. 120-21.

6 Cone, *God of the Oppressed* (New York: Seabury Press, 1975), pp. 135-37.

Cone believes that Cleage's black Messiah Jesusology is "distorting history and the Christian gospel".[7] In contrast, Cone brings together both the Jesus of history with the Christ of faith to complement the liberation theme; we cannot have one without the other. Similar to Cleage, Cone does argue that we know what and where Jesus is today based on what Jesus did while on earth. But moving beyond Cleage, Cone creates new political meaning in the crucifixion and resurrection around the thread of his liberation axis. Calvary and the empty tomb prove key in Cone's Christology. Jesus' "death and resurrection" reveal "that God is present in all dimensions of human liberation."[8] In contrast, Cleage recognizes emancipation from oppression because Jesus carried out liberation on earth before death.

Finally, Cone's Christology underscores the poor. Christ died on the cross and rose from the dead in partiality to the liberation of the poor and the oppressed. The being and work of Christ express the divine intent to free the oppressed. Christ rescues the downtrodden from the material bondage and 'principalities and powers'. In this liberation process the "oppressors" also realize their freedom because the object of their oppression–the now freed poor–no longer occupies an oppressed status.[9]

Cone's image of the divine comes from that part of the black cultural orientation that called for a universal note of liberation arising out of the particularity of the black renaissance. For instance, Cone represents a perspective, during his time period, of forces that never called for going back to Africa or building a black nation. From his very first book, he offers argumentation that he was an American and this was his country too; a position held by the majority of black Americans then and now.

Cone looked at Christ and concluded the following: if the risen Christ is for liberation and the oppressed and black people are the oppressed who are organizing for liberation, then Christ must be *theologically* black. The Christ has to be with the oppressed blacks by force of a theological argument, not because of skin color. This effort to unite particularity with universality–divinity imaged as both for the particular one and for the all–enabled Cone to say, even in his first book (1969), that his Christological title was subject to change as contexts and situations changed in the future.

To restate, for Cone the image of the divine black Christ results from *theological logic*–i.e., if Christ is for the poor and the oppressed and blacks are poor and oppressed then Christ is black, poor, and oppressed. In addition, the image of the divine black Christ results from *social location*. Because the mission of Christ is to be present with the poor and oppressed and because blacks exist in poor and oppressed conditions, then Christ reveals Christ's spirit in the physical location of the black poor and oppressed. Hence, Christ is black by virtue of his revelation

---

7 See Cone, *For My People* (New York: Orbis Books, 1984), p. 36.

8 Cone, *A Black Theology of Liberation*, pp. 110-24.

9 *Black Theology and Black Power*, pp. 37, 42-43.

in the materiality of black people's condition. For Cone, only a black messiah would live with the black marginalized communities.

J. Deotis Roberts was 11 years older than James H. Cone. Roberts participated in the old reconciliation civil rights movements of the 1950s. Yet, while teaching at Howard University in 1966, the year that the black power slogan was enunciated (June 16, 1966 in Greenwood, Mississippi), Roberts was caught in the hot bed of the new cultural renaissance. Thus his Christology attempts to bridge the turn-the-other-check philosophy of the Martin Luther King, Jr. civil rights era and the youthful by-any-means-necessary thrust of the new black cultural renaissance.

Roberts seeks to place Cleage's and Cone's Christology in proper perspective. Cleage argues for a literal black Jesus and Christ. Cone believes Christ assumed his blackness by theological logic and by his presence among the oppressed African American community. In *Liberation and Reconciliation*, Roberts also adheres to a black Messiah, though not in the literal historical sense. For him the black Messiah speaks to a *psychocultural* crisis engendered by white American religion's demand that only the white Christ is worthy of adoration. In other words, for him, years of worshipping images of a white Christ have caused psychological damage to black Americans. To correct this damage, one has to now propose black Christological images. In Robert's opinion, one must not limit Christianity merely to the white Christ's worthiness. The black experience has to also be a major source for contemporary Christology. A need materializes to make Christ and the gospel address the black person directly. As a black image, Christ becomes one among black people, and the black person retrieves his or her own dignity and pride. That is to say, psychological healing materializes. With psychological healing achieved, blacks can better reconcile with their fellow white citizens.

Furthermore, Roberts does not wish to challenge white Americans to worship a black Christ. Thus Roberts does not demand a vengeful repentance from them for worshipping a white Christ. This type of "revenge" would dehumanize white citizens. Besides, affirmation of a black Christ, for Roberts, includes room for a white Christ. At the same time, Roberts hopes, if whites could overcome their superior-inferior state of mind and color-consciousness and could worship a black Messiah, then reconciliation would be nearer. Still, Roberts claims, real reconciliation through black and white equality would allow American blacks and whites to transcend the skin color of Christ and reach out to a "universal Christ" without color.

At this point, Roberts clarifies the black Messiah-colorless Messiah relation in his liberation-reconciliation paradigm. The black Messiah functions in a symbolic and mythic capacity. In the African American experience the black Messiah liberates blacks. At the same time, the universal Christ reconciles black and white Americans. Jesus Christ the Liberator offers liberation from racial discrimination and forgiveness from sin and exploitation within the black community. Jesus Christ the Reconciler brings black people together and black and white citizens together in "multi-racial fellowship."

Roberts' *A Black Political Theology* further elaborates his Christology. In this text, (a) Christ operates above culture and in culture while liberating the whole person and speaking to the need for peoplehood. Christ is the focus of a theology of social change and political action. And Jesus is the liberator who casts his lot with the oppressed. (b) Along with "mainstream Protestantism", Roberts agrees that the *essence* and *substance* of Christology are located in the universal Word—the lordship of Christ over each people. Black Christology takes for granted this universal definition and particularizes it in the *form* of the black experience. (c) The existential and personal Christ liberates and the universal Christ reconciles all Americans.[10]

2. The Image of the Divine in South Africa

As we turn to the image of the divine in South Africa, we begin with Manas Buthelezi, a member of the Evangelical Lutheran Church. Buthelezi was the leading proponent of black theology in South Africa of the 1970s. His texts reflect a specific problematic: How to uphold black dignity under apartheid while pursuing some type of Christian relationship with white fellow church members in the midst of the (1960s and 1970s) Black Consciousness Movement of South Africa? His response is that the image of the divine is revealed in Racial Fellowship demanded by Christ.

Buthelezi sees his Christological claims centered in the Bible. The Bible depicts humanity as a body in Christ. Unity in Christ serves as the starting point for racial interaction and not for the apartness of apartheid Christology, which preaches an incarnation of division and dissension. "The Church drives the shape of its life not from the divisions of sin but from the unifying salvation in Christ."[11] God's revelation in Christ resolves the tower of Babel predicament in the Old Testament. In the body of Christ human identities and differences come together to complement one another and to enrich fellowship. Thus, the appropriate Christology brings together differences in unity, not in discord.

Buthelezi's Christology of unified differences argues strongly for more than simply ecclesiological unity. Primarily, he fights for unity in Christ in order to live out the uniqueness of the gospel.

In Christ mankind becomes a family, a brotherhood. This is the uniqueness of Christianity.... This is the uniqueness which, according to my diagnosis, the South African way of life has done its share to undermine and almost destroy.[12]

God expresses God's love for humanity through Christ's work of transforming human enmity into love, fearful neighbors into affectionate siblings. In Buthelezi's

---

[10] For an account of his Christological claims, that is, black messiah, colorless Christ, libertine and reconciliation, see Roberts, *Liberation and Reconciliation* (Philadelphia: Westminster Press, 1971), chapter 6.; and his *A Black Political Theology*, (Philadelphia: Westminster Press, 1974), chapter 5.

[11] Buthelezi, "The Relevance of Theology," *South African Outlook* 104, no. 1243 (December 1974), p. 198.

[12] Buthelezi, "Christianity in South Africa," *Pro Veritate* (15 June 1973), p. 4.

opinion, Christianity's sacred ground and line of demarcation materialize in Christology—the incarnation of Christ's unifying activity among humankind.

For black South African Christians, Christology suggests the sobriety of crossbearing. The essence of Jesus Christ's message, from Buthelezi's vantage point, revolves around Christ's pain in being one with another, even after the other has turned his or her back on him. Christ bore the burden of his accusers, even as they mocked him and nailed him on the cross in his own blood. Therefore Christ's cross symbolizes his person and presence among humanity. To be one with those who cause pain is to follow the way of the cross toward racial fellowship. Buthelezi emphasizes:

> As far as the racist is concerned, I take this to mean that I should try to be one with him in love, even if it is unilateral, unreciprocated love and to contine to minister to him even while he carves for himself a racist church.

Buthelezi knows that to travel this path involves trepidation and tremendous risk. He resumes:

> This is a hard thing to do. I believe that it is for this reason that it is called the taking up of the cross and bearing one another's burden.[13]

Christology pushes black Christians into a pastoral role of ministering to racist Christians in a unilateral and unreciprocated fashion. Indeed for Buthelezi, Christ demands that blacks initiate reconciliation.

Allan A. Boesak, another founder of South African black theology, was a leader of the "Colored" Dutch Reformed Church in South Africa and he also held the distinguished position of president of the World Alliance of Reformed Churches in the early 1980s. Like Buthelezi, Boesak concentrates on the evils of apartheid theology. Evenmore, he is motivated by his theological project to dethrone the theological support given by the white Dutch Reformed Church to apartheid political policies. For instance, when the white National Party came to power in 1948, it adopted the apartheid practices already existing in the white Dutch Reformed Church.[14]

Boesak is driven, therefore, to undermine his church's theological backing for the apartheid state because the Afrikaner government was literally a collection of self-identified white racist politicians of the Dutch Reformed Church. For Boesak, every Christology has to undergo the core test of the Word of God, which, for him anchors the Reformed tradition. The image of the divine, consequently, is the Word of God.

---

[13] Buthelezi, "Church Unity and Human Divisions of Racism," *International Review of Missions* (August 1984), pp. 424-25.

[14] See Charles Villa-Vicencio, "An All-Pervading Heresy: Racism and the English-speaking Churches," in Apartheid Is a Heresy, ed. John W. de Gruchy and Charles Villa-Vicencio (Grand Rapids, MI: Eerdmans Publishing Co., 1983), p. 59.

In Boesak's Christology, emancipatory practice reveals under the Word of God. And the liberating work and person of Jesus Christ pinpoint the substance of the Word. In the final analysis, the gospel of Jesus Christ judges all reflection and all action; the Word is the gospel.

Boesak argues that Christ judges in the person of the Poor One and the Oppressed One. In Boesak's Christology, Christ's birth in a barn and his parents' financial inability to bear him at an inn reveal him as the Son of the Poor. And his lacking a place to "lay his head" (his homelessness) reveals a state of destitution. At the same time, Christ suffered oppression at the hands of the political state for preaching the Word of God. He even bore unearned punishment from the wicked of his own people. Yet, his person (divinity assuming Poverty and Oppression) lay the basis for his work on behalf of all poor and oppressed. He sounded good news for the marginalized. He sided with the dispossessed. He effected liberation. And he fulfilled Yahweh's promise of deliverance for the captives.[15]

To the lordship of this Person and Work, Boesak pledges paramount allegiance. At all costs one clings to the confession of Christ as Lord. Consequently the laws of the state and of self-preservation do not undermine the authority of Christ's Person and Work. Neither do the intimidating demands of any people, status quo or ideology dictate to the followers of Christ. Here, drawing on progressive strands within his Reformed tradition, Boesak theologically justifies disobedience to apartheid and commitment to the Word in the liberation movement.

Divine lordship thrusts the faithful completely into the political arena. One has to trek the political path because even the "slightest fraction of life" falls under the lordship of Christ. Boesak employs a theological rationale for his lordship Christological claim. God created life and God is indivisible. Hence life is indivisible. Since the substance of the Word of God is the liberating lordship of Christ, Christ reigns over all life. Buthelezi's Christology situates its uniqueness in drawing black and white into racial fellowship. Boesak sees this Christological function, but within the context of apartheid theology submitting to Christ's absolute lordship.

In this lordship, Boesak also perceives faith and hope for the church. The certitude of Christ's past resurrection confirms his current reign. If Christ rose, he lives and rules over us today. Therefore, having risen from the dead, Christ guarantees us a future life in the eschaton. The ecclesia, then, witnesses as a church of the resurrection. Moreover, the resurrected lordship cosmologically altered the balance of forces over sin's dominion. So the kingdom of sin likewise submits to the kingdom of Christ. This knowledge provides faith and hope for the church in the struggle between disloyalty to sin and unswerving allegiance to the kingdom.

---

15 See Boesak, "Coming in Out of the Wilderness," in The Emergent Gospel: Theology from the Underside of History, ed. Sergio Torres and Virginia Fabella (Maryknoll, NY: Orbis Books, 1978), pp. 82-83.

In summary, Boesak sees Christ's lordship of liberation (i.e., the Word of God) defeating the devil in political places. Christ rose from the clutches of evil persons and forever placed the faithful in God's kingdom of liberation.[16]

A member of the Evangelical Lutheran Church of South Africa, Simon S. Maimela, like Buthelezi and Boesak, develops his black theology in a white church during the apartheid era. Maimela establishes the context for his Christology by confronting the treacherousness of the anthropology proclaimed by both Afrikaners and English-speaking whites under apartheid. He charges "white" anthropology with the sin of falsely portraying the created reality of humankind. Humanity, in white anthropology, has fallen prey to self-centeredness, a drive to accumulate absolute power and wealth for a particular individual, group or class. This negative anthropology attributes a utilitarianism to human contact. In particular, the neighbor becomes a mere tool for the personal gratification of the individualist. Different peoples, then, pose an immediate danger to one another and can never experience creative interrelation. "It is against the background of this extremely negative, cynical, and pessimistic anthropological presupposition of the human self," writes Maimela, "that we should try to understand White praxis in [apartheid] South Africa."[17]

Maimela, therefore, claims that such a deep, socialized, indoctrinated anthropology causes whites to automatically discourage contacts between diverse black ethnic groups, and between whites and blacks, hence the apartheid policy of separate development; that is, Maimela accuses white anthropology of creating apartheid. Among black South Africans, Buthelezi targets the breach in Christ's love in racial fellowship, and Boesak unveils the incorrect use of the Word of God in the Reformed tradition to support apartheid. For Maimela, the heart of the matter is a heretical theological anthropology.

This heresy fractures genuine reconciliation. But, for Maimela, the Christian message of reconciliation ultimately rests on what God has brought about in the incarnation of Jesus of Nazareth, the Christ. The man Jesus leaves us no alternative but to have faith in a positive anthropology. Yes, we take seriously the perversion of sin in the human reality, but not to the conclusion of negating God's redemption for all humanity in Jesus Christ. Christ brought redemption expressly to heal the most serious "diseases of the heart" and of human works such as lack of love and fellowship. In fact, Maimela continues, the complete Christian message of "conversion and reconciliation" reveals an understanding and a faith "that humans have been and continue to be changed by God [through Christ] who continues to fashion them into new creatures."

Why did Christ die on the cross? According to Maimela, Christ gave his life in order for us to undergo a healing and renewal from the perverted life of sin and the products of sin. Christ's death brought regenerated and reinvigorated life and love to distorted human relations. To say otherwise, in the manner of white

---

16 Boesak, If This Is Treason, I Am Guilty (Grand Rapids, MI: William B. Eerdmans Publishing, Co., 1987), pp. 14-15.

17 Maimela, "Man in 'White' Theology," *Missionalia*, vol. 9, no. 1 (April 1981), pp. 68-69.

anthropology, signifies a cynical attempt to a) take the jugular vein out of the crucifixion and b) blasphemously mock God's power in the resurrected Christ to intervene in the affairs of God's created humanity.[18]

While affirming the power of the cruxifixion, Maimela cautions against an abstract or esoteric atonement. Such an incorrect view depicts "the problem of man largely in spiritualized terms." Even with the atonement, Maimela approaches from an anthropological persuasion. He begins with Christ's atoning work from the perspective of humanity entangled in the concrete web of sociopolitical oppression. Though Christ's death and resurrection did resolve the need for a general and spirutal forgiveness of sins and guilt, this confession alone ignores the more exact Christological picture of humanity's material reality. Hence, Christ's basic work accomplished the physical transformation of humanity.

Here Maimela's introduction of the work of Christ with physical change shows us how his Christology bridges theological anthropology (Christ's transformation of material humanity) and reconciliation (Christ's atonement in sociopolitical oppression) with liberation. He includes liberation in such a construction by the correct juxtaposition of Christological activity to salvation and historical liberation. The former, salvation, Christ has achieved and promised to humanity. The latter, historical liberation, remains the joint project of both God (in Christ) and Christians. While ultimate salvation of the kingdom is a divine gift, co-creators–God in Christ and humankind–forge alienating social conditions into a more humane and just social relation. In short, salvation preconditions historical liberation, and Christ's work links both to anthropology and reconciliation.

Maimela succinctly states the intricacies of his entire theological enterprise:

> Put differently, the fundamental message of liberation is that the life, death and resurrection of Jesus Christ [Christology] were aimed at the total liberation (salvation) of humanity [liberation] from all kinds of limitations both spiritual and physical, and that this liberation is a dynamic historical process in which man [theological anthropology] is given the promise, the possibility and power to overcome all the perverted human conditions [reconciliation] on this side of the grave.[19]

In Christ, it seems for Maimela, all things are possible: a healed theological anthropology, a just fellowship of reconciliation, and both a penultimate and ultimate liberation/salvation. Like Buthelezi's Christology, Maimela discovers racial fellowship but sees Christ's resurrection providing the condition for both races working together in radical social transformation-creation. And when Boesak advocates total submission to Christ's liberating lordship as the Word of God, Maimeal links this to Christ's work of healing sinful anthropology between white and black.

---

[18] Maimela, "An Anthropological Heresy: A Critique of White Theology," in de Gruchy and Villa-Vicencio, pp. 48-58.

[19] Maimela, "The Atonement in the Context of Liberation Theology," *South African Outlook* (December 1981), pp. 184-85.

3. Conclusion

In this critical comparative conversation, we advance a variety of images of the divine. On the USA side of the Atlantic, we encounter Christology as a literal "black skin" Messiah, Jesus as Liberator, and Christ Liberator-Reconciler. From the South African debates, there emerges a Christology of Racial Fellowship, Word of God, and Liberation Anthropology.

An inter-continental and inter-contextual discernment of Christology as the image of the divine in the USA and South Africa offers us some suggestive possibilities for further academic and broader public scrutiny.

(i) The image of the divine in various manifestations of global black theology indicates human cultural orientation imagining ways and methods of interpreting and naming the Spirit in the Christian religion.

(ii) These imaginations, interpretations, and naming flow from the time-bound, local, and context of particular cultures.

(iii) Human beings do theology, not God. Human beings do cultures. Thus human cultures create divine images from human cultures.

(iv) Once one acknowledges the centrality of cultural orientation, then the human realm cries out for an interdisciplinary study in order to grasp more deeply and comprehensively the many dimensions of divine images.

(v) And, moreover, if the human creates the cultural orientation from which divine images emerge, a better grasp of the divine imaging might result from a better understanding of the context and character of the theologian who is imaging. Perhaps out of these many particularities of human cultural orientations, we might one day obtain a universal set of divine imaging as a contribution to the well being of all humanity, religions, spiritual practitioners.

Contributors

Alfred Bodenheimer is Professor of the History of Religions and Jewish Literature and Director of the Center for Jewish Studies at the University of Basel, Switzerland.

Sarah Coakley is Norris-Hulse Professor of Divinity at the University of Cambridge, UK.

Susanne Enderwitz is Professor of Islamic Studies at the University of Heidelberg, Germany.

Michael Fishbane is the Nathan Cummings Distinguished Service Professor of Jewish Studies at the University of Chicago Divinity School, USA.

Paul Mendes-Flohr is the Dorothy Grant Maclear Professor of Modern Jewish History and Thought at the University of Chicago Divinity School, USA.

Johannes Heil is Professor of Religion, History and Culture of European Judaism and President of the Hochschule für Jüdische Studien in Heidelberg, Germany.

Susannah Heschel is the Eli Black Professor of Jewish Studies at Dartmouth College in Hanover, USA.

Dwight Hopkins is Professor of Theology at the University of Chicago Divinity School, USA.

Baber Johansen is Professor of Islamic Religious Studies at Harvard Divinity School in Cambridge, USA.

Angelika Neuwirth is Professor of Arabic Studies at the Freie Universität Berlin, Germany.

Friederike Nüssel is Professor of Systematic Theology and Principal of the Ecumenical Institute at the University of Heidelberg, Germany.

William Schweiker is the Edward L. Ryerson Distinguished Service Professor of Theological Ethics at the University of Chicago Divinity School, USA.

Kathryn Tanner is the Frederick Marquand Professor of Systematic Theology at Yale Divinity School in New Haven, USA.

Michael Welker is Senior Professor of Systematic Theology and Director of the Research Center International and Interdisciplinary Theology (Forschungszentrum Internationale und Interdisziplinäre Theologie, FIIT) at the University of Heidelberg, Germany.